How Women Can Make It Work

How Women Can Make It Work

THE SCIENCE OF SUCCESS

Eden King and Jennifer Knight

Women and Careers in Management
Michele A. Paludi, Series Editor

PRAEGER

AN IMPRINT OF ABC-CLIO, LLC
Santa Barbara, California • Denver, Colorado • Oxford, England

BP53

Library of Congress Cataloging-in-Publication Data

King, Eden.
  How women can make it work : the science of success / Eden King and Jennifer Knight.
      p. cm. — (Women and careers in management)
    Includes bibliographical references and index.
      ISBN 978–0–313–39309–9 (hbk. : alk. paper) — ISBN 978–0–313–39310–5 (ebook)
  1. Women—Vocational guidance. 2. Women—Employment. 3. Career development. I. Knight, Jennifer L., 1978– II. Title.
  HF5382.6.K55   2011
  650.1082—dc22   2010054531

ISBN: 978–0–313–39309–9
EISBN: 978–0–313–39310–5
15 14 13 12 11   1 2 3 4 5

This book is also available on the World Wide Web as an eBook.
Visit www.abc-clio.com for details.

Praeger
An Imprint of ABC-CLIO, LLC

ABC-CLIO, LLC
130 Cremona Drive, P.O. Box 1911
Santa Barbara, California 93116-1911

This book is printed on acid-free paper ⬁

Manufactured in the United States of America

5/25/12

For our families, who shaped us.
For our mentors, who support us.
For our partners, who stand beside us.
For the women and men who worked for equality before us.
And for the friends, students, and strangers in the generation of women for whom this book was written, who inspire us.

Contents

Series Foreword

Ma muaka kite a muri
Ma muri ka ora a mua
(Those who lead give sight to those who follow,
Those who follow give life to those who lead)

—Pauline Tangiora

Welcome to the *"Women and Careers in Management"* Series at Praeger.

This series shares Tangiora's sentiment in that it examines the status of women in management and leadership and offers discussions of issues which women managers and leaders face, including:

Differences in leadership styles.

Traditional gender roles reinforcing women's subordinate status in the workplace.

Obstacles to advancement and pay.

Benefit and resource inequity.

Discrimination and harassment.

Work/life imbalance.

This series acknowledges that gender is one of the fundamental factors influencing the ethics, values, and policies of workplaces and that the discrimination against women managers and leaders explains the pervasiveness of institutionalized inequality. This series also discusses interconnections among equality issues: sex, race, class, age, sexual orientation, religion, and disability. Thus, this series brings together a multidisciplinary and multicultural discussion of women, management, and leadership.

"*Women and Careers in Management*" encourages all of us to think critically about women managers and leaders, to place value on cultural experiences and integrate empirical research and theoretical formulations with experiences of our family, friends, colleagues, and ourselves. It is my hope that the books in "*Women and Careers in Management*" serve as a "life raft" (Klonis, Endo, Crosby, and Worrell 1997), especially for the millennial and subsequent generations.

The present book, *How Women Can Make It Work: The Science of Success*, by Dr. Eden King and Dr. Jennifer Knight, is the first book to be published in the "*Women and Careers in Management*" series at Praeger. Drs. King and Knight offer readers an opportunity to value ourselves and look at what factors outside of ourselves contribute to obstacles we face in our jobs and careers. This book underscores the need to have change occur at the organizational level so that women and issues confronting women in the workplace are not marginal, but central, e.g., integrating work and life roles, offering mentoring opportunities to and for women, shattering the glass ceiling, valuing leadership and communication styles.

I am honored to have this book published in the "*Women and Careers in Management*" Series. Drs. King and Knight express the sentiment of Secretary of State Hillary Rodham Clinton who is quoted as stating: "*Talent is universal, but opportunity is not.*" Drs. King and Knight's book provides strategies for leveling the playing field for women in careers. Their book is a "life raft" or (wo)mentor for its readers in that it empowers women to "make it work."

Reference

Klonis, S., Endo, J., Crosby, F., and Worrell, J. (1997). Feminism as life raft. *Psychology of Women Quarterly* 21: 333–345.

—Michele A. Paludi
Series Editor

Introduction

Make it work.

—Tim Gunn

For a book aimed at helping young women harness a huge body of social science research to survive and thrive in their jobs, it might seem counterintuitive to begin with a quote from *Project Runway's* resident male advisor, Tim Gunn—but for our money, nothing sums up our approach to this book better than Tim's dictum. We were raised to believe that we can have it all . . . or at least have the choice to have it all. So if you want to try to always be the perfect über-woman who nails the big client contract in the morning, brings homemade, organic snacks to her daughter's soccer game in the afternoon, and chairs the city council meeting at night, all without breaking a sweat—then by all means, go for it (and then please tell us how you did it). But if you are like us, this scenario probably seems aspirational at best and overwhelming at worst. As such, we look forward to providing some tools based on social science research to help you "make it work"—whatever that looks like for you.

First a note about who "we" is. *Dr. Eden King* is the child of genuine hippies who ended up being passionate about the science of social justice. To pursue this passion, she joined the faculty of the Organizational Psychology program at George Mason University after earning her PhD from Rice University in 2006. Eden's research has been published in a number of scholarly outlets, and has been featured in the popular media, including *Good Morning America,*

The New York Times, and the *CBS Evening News*. When she's not working, Eden tears it up on the flag football field, bakes up a storm, and watches just about every television show that features a strong woman kicking butt (*Buffy, Bones, Alias*) plus a few other guilty pleasures (*Grey's Anatomy, True Blood, Weeds*).

 *Dr. Jennifer Knight* grew up in small-town West Texas (think *Friday Night Lights*), graduated Phi Beta Kappa from Southwestern University in Georgetown, Texas, with a degree in psychology with minors in sociology and music, and earned her PhD in Organizational Psychology in 2004 from Rice University. Her research on diversity and discrimination has been featured in several media outlets, including *The New York Times, Allure*, and *CNN's Anderson Cooper 360*. Dr. Knight's consulting has taken her to workplaces across the nation and to more exotic locales such as the Middle East, South and East Asia, the Balkans, Oceania, Latin America, and western Europe. She currently works for Uncle Sam in Washington, D.C.—that's right, she's from the government and she's here to help.

Purpose of the Book

Our goal is to use state-of-the-art social science studies to help *you*: that is, Gen-X, Y, and Z women who are recent high school or college grads, women in their first or second job, new moms who are weighing decisions about work and life balance, and/or the managers and counselors who work with young women and want to understand the issues they may be facing. We'd like to help you navigate the mountains and molehills you may encounter in the workplace. Although women have overcome many barriers at work, research indicates that we still encounter subtle obstacles that can have a huge impact on the careers and lives of the youngest generations of women. We will point out potential problems that can emerge at the intersection of gender, work, and family and offer strategies for their resolution.

Each of the following six sections will mix empirical findings with personal stories and pop culture references to describe a particular issue before presenting narrower problems and science-based tools for fixing them—we believe this format will allow you to focus on particular issues as needed or to read the entire book from start to finish.

1. **How to Make It Work When Finding the Job: Moving Beyond the Want Ads**

   In this opening section, we will focus on challenges that women should keep in mind when they are looking for a job. We'll discuss factors women might weigh when deciding what they want to be when they grow up (choosing a career path), what organizational features might be particularly important to look for and how to look (work-family policies), and how women can get the jobs they decide they want (interviewing tips, dealing with résumé "gaps" after off-ramping to raise a family, utilizing informal networks, succeeding in a down economy, and negotiating a salary).

2. **How to Make It Work When Navigating Interpersonal Relationships: Why the People Make the Place**

   As social beings, our interpersonal relationships are critical to our happiness. One central set of relationships is that which emerges in our workplaces. This section of the book will describe challenges and benefits that occur when young women work with men, other women, and older workers, including topics such as romance at work, the old boys network, queen bees, mentoring, sexual harassment, gender discrimination, networking, and the gray to green shift.

3. **How to Make It Work While Communicating on the Job: Speaking Up and Standing Out**

   To make it at work, women must communicate effectively with supervisors, coworkers, and subordinates. We will describe research on gendered styles of communication (like sports metaphors in the office and "metaperceptions," or what I think you think about me) and specify techniques for capitalizing on verbal and nonverbal communication, including what your clothes and workspace say about you. We'll also discuss issues that have arisen in the digital era, such as communicating at work via instant messenger, e-mail, text message, and emoticons.

4. **How to Make It Work While Advancing in the Job: Getting Beyond the Glass Ceiling, the Glass Cliff, and the Sticky Floor**
Women who want to get ahead at work need to be aware of several potential roadblocks that may get in their way. We will discuss issues related to compensation, performance appraisal, feedback, developmental work opportunities, and leadership. These aspects of advancement are affected by how women are perceived by organizational decision-makers and by how women see themselves. Additionally, we will point out these barriers to advancement and offer tips for avoiding and overcoming them, such as time management and planning practices.

5. **How to Make It Work While Balancing Work and Family: The Grand Canyon or a Line in the Sand?**
One of the aspects of work that can be particularly tricky for young women is the intersection of work and family. We will consider a wide range of family issues including concerns related to marriage (changing your name professionally, balancing dual careers), pregnancy (disclosing pregnancy, negotiating maternity leave, return-to-work), and motherhood (possibility of changing priorities, questions about working mothers competence and commitment, balancing childcare and eldercare, commuting and telecommuting, working abroad).

6. **How Women of All Stripes Can Make It Work: Special Issues for Subgroups**
The experience of women at work is affected not only by their gender but also by other visible and not-so-visible aspects of their identities. We will devote this section of the book to issues that may be central to women with potentially stigmatized identities. Being both a woman and a member of another stigmatized group can be doubly difficult. We will consider the unique experiences of lesbian and bisexual women, disabled women, single working moms, and women from ethnic minority backgrounds and show how women of all backgrounds can be allies of one another.

As a whole, we hope this book will help serve as your guide to achieving personal and professional success.

You Take the Good, You Take the Bad, You Take Them Both, and There You Have the Facts of Life

This first decade of the new millennium, of course, has brought a number of kick-ass developments for women in the workplace that are worth lauding and celebrating:

- The first viable female Presidential candidate (Hilary Clinton), the second Vice Presidential female candidate (Sarah Palin), and the first female Speaker of the House (Nancy Pelosi).[1, 2] It is also the first time three female Supreme Court judges have simultaneously served on the bench (Ruth Bader Ginsburg, Sonia Sotomayor, and Elena Kagan). Additionally, two of the three major primetime news anchors are now women (ABC's Diane Sawyer and CBS's Katie Couric).

- 2010 marked the first time that there were more female than male nonfarm employees (though we'll talk about why this is a bittersweet development and double-edged sword in a chapter in our first section about finding a job in a tough economic climate).[3]

- Women now earn 60 percent of master's and bachelor's degrees, half of law and medical degrees, and 40 percent of MBAs.[4] Though as Gloria Steinem astutely notes, these advances may not be as exciting as they sound, since women *need* higher education to keep up economically with less-educated but higher-earning men who are in trade professions that are traditionally not open to women, such as construction, mining, and manufacturing.

- 94 percent of young professional female millennials believe they will have "rewarding careers balanced with fulfilling personal lives," and they identified having "a job where they can make a difference" and "the ability to balance personal and professional lives and a job" as the two biggest keys to their workplace success.[5]

- President Obama in 2009 signed into law his first bill, the Lilly Ledbetter Fair Pay Act, which was designed to restore "workers' rights to challenge illegal wage discrimination in the federal courts."[6]

- Both academic and consulting research shows that female representation in senior leadership positions (as board members, high-level managers, and in the so-called "C-suite" of CEOs, COOs, and CIOs) is positively related to a firm's financial performance.[7, 8]

With so many groundbreaking workplace achievements, then why is this type of book, sadly, still necessary?

- According to the US Department of Labor, women in full-time year-round jobs continue to make only 77 cents for every dollar that men earn.[9] This pay gap is particularly pronounced at the highest levels of compensation, with top female CEOs earning on average $3.9 million as compared to male CEOs who brought in on average $11.9 million.[10]
- Of the top 100 largest firms in the United States, 20 did not have *any* top female officers and only 7 had a female CEO; furthermore, only 13 percent of people in the top management teams in these corporations were women.[11]
- Only one-third of organizations surveyed by the consulting firm McKinsey cited gender diversity as a priority, and 40 percent say it's not important to their strategic agenda.[12]
- An Accenture survey finds that young, working female millennials, age 22 to 35, continue to cite a number of gender-related barriers to their current and future careers, including the pay scale for women (30%), a corporate culture that favors men (28%), general stereotypes (26%), day care availability (24%), lack of women in the top echelons of their organization (20%), and wanting to start a family (20%).[13]

Caveat Emptor

Throughout the book, when we discuss the social scientific literature we'll often use phrases such as "Women were more likely to ..." or "Research shows that men tend to ... " This is in no way meant to stereotype or imply that *all* women act one way and *all* men another. In fact (and we'll emphasize this for effect): *There is more variation within each gender then between them.* For example, *on average* men are taller and weigh more than women, but there is certainly a wide diversity of height and weight within each sex. And you remember how the somewhat crude but memorable warning goes about averages related to gender: "The average person has one testicle and one ovary." So for every "traditional" woman you might encounter who fits neatly into these averages, there is a super-hacker badass like Lisbeth Salander—the unconventional heroine of Stieg Larsson's wildly popular "Millennium Trilogy" and protagonist who has been labeled by ForbesWoman as "The Girl Who Started A Feminist Franchise"—to remind you to look beyond the numbers when interpreting data and research.[14]

Now let's get started to show how young women can make it work. . . .

Section One

How to Make It Work When Finding the Job: Moving beyond the Want Ads

If you ever want to get an organizational psychologist's attention, all you have to do is say two words: Job and Satisfaction. Job satisfaction is, in some ways, the holy grail of organizational psychology. We sit at our desks and in our laboratories and we try to come up with ways that we can make people happier with their jobs. Not a bad gig, eh?

So what have we learned about this ultimate goal? Job satisfaction begins with the match between the person and their job and company. Dissatisfaction can result from mis-matches in either category. In this section of the book, we will discuss the research findings that point to ways that you can maximize job satisfaction by finding the job and organization that is a good fit for you.

This may seem like a daunting task. You may be thinking, "It was hard enough trying to find a paycheck. Now I'm supposed to try to find everlasting job satisfaction?" But this goes back to the idea that you should be looking for whatever is the best fit for what will make *you* happy—sometimes a paycheck is all it takes. Think about *(Good) Will Hunting*—a genius who was happy to be a night janitor and hang out with his Southies (i.e., guys from South Boston to you non-Yankees) on the weekends.

Take, for illustration purposes, Eden's flag football team. The founding members of Cobra Kai (Karate Kid reference) represent an interesting cross-section of the job and career issues facing people in their 20s and 30s. Here's the lineup with a caveat: these descriptions are based entirely on Eden's understanding of her teammates' jobs and may have little to do with reality:

Quarterback/Safety: *Roger*—computer dude extraordinaire who recently changed jobs. Favorite feature of the new job: proximity to his family. He has lunch with his wife and kid every day.

Wide Receiver/Running Back/Safety: *Winston*—newly certified family physician. Favorite feature of his job: talking to patients and medical students/residents about music, sports, and, oh yeah, medicine.

Wide Receiver: *Shelley*—high school Spanish teacher. Favorite features of her job: sharing Spanish, travel opportunities, and summer vacation. Least favorite part: having to go to prom year after year.

Wide Receiver: *Jared*—actuary. We're still trying to understand what an actuary does. Best part of this job: working from home and looking at numbers.

Tight End/Linebacker: *Phoebe*—grant budget coordinator at a law school, soon to be law student. Best part of the job: overlap with career/life goal of advocating for underdogs.

Tight End/Corner: *Steve*—computer dude extraordinaire who recently changed jobs #2. Favorite feature of the new job: recognition for his ideas and enthusiasm.

Center/Corner: *Ryan*—works for the government. Favorite feature of his job: met his wife, Jenny (see below).

Offensive Line: *Guillermo*—computer dude extraordinaire. Favorite feature of his job: he used to share a cubicle with Steve (see above).

Offensive Line/Linebacker: *Jenny*—works for the government. Favorite feature of her job: telling other people what to do and meeting Ryan, of course.

Linebacker: *Julie*—technical editor. Favorite feature of the job: any writing she gets to do is a good thing.

Defensive Line: *Dan*—computer dude extraordinaire. Favorite feature of the job: biking to work.

Offensive Line: *Lindsay*—occupational therapist for special needs kids. Best part of the job: seeing change in the kids.

Offensive/Defensive Line: *Eden*—psychology professor. Favorite parts of the job: flexibility, mentoring students, and feeling like the work matters.

A few themes can be extracted from this cross-sectional view of young people's jobs that are reflected in the research literature.

Jobs can be about a lot more than the tasks you do. For Lindsay, her job satisfaction is almost entirely related to the kids who she helps—when she feels like she is making a difference, she is satisfied with her job. But for many other members of Cobra Kai, the tasks of the job are secondary to many other characteristics of the job. For Roger and Jared, convenience is key. For Steve, recognition for hard work is important. For Eden, flexibility in what she studies and when and where she works is huge. For many of us, the people who we talk to while we are at work are big pieces of our satisfaction pie. This variability in what is important to you, taken with the variability in what jobs and companies can offer, makes it important to figure out what kind of job will make *you* happy.

You CAN find a job. Every one of Eden's teammates worried about finding a job after college. We all got rejection letters. We were all scared that we would have to move in with our parents for the rest of our lives. But we took the leaps that we needed to take. For example, none of the 13 of us is actually from the D.C. area—we all moved here for work. We understand your fears, but we encourage you to take the leaps like those described in the following chapters that might help you land a great job.

Sometimes your job doesn't match exactly what you'd like to do. Your first job may not be your dream job. Just think about Andrea (Anne Hathaway) in *The Devil Wears Prada*. Of the four computer dudes on the football team, only one is really *into* being a computer dude. Julie is a writer, through and through. She gets to do some of this at her job, and she gets paid—two key characteristics of Julie's job satisfaction. But in her dream world, she might be writing fiction or poetry rather than technical manuals. So maybe she'll do fiction writing on the weekend to improve her life satisfaction, or maybe she'll negotiate for more writing opportunities at her job. Or eventually, she may even change jobs altogether.

You CAN (usually or eventually) change jobs. The overwhelming majority of people will not work for the same company or even in the same job for their entire working life. Roger and Steve both changed jobs in the past year. Winston loves being a family doctor now, but he may eventually want to use his background in and passion for public health to work for the government (put your hands in the air for the future surgeon general . . .!). Phoebe is going to law school for the specific purpose of changing her career path. This is all to say that if you find that you are not getting what you want in a job—that it is no longer a good "fit"—you *can* make changes either at the job itself by asking for different responsibilities/ opportunities or by finding another job while carefully maintaining the current one.

This section of the book is devoted to helping you find the job and company that will make *you* happy. We'll use all the resources we can find to help you:

- *Find out what kind of personality and aptitudes you have and the jobs that may be the best fit.* We'll link you up to lots of great resources for self-assessment.

- *Find out the kinds of jobs that are available.* Did you know that it is actually our acquaintances that often end up giving us successful leads more than our close family and friends?

- *Find a company that is a good fit for you.* Research suggests that women may want to keep some specific ideas about numbers and policies in mind when getting a feel for "fit."

- *Prepare résumés, cover letters, and interviews.* Studies suggest that some tricks like simply including competency statements in your materials can increase your likelihood of getting an interview offer.

- *Overcome your own stereotypes about women at work.* Research on stereotype threat suggests that women sometimes confirm our own worst fears! Read on for strategies for avoiding these traps.

- *Get the offer you're entitled to.* We'll talk about the tendency of men to negotiate more often and better than women, and point out findings that show women can be more successful in negotiations by emphasizing their competence and niceness.

- *Cope with changing economies.* Our research suggests that policies and programs supporting women, minorities, and families may be the first to go in tough economic times. We'll tell you about what stressors to look out for and how to cope.

According to Confucius, "Choose a job you love, and you will never have to work a day in your life." We hope to help you find this kind of job satisfaction in the following pages.

I

Who Are You? Who-Who-Who-Who? Understanding What You Bring to the Table in the Workplace

Though many of you may be too young to remember this iconic song by The Who, an important first step in choosing your career path is knowing what you like and what you are good at and understanding how to move forward anyway if the two aren't related. Almost all university career service centers have a variety of self-assessment tools available to students and alumni to help them discover more about what makes them tick—the following four types of psychological tests might help you navigate that career minefield:

Work Personality

Some of the most common personality tests include the Myers Briggs Type Indicator, Clifton Strengths Finder, the 16PF Questionnaire, the Birkman Method, and the DiSC Profile. Despite the commercial popularity of these instruments, one of the most frequently used personality assessment tools among organizational psychologists like us is what's often known as "The Big Five," so named because a number of statistical analyses consistently find that someone's work "personality" can be boiled down to the following five traits (which you can remember using the catchy mnemonic device OCEAN):

Openness to Experience—Do you value new experiences, have a strong imagination, and enjoy spending time on scholarly, artistic, or literary pursuits, or do you consider yourself more conventional, conservative, and practical? Women who score high on the Openness to Experience scale might look for careers where they can express themselves creatively, whereas those low on the scale might prefer very structured work settings with established protocols. A good example of a woman who would score high on this scale? Carrie Bradshaw from *Sex and the City*.

Conscientiousness—When you have a task to complete, do you create to-do lists and tackle the job well before the due date, or do you prefer to work more spontaneously on the task and use the pressure of deadlines to spur you? If you are high on this conscientiousness scale, you probably would enjoy jobs where deadlines are generally laid out far in advance, whereas if you are low, you probably want to look for jobs where details and deadlines aren't as important. A woman high in conscientiousness? Hermione Granger from the "Harry Potter" series.

Extraversion—When you walk into a room full of people you don't know, are you filled with anticipation, thinking of all the new friends to be made, or filled with dread, worried about having to make small talk with strangers? High extraverts will want to look for jobs where they can think on their feet and be in frequent interaction with clients and coworkers, whereas those who score low on this scale should find work environments where they can have "downtime" and opportunities to reflect before having to make decisions. Who might be considered a strong extravert? Elle Woods from *Legally Blond*.

Agreeableness—When forced to work with ornery coworkers, are you more likely to try to just go with the flow and create team harmony or to confront your colleagues and directly tell them what you think their problem is? Women high in agreeableness might want to seek out office environments where a premium is placed on team cohesion, whereas women low in agreeableness would probably do better in an office culture where emphasis is placed on individual accomplishments. A good example of a woman low on the agreeableness scale? Sue Sylvester from *Glee*.

Neuroticism—When encountering a stressful situation, are you generally more likely to be very anxious, moody, and panicked or relaxed, confident, and calm? If you have a low Neuroticism score, you will probably do well in most work environments, whereas those with a high score probably need to find jobs with a minimum number of surprises and high-stress situations. Someone who probably would score high on this scale? Jenna Maroney from *30 Rock*.

Interested to know how you rate on these five traits? Check out this Web site, www.outofservice.com/bigfive, to complete your own (free!) self-assessment.

So what do your scores on these five scales mean for your career path? Well, across almost all jobs, conscientiousness is a great trait to have, as it predicts success in many different occupational groups; conversely, having an extremely high Neuroticism score can be something of a stumbling block, though it can be somewhat compensated for by strong scores in other personality traits.[1] Interested in management or sales? In addition to having high Conscientiousness and low Neuroticism, Extraversion is an important trait to have in these two fields.[2, 3] Agreeableness can also be useful for managers and other workers who lead teams, teach students, perform customer service, or work in a nurturing environment, whereas Openness to Experience often serves workers well in who are in creative or entrepreneurial jobs.[4]

Psychological research has found that—when comparing the sexes on these five scales, there are often more differences within each sex than between them.[5] However, there do seem to be small but consistent findings showing that women report being higher in Neuroticism, Agreeableness, Warmth and Gregariousness (subscales of Extraversion), and Openness to Feelings and Aesthetics (subscales of Openness to Experience), whereas men report higher scores in Assertiveness and Excitement Seeking (subscales of Extraversion) and Openness to Ideas (a subscale of Openness to Experience). Interestingly, these gender differences are even larger in prosperous nations like the United States than in less developed nations.[6]

Work Interests

In addition to knowing your personality type, it can also be instructive when picking a career field to know what interests you. Most work in this field has centered around the Holland Interest Inventory, which assesses the following six types of interests:

- **Realistic**—Do you consider yourself practical, good at solving hands-on, mechanical problems, and interested in using your hands to build things? Think Marisa Tomei's fast-talking Mona Lisa Vito from *My Cousin Vinny.*

- **Investigative**—Do you consider yourself analytical, good at processing multifaceted or abstract data, and interested in using theories to solve scientific or complex problems? Think Temperance "Bones" Brennan from *Bones.*

- **Artistic**—Do you consider yourself innovative, good at writing, art, drama, music, acting, or dancing, and interested in expressing yourself creatively? Perhaps not surprisingly, these Artistic types also tend to score high on the Openness to Experience personality measure from above.[7] Think Rachel Berry from *Glee.*

- **Social**—Do you consider yourself friendly, good at cooperating with, leading, and training others, and interested in helping individuals and teams? Think Carla Espinosa from *Scrubs.*

- **Enterprising**—Do you consider yourself persuasive, good at convincing others, and interested in sales, political, public speaking, competitive, or leadership positions? As you might guess, enterprising interests often score highly on the Extraversion personality measure.[8] Think Tracy Flick from *Election.*

- **Conventional**—Do you consider yourself methodical, good at keeping accurate records, and interested in working with data, numbers, systems, and details? Think Angela Martin from *The Office.*

You can tally your work interests at the O*Net, or Occupational Net, Resource Center's Interest Profiler, brought to you at no cost courtesy of your very own federal government (specifically the U.S. Department of Labor, Employment and Training Administration): www.onetcenter.org/IP.html.

What kind of gender differences have psychologists found with regard to work interests? Some argue that it can be reduced to this motto: men and things, women and people (though as with personality, there is often more variation on these scales within the sexes than between). Specifically, these researchers discovered that men often had higher scores on the Realistic and Investigative interest scales, whereas women were higher on the Artistic, Social, and Conventional scales.[9]

Work Values

Another consideration in thinking about a career path is whether that job's values align with yours. Based on early work by two prominent psychologists,[10, 11] The Department of Labor has also has put together a tool on the O*Net Work Importance Profiler Web site to help you decide what your highest priorities are in a work environment: www.onetcenter.org/WIP.html. These values include:

- **Achievement**—Do you enjoy work environments where you can really utilize your skills to gain a feeling of worth and accomplishment from your efforts?

- **Independence**—Do you prefer being able to set your own timelines, make your own autonomous decisions, and implement your own ideas at work?

- **Recognition**—Do you seek to work in places where you are likely to advance quickly, where you can direct others, and receive credit for your work?

- **Relationships**—Do you like to work in settings where your colleagues are friendly, where you can help others, and where you don't have to compromise your moral values?

- **Support**—Do you prefer settings where your managers will give you opportunities for professional development, where they will stick up for you, and treat you fairly?

- **Working Conditions**—Do you most value certain aspects of the job, such as your pay and benefits, job security, and safety and do you value specific ways of working, such as working alone, keeping a fast pace, or having variety?

Interestingly, psychologists found that working women tended to value the intrinsic enjoyment and value of work (the personal satisfaction that comes from working above and beyond extrinsic factors such as competition, evaluation, or compensation) more than working men do.[12]

Looking for even more of that buzz word *synergy* when seeking a career field? Then this document will be *epic*—the PDF at this link combines the results of your work values and work interests scores with your desired level of ultimate education to provide even more focused ideas about potential career paths: www.onetcenter.org/dl_tools/WIL_zips/CL-deskp.pdf.

Work Knowledge, Skills, and Abilities

If Hollywood Week on *American Idol* has taught us anything, it is that many Americans have a very distorted sense of the true nature of their skills and abilities. For an objective and accurate assessment of some of your strengths, the following Web site—yes, again brought to you by the U.S. government by way of the O*Net Ability Profiler (www.onetcenter.org/AP.html)— allows you to accurately assess your skills in the following domains:

- **Verbal Ability**—How articulately and effectively can you communicate when writing or speaking?
- **Arithmetic Reasoning**—How proficient are you at logical reasoning and basic mathematical functions like addition, subtraction, multiplication, and division?
- **Computation**—How competent are you at basic mathematical functions like addition, subtraction, multiplication, and division?
- **Spatial Ability**—How well are you able to form and rotate images of objects in your mind?
- **Form Perception and Clerical Perception**—How quickly and accurately can you notice small details and minute differences in objects and pictures or in printed text and numbers, respectively?
- **Motor Coordination, Finger Dexterity, and Manual Dexterity**— How strong is your hand-to-eye coordination, and do you have precise motor skills when manipulating objects with your fingers?

Don't want to go to the trouble of taking all those tests? If you think you have a really good handle on your own skills already, the Department of

Labor's Career One Stop Web site (www.careerinfonet.org/skills) allows you to subjectively assess your abilities in areas such as social skills, problem solving abilities, technical skills, judgment and decision-making, managing resources, active listening and learning, critical thinking, scientific skills, reading comprehension, and computer skills. From there, the Web site crunches your input to display what job types would be a strong match for your abilities, ranked by how good a match it expects given your self-rated skill set.

For each of these four types of work self-assessments—personality, interests, values, and skills—they should be looked at as part of a larger body of data about yourself, including honest feedback from coworkers, bosses, family, friends, mentors, and guidance counselors about your strengths and weaknesses. We encourage you to not get too wrapped up in any one result from these self-assessment tests and particularly to not focus too much on any of the general gender differences described above, lest they deter you from exploring a career path that might be extremely rewarding. As Mark Twain, channeling Socrates, said, "The unexamined life may not be worth living, but the life too closely examined may not be lived at all."

2

What Would You Do If You Had a Million Dollars and Didn't Have to Work? Deciding What You Want to Be When You Grow Up

Peter: Our high school guidance counselor used to ask us what you would do if you had a million dollars and didn't have to work. And, invariably, whatever you'd say, that was supposed to be your career. So if you wanted to fix old cars, then you're supposed to be an auto mechanic.

Samir: So what did you say?

Peter: I never had an answer. I guess that's why I'm working at Initech.

Michael: No, you're working at Initech 'cause that question is bullsh*t to begin with. If that quiz worked, there would be no janitors, because no one would clean sh*t up if they had a million dollars.

Many recent and not so recent graduates are faced with a dilemma similar to Peter's in *Office Space*—maybe you are like him, stuck in a mindless job writing TPS reports, or maybe you are finishing up that liberal arts degree and are wondering how to translate that diploma into a career. In either scenario, you are likely trying to figure out how to maximize your strengths and career interests while avoid being forced into a McJob. Here are a few steps that might help you decide what you want to be when you grow up:

Use the Interwebs

A useful and free resource, compiled once again on the federal government's dime by the Department of Labor, is O*Net (for Occupational Net), which can be found here: http://online.onetcenter.org. This Web site will give you an astonishing amount of data about almost any given profession, from accountants to zoologists, including:

- the tasks and activities you would be required to perform,
- the tools and technology you would need to use,
- the knowledge, skills, and abilities you would need to possess,
- the type of context you would work in,
- the education and experience required,
- the types of work interests and values (remember these concepts from the previous chapter?) that are best suited for the job,
- the wage you could expect to earn, and
- the occupational outlook (how many people in the U.S. and in your state currently work in the field and how many openings are expected over the next year) plus links to additional information.

A number of other commercial Web sites also provide information about specific professions and companies—for example, Web sites like www .thevault.com and www.glassdoor.com offer "career intelligence." Always wanted to know what it would be like to work at Apple? Is the organizational culture at Vogue really as depicted in *The September Issue*? What kind of questions could you be expected to answer during an interview at St. Jude's Children's Research Hospital? These Web sites offer unvarnished—and unsolicited, so take it with a grain of salt—insight from insiders who have been there, done that, in the organization and have lived to tell and tweet about it.

Though collecting information and leads on the Internet can be a good investment of time, don't kid yourself into thinking this is all you can and should be doing. Career coach Michael Melcher encourages job seekers to "lessen your dependence on the Internet,"[1] as even highly qualified folks submitting applications online are going to have a hard time getting hired without first connecting with an actual person in the company. Which is where our second point comes in . . .

Harness the Strength of Weak Ties

An older but incredibly impactful and somewhat counterintuitive study by sociologist Mark Granovetter demonstrated that when searching for jobs, it is actually our acquaintances or our "weak ties" that often end up giving us successful leads more than our close family and friends, our "strong ties."[2] Think about it—if you are looking for a job as a museum curator and your best friend is a mechanical engineer, she will certainly *want* to help you out, but probably doesn't have the career connections in that field to do so. Moreover, because you two are so close, you probably share a lot of mutual friends, so there is a high degree of overlap in your networks, meaning she probably doesn't have a lot of unique contacts to share with you anyway, despite her best intentions.

However, the people you know only casually or fleetingly might instead be able to provide whole new networks outside of your own for job leads. Maybe a guy that you played coed soccer with last season happens to be married to the director of development for a local museum. Through that "weak" tie, she might be willing to introduce you or get your résumé in front of a hiring manager at the organization.

- This approach worked for a young woman who recently graduated from college and was having trouble finding a job in construction management until a fortuitous encounter at an aunt's tennis party: "A friend of my aunt's said, 'You seem like an intelligent young lady. One of my brother's friends owns a construction company in DC.' "[3]
- By the way, the power of this idea doesn't apply only in the business world—another body of research shows how weak ties more often than not can lead us to our significant other and can significantly influence our health, including our weight and smoking behaviors.[4]

There are whole business and online communities set up to help you mine these weak ties—for example, LinkedIn and, of course, the ubiquitous Facebook (though make sure you clean up those Cancun beach shots and any salty postings before beginning the job search since employers are almost certainly going to search for YOU). Additionally, most universities' career service centers maintain databases that you can use to search for alumni contacts in your same field. There are also myriad professional conferences, career fairs, trade shows, and other sundry networking events that ambitious women can attend to meet the very acquaintances that might help them nail a job down the road. Even in your personal life, activities such as religious gatherings, book clubs, weddings, happy hours, sporting events, gym workouts, volunteer work, and reunions can all provide casual but critical opportunities to expand your network.

The most important thing to remember is that network building isn't a one-time experience, and it's not a one-way street. For every lead and bit of helpful career advice you receive, always be willing to "pay it forward" to others through maintaining a vibrant and dynamic network. As business school professor and networking guru Herminia Ibarra has said:

> Most people are not very good at building networks and only start doing it when they really need it, like when they are feeling isolated or they need a job. Network building is huge for people moving into bigger leadership roles. It's very important both for perspective and for getting things done.[5]

Informational Interviews

Once you've solidified your strong ties and found ways to proliferate your weak ones, you are probably in a position of having the contact information for a couple of individuals currently working in your dream field. Our own former career service center at Rice University offers the following questions to ask during this interview, along with advice for how to make that initial cold call and how to properly follow up with a thank you note[6]:

- **Job description:** What are the typical responsibilities and duties of this job? What would a typical day be like? What do you most like about what you do? Least?

- **Qualifications:** What skills, education, training, attitude, or experience are necessary? What type of personality does it take to perform this job well? How well suited is my background for this type of work?

- **Work environment and conditions:** What is the psychological environment like? Will I have my own office? In what part of the country am I most likely to be located? Is frequent travel required?

- **Organizational structure:** What would my place be in the company hierarchy? Who would my boss be?

- **Entering the field:** Is there a training program, or would I have to work my way up from the mailroom? Is there a professional association for this field that you would recommend I join? Do you know the entry-level salary ranges for this type of work?

- **Earnings and outlook:** What are the typical long- and short-term earnings? Will opportunities in this field continue to grow? What are the toughest problems facing the industry?

- **Preparation:** If you were a college graduate today, how would you approach the career search in this field? What publications or periodicals do you suggest I read to learn current trends in this field? What kind of work experiences, paid or unpaid, do you recommend?

- **Contacts:** Who are some of the employers who hire entry-level graduates in this area? Where are they located? Do you know of employers who offer internships to college students interested in this work? How did you learn about this job? Is that the way others have learned of job openings in this field? Based on our conversation today, what other people would you recommend I speak with? May I have your permission to use your name as a referral in contacting them?

Of course, this goes without saying, but treat this as a real interview, even though you are the one asking the questions. That is, be on time, well-dressed, polite, engaging, proactive, and always follow up with a thank you note . . . because even if you're just going in to gather data, you never know how the interview might pay off down the road if you impress the boss. Take this story, relayed by Nell Minow, the co-founder of the company Corporate Library:

> I once hired somebody who wasn't looking for a job. A guy called me to ask me some questions about some corporate governance issue and I just thought he was so bright. I said, "I'll put some materials together for you, and put them in the mail." And he said, "Can I come over and pick them up right now?" And I said, "Wow, are you looking for a job?" And he said, "Well, I'm in an internship right now." And I said, "If you are looking for a job when the internship ends I'm going to

hire you." And I did. I just like that kind of initiative. That's really important to me.[7]

A Day in the Life

So maybe you've outgrown "Take Your Daughter to Work Day," but there's no reason not to participate in internship or shadowing programs or to take an entry-level position in a company to see what knowledge, skills, abilities, and interests are needed to succeed in certain positions. Though not terribly glamorous, these positions can get your foot in the door of organizations and give you unique insights that you would never be able to get from an informational interview or any other type of data gathering.

For example, Susan Lyne, the C.E.O. of Gilt Groupe, had this to say when asked about how to really learn a trade by being an underling:

> In my early 20s, I talked my way into a job as the assistant to the editor in chief of City Magazine. It was a really useful role to be in, being able to watch someone doing the job you wanted was hugely valuable. It's actually something that I have urged a lot of younger people to do. What I always ask is, whose job interests you? Try and get a job as their assistant. Just to have a seat at the table, be able to listen in, listen in on the phone conversations, understand how their day works, what the job really entails. And one of the interesting things is that many times people discover, "I really don't want to do that." So it's useful on many levels to either allow you to see what kind of skills you'll have to develop and to be imprinted with a good leadership style, or it's going to tell you that you've got to rethink where you're going.[8]

3

Finding a Company That Fits Just Right

The story of Goldilocks and the Three Bears has been interpreted as a cautionary tale intended to convince little girls to be good and stay out of the woods. An alternative interpretation, however, is that Goldilocks was a feminist pioneer who got exactly what she wanted and survived an encounter with three bears. One message you might take away from the golden-haired protagonist's endeavors is that you too can and should find a place that isn't too big or too small, too hot or too cold—a place that fits just right.

Organizational psychologists have studied an idea called "person-organization fit" (P-O fit) that captures the compatibility between a person and a company.[1] The basic notion is that the more a person "fits" with their organization, the happier they will be when they work there and the less likely they will be to want to leave their jobs. Yes, this is essentially the workplace equivalent of the happy ending of relationship compatibility espoused by date-makers like eHarmony and Match.com. The research backs this up—across 21 studies, the extent to which workers experienced P-O fit was positively related to their commitment to the organization and intention to stay in the company.[2] So how can you find a company that is the right "fit" for you?

First, you need to decide what is important to you. P-O fit is defined in large part by the relationship between your values in relation to a company's values. Take as an oversimplified example the following question: are you a Mac or a PC? Some people value the graphical interface, sleek design, and anti-virus features of the Mac. Others prefer the more cost-efficient, software compatible, and ubiquitous PC. In the case of companies, organizational values might include the degree to which the company endorses the importance of people as individuals, informality in communication, innovation, profit-orientation, and socially responsible business practices.[3] A Mac working in a company of PCs might not be happy, just as an individual who values innovation and flexibility might not be happy in a company with a traditional model of work.

One way to get a sense of your work values (if you don't want to use the formal assessment tools we mentioned in the first chapters in this section) is to think about a time when you were happy at a job and ask yourself some probing questions: What are the tasks that you were doing? Who were you working with, if anyone? Where were you physically—an office, a meeting, off-site? What were the products or outcomes of the work you did? What rewards, incentives, or motivations were in place? Once you've pinpointed the elements of the job that made you happy, you may get a sense of what to look for. A less optimistic approach would be to ask yourself these questions in relation to a time when you were unhappy at work, but we are glass-is-half-full kind of gals. Nevertheless, if you are miserable at your current job, the thinking of an unhappy time approach might actually be more effective for you.

Second, you need to go into data-collection mode—yep, whether you like it or not you have now become an honorary organizational psychologist! Once you know what you want, you need to find out which companies can offer it to you. Several questions arise regarding the ways in which to get this information:

1. **Who can tell me about an organization's values?** If you are seriously considering a particular job, you should talk to as many people as possible about the organization. This means going beyond the recruiter or interviewer, who will hold only a single perspective, which will probably feel a little like the stereotypic car salesperson perspective, "selling" you the company by emphasizing its strengths and benefits. You should have informational interviews with other people who are currently working for the organization, people who left the organization, people who work in competing companies, and even clients or customers of the organization.

   Use your social network to find these friends and friends-of-friends. These people are experts in the subject matter that is your potential company and can tell you about the times that they have been happy and unhappy at the company. Weighing this information can help you to evaluate whether the values that lead to your happiness will be met at the particular company. Note of caution: If you are currently employed and haven't told your company you are considering a change, take care to choose conversation partners that are trustworthy and will keep the secret of your job exploration.

2. **When can I ask?** Your data collection process could start before you even apply for a job. Why waste your time in the application process if you can find out ahead of time that the organization isn't a good fit? In you decide to move forward with an application, you need to prioritize making a good impression that would facilitate getting the job. Nevertheless, you should certainly come to interviews prepared with questions that will help you get a sense of P-O fit.

   This means you probably shouldn't demand that an interviewer tell you how many days a week you can work from home or leave work early to pick up your kids from school, but you should feel free to ask an interviewer a broader question like, "What is the typical work day like for most people in this company?" Hold off on the more specific questions until you get the offer (see also the chapter on negotiation), except with trustworthy subject matter experts. It is in your best interest to manage the impression you are making in the interview process, and then to have a realistic preview of a job before you accept an offer.

3. **Where else can I look?** The Internet has opened up a whole new world of company-relevant data collection possibilities. Get to know the company's Web site backwards and forwards, paying particular attention to what is and what may not be part of the company's mission, strategic vision, and/or goals. These statements are generally carefully crafted sentiments of top management teams, and are designed to reflect something similar to the values of the company. Remember how passionate Tom Cruise/Jerry Maguire became when writing the mission statement that reflected his ideas about changing the business model in sports management?!

   The main purpose of these sometimes-hokey statements is to provide direction and guidance regarding the company's future policies, practices, and procedures. Indeed, research suggests that mission/vision statements can be related to actual behaviors of leaders in organizations. It may be valuable to know, for example, whether "valuing diversity" is a component of your potential company's strategic plan, as this could be evidence that there is money and support behind diversity-related efforts. Additionally, *Working Mother*,[4] MSN,[5] *USA Today*,[6] and NAFE[7] have also compiled lists of "best places to work" for working mothers and executive women.

4. And perhaps the most important and least-considered question: *What should young women look for in a company?* Given the unique challenges of sexism, stereotypes, and work-life balance that will be discussed throughout this book, you may want to pay close attention to both formal and informal aspects of the company that are unique to women.

Gender-Specific Formal and Structural Cues

How Many Women Are There in the Company?

Compared to women who work in organizations that have similar numbers of male and female employees, women who work in organizations that are predominantly male tend to encounter more challenges. These "token" women feel very aware of their gender and wonder whether they were hired because the company needed to fulfill a quota rather than because they were qualified for the job.[8] Coworkers and supervisors sometimes see token women as uber-feminine, and gender differences in work styles and preferences can become exaggerated. Because there are few other women to connect with, token women sometimes feel socially isolated.[9]

If the company you are courting is overwhelmingly male, you should consider whether that environment is one in which you are likely to be happy and successful. We are *not* suggesting that women should avoid male-dominated organizations entirely; indeed, the effects of such decisions en mass could be problematic. Some women prefer to work with men and find that this kind of environment fits their work style perfectly. Eden's friend Hannah is an orthopedic surgeon and has worked for the past five years in an all-male residency program in a field that is overwhelmingly male, sports-oriented, and just generally guy-ish. And Hannah LOVES this job. She is a take-no-prisoners kind of person, she has a direct style of communication, and she loves power tools like the ones they get to use in orthopedic surgeries.

So the ultimate question goes back to the issue of fit—will you as an individual person with your own particular views and values be comfortable working in a male-dominated company?

What Kind of Positions Do Women Have in the Company?

In addition to overall representation in the company, you might also consider the kinds of positions that women have in a company. A company could have a lot of women but not actually promote many women into top-level positions; this is actually fairly common. On average, women are hired into companies at about the same rate as men, but over time women are substantially less likely to be promoted and thus are underrepresented in positions of power.[10]

If you are interested in moving up the ranks of an organization to management positions, you should take a closer look at the representation of women in those kinds of roles at your potential company. A study of Fortune 500 companies by Catalyst, a nonprofit research firm, found that the number of women on the boards of directors in 2001 predicted growth in the percentage of female corporate officers in those companies five years later.[11]

What Are the Organization's Formal Policies That Are Relevant to Your Personal and Professional Goals?

Even beyond salary and retirement plans, the benefits offered by companies vary as much as the amenities offered by hotels—you should find out whether your potential company is more like a Holiday Inn Express or a Crowne Plaza. Also keep in mind that not all amenities mean the same thing to every person; the "Express" kind of company may suit you fine, as long as it has what you really need to be happy (e.g., telecommuting). The following is a list of formal benefits and questions to consider:

- **Flextime:** Can you come to work at 10 and leave at 6 or come at 7 and leave at 3?

- **Compressed work week:** Can you work 10-hour days and get every other Friday off?

- **Telecommuting:** Can you work from home? How often? Does the organization pay for home office equipment?
- **Part-time work:** If at some point you want to go part-time, is this possible?
- **Concierge services:** Can you drop off your dry cleaning or packages to mail at your office?
- **On-site athletic facility:** Can you work out during your lunch break?
- **On-site child care center:** Can you bring your kid to work with you and have lunch with them?
- **Subsidized local child care:** Is there financial support for families?
- **Child care information/referral:** Will the company help with the difficult task of finding a quality child care provider?
- **Emergency child care services:** Does the company provide help when your typical source of care falls through?
- **Paid (or extended) maternity leave:** Does the company go beyond what is required by law (12 weeks unpaid)?
- **Paid (or extended) paternity leave:** Do men get to take it too? This could help curb coworkers' resentment.
- **Elder care options:** What kind of support for eldercare does the company offer?
- **Health insurance:** Who can be covered? What level of coverage? What is the employer/employee responsibility?
- **Sexual harassment policies:** Are there formal, written policies in place? Are the procedures for dealing with harassment clear and reasonable?
- **Sexual harassment training:** Are people actually aware of the policies?
- **Diversity training:** Does the company attempt to develop employee cultural competence? Do the company leaders attend?

Are Structures of Responsibility in Place?

Having policies that support women and families is a great start, but research suggests that these policies may be more influential when they are supported by structures of responsibility. These structures ensure that a specific person, group, or office in the organization is directly accountable for equal employment goals. In a longitudinal study of over 700 companies, having a specific position (e.g., a director or executive officer for diversity) or group of people (e.g., a diversity committee or task force) who were responsible for diversity efforts was correlated with growth in the proportion of women and minorities in managerial roles.[12] In other words, companies with structures of responsibility helped women to advance.

Gender-Specific Informal Culture of the Organization

Policies and structures won't do you much good unless you feel comfortable making use of them. For example, does the fact that the company has a policy of "casual Fridays" mean that the organizational culture is supportive of a relaxed work environment, or that you can talk to your boss in a casual manner? Watch the movie *Office Space*, and you'll know the definitive and resounding answer to this question is absolutely not!

Is the Company Supportive of Women?

Once you have the job offer in hand, it may be time to ask some of your trusted female subject matter experts, such as current or past employees, to give you the scoop. Use the data you collected about the company to help start the conversation by asking an open-ended question: "I noticed that there are [or aren't] a lot of women here. How do you feel women are treated relative to men?"

Is the Company Supportive of Work-Life Balance?

Whether or not you plan to have kids or take care of your aging parents, you will certainly have a life outside of work. And because women who hold jobs spend more of their nonwork hours on household labor than do men who hold jobs,[13] it may be particularly important to understand whether employees can feel comfortable taking advantage of programs that are offered. One item from a popular work-family culture scale exemplifies this dilemma: "Employees who use flextime are less likely to advance their careers than those who do not use flextime."[14] Ask your subject matter experts what proportion of employees use the policies that are most important to you (e.g., onsite child care) and whether other employees are resentful. This kind of information is a critical part of understanding what it is *really* like to work in the company you are considering.

Keep in Mind

The company culture may or may not be aligned with the culture of the particular department/division/workgroup in which you will be working. The company could be male-dominated and unfriendly to families, but the "operations" division could have a lot of women with kids who have developed a mini-culture that helps them make it work. Make sure you ask the same questions about both the company overall AND the specific area in which you will be working.

Happily Ever After?

Once you've completed your stint as an honorary organizational psychologist by collecting every piece of data about the company you can, you should compare your personal values and characteristics to those of the organization. Is there a good amount of P-O fit?

Let's face it. Life isn't a fairy tale and there's a reason why "work" is called "work." But like the golden-haired adventurer-protagonist of the Goldilocks story, finding a company that fits just right might make the hours you spend at your job a bit more *bear*able.

4

Preparing a Picture Perfect (but Not Pink) Application Package

Professor Callahan: Do you have a résumé?

Elle Woods: Yes, I do. Here it is.

Professor Callahan: It's pink.

Elle Woods: And it's scented. I think it gives it a little something extra, don't you think?

—From Legally Blond

So you've figured out who you are and what you want, you've done your research to know what kind of industry and company you want to work in, you've developed and leveraged your network, and you're finally ready to conquer the world. *How can I lose?!* Despite all this admirable effort, you still haven't passed the first hurdle—getting your résumé in front of folks who actually have the authority to hire you and then impressing them in an interview.

There is an (over)abundance of Web sites, books, blogs, and well-meaning but sometimes misguided friends and family members who will give you an endless amount of advice about how to create the perfect application package; for example, whether to create a functional vs. chronological résumé, what are the best "action verbs" to use, and how long it should be. We are not about to try to compete with this full panoply of literature and counsel, primarily because the research hasn't fully addressed these questions. Instead, what we'll try to do is give you the lowdown from a social science perspective of what seems to work and what doesn't.

Getting someone to actually read your application may be one of the hardest parts of the job search these days with the burgeoning use of scanbots that many large organizations and government agencies now use to efficiently—if not effectively—screen thousands of applications electronically.[1] C.E.O. of Macy's Terry Lundgren discusses this new reality, giving these brilliant suggestions when asked to provide job-seeking advice for young applicants:

> No. 1, don't be so specific about what you want in this environment. Don't be so choosy. You should get your résumé out there to a fairly broad number of companies and businesses to give yourself a chance.
>
> No. 2, use every single contact you can come up with. Use your friend's father's uncle who knows somebody who's an assistant to the college recruiter. Use whatever contact you have to try to get your résumé read. That's the most important thing—just to get it in front of people.
>
> Because we're all flooded with, of course, thousands and thousands of résumés in a company of our size, and getting your résumé read is not an automatic. And so do what you can do to get it in front of the people who matter who will read it. It's not the C.E.O. typically, by the way; it's the H.R. person or the head of recruiting or head of training or whatever.
>
> Third, don't stop there. Don't just do it online, because it's easy to do it online. Do it online and then put it in an envelope and send it to the top company that you're interested in pursuing. And then follow up with a phone call, and talk to the assistant and say: "I just want to make sure that my résumé's getting read. I'm very interested in your company, and it's really important to me. And I just want to know—can you give me advice?—is there anything that I can do to get my résumé in front of your boss?" Whatever you have to say, just to show the most important thing—that you're hungry. And to convince them, maybe you use a little of your acting skills.[2]

Résumés

Now that you've internalized that advice, start thinking about what types of résumés will work best for the career field you are hoping to join. Take advantage of this opportunity! It is really the one and only time you have complete control over the image and impression you give to the company, so says a psychologist from down under, Jim Bright. His main take-aways include[3]:

- Sentences are generally more useful than choppy bullet points, and simultaneously show that you actually understand subject-verb agreement and can avoid dangling participles.

- Don't use colored résumé paper because it looks gimmick-y (sorry, Elle).

- Including hobbies makes you no more or less likely to get short-listed and since space is at a premium, he suggests omitting them. We agree, as other research seems to indicate that including them might make women look like a dilettante.[4]

- Being "flexible, open to opportunity, persistent, and optimistic" are more important than rote goal-setting when looking for jobs. As the founder of Southwest Airlines, Herb Kelleher, said, "We can train people to do things where skills are concerned. But there is one capability we do not have and that is to change a person's attitude. So we prefer an unskilled person with a good attitude . . . to a highly skilled person with a bad attitude."

- The top factors that reviewers like most in résumés are whether the applicant has relevant experience, whether the layout is easy to read and presented well, and whether the candidate has appropriate qualifications. Conversely, the three biggest concerns often cited in poor résumés are having a lack of or irrelevant experience, having a poor format that is difficult to read, and having a résumé that is too brief, that lacks information.[5]

Another organizational psychologist, Michael Cole, has also looked at how recruiters view applicant résumés and his research reveals that:

- Recruiters will look at biodata (psych speak for "info you put on your résumé") such as GPA, list of academic honors, and membership in scholastic societies to surmise your intelligence and your level of conscientiousness . . . so think twice before leaving off a too-low GPA.[6]

- Additionally, they will be looking at your social/extracurricular activities, such as community volunteer work, Greek society membership, holding elected office, to determine whether you are high in extraversion and low in neuroticism.[7]

- Obviously, having strong academic, extracurricular, and work experience credentials is useful for heading out into the job market if you are a recent graduate, but even if you have poor academic record, the other two factors might be enough to compensate.[8]

- If a recruiter is looking to fill a job that matches on to the Conventional work interest (remember the six occupational interests from the self-assessment chapter?) like accounting, they are going to be focused on information in your résumé like GPA and academic achievement, which shows you are high in conscientiousness. Conversely, if they are trying to fill an Enterprising work interest type of job like sales, they are going to focus more on extracurricular and social activities in your résumé to determine your level of extraversion.[9]

- Finally—and falling into the category of we can be our own worst enemies—professional female recruiters in one study were more likely to rate male applicants as having more work experience than female applicants. Additionally, following the stereotype of women as caring and social, male recruiters were more likely to rate female applicants as having more extracurricular activities than male applicants.[10]

And, of course, advice that we hope goes without saying: don't lie, fudge, or otherwise distort information on your résumé; tailor it to fit the specific job you are applying for; and have a trusted colleague or friend take a critical eye to it to catch typos, assess readability, and make sure it is an accurate and positive reflection of you and all your experiences and qualifications. Moreover, some résumé experts suggest quantifying your performance (e.g., "automated internal record-keeping processes, resulting in a 27 percent reduction in annual operating costs"), listing education after work experience unless you are a very recent graduate, keeping them "tight, lean, and mean," and free from big blocks of text.[11]

Mind the Gap: Dealing with Résumé Gaps When Reentering the Job Market

Many women who have left the workforce for an extended period of time to raise a family wonder how to craft their résumés to explain the gap in employment while still remaining competitive. One option is to have a functional rather than chronological résumé that highlights your skills rather than the dates you've been employed, although trying anything too sneaky with fuzzy math will probably backfire on you. We think a better solution is to highlight all of the important ways you maintained connections and developed new skills while off-ramping. For example, you could highlight:

- that you maintained your certification or license if these are relevant to your industry while you were a full-time mom because your professional identity was important to you

- that you took continuing education credits, attended professional conferences, read relevant trade magazines and publications, and/or maintained membership in professional associations or networking events to remain current in developments in your field

- that you developed new skills while doing volunteer work, such as balancing the budget as treasurer for a local civic group or running a successful music club for your child's school that increased membership by 75 percent and doubled the club's budget through fundraising activities

No matter how long you've been out of the paid employment world, it is *never* too late to on-ramp or reenter the workforce when you feel the time is right. One of the proudest moments of Jennifer's life was sitting with her sisters and mom, Nancy, over the Christmas holiday a few years ago—her mom decided to apply for a job as director of discipleship ministries at her church and needed to prepare a résumé. As the family brainstormed all the accomplishments she had achieved over the last several decades (PTA president, the American Cancer Society's Relay for Life chair, treasurer of her Sunday school class, head of the school soccer club, volunteer of the year at the local therapeutic riding stable), the list went on and on and on. Needless to say, she got the position and is doing a phenomenal job in a role she was born for (and now that Jennifer's father is retired, she gets a certain kick out of being the primary breadwinner in the family again).

Cover Letters

For most applications, however, having a solid résumé as part of the package isn't enough—you'll probably have to create a cover letter. Sadly, there isn't too much psychological research on this topic, mostly because it is so hard to objectively score them—other than providing a writing sample, most cover letters simply provide information that is covered in your résumé and that you will cover in your interview. However, one cofounder of a small software firm claims that they ignore résumés outright because they are:

> "full of exaggerations, half-truths, embellishments—and even outright lies" and instead focus on cover letters because "they immediately tell you if someone wants this job or just any job. And cover letters make something else very clear: They tell you who can and who can't write."[12]

Despite this dearth of research, there are a few take-aways from the social science literature:

- Including competency statements—that is, specific information about your knowledge, skills, and abilities—in cover letters and résumés is generally a good way to increase the likelihood that you will get short-listed for a job.[13] One study manipulated the number of competency statements included by putting in sentences into applications for a sales analyst position in a pharmaceutical company to show competencies like sales market knowledge ("I keep in touch with the market by reading sales journals and magazines, as well as visiting supermarkets and other points of sale where products are sold. Last year I completed a research project entitled 'What makes a supermarket tick: Best placement or best product?' which looked at the dynamics of product placement in stores and the impact on sales."), as well as organization skills, motivation, communication skills, responsibility, and high energy. As expected, the more competency statements included in the application, the higher the reviewers ranked them and the more likely the candidates were to get called in for an interview.
- Because cover letters are a form of impression management,[14] some studies have tried to determine what type of ingratiation strategies

work best in cover letters. Specifically, they looked at *self-enhancement* (touting your academic credentials, record of responsibility, strong teamwork), *other enhancement* (discussing how much you respect the work of the person you are applying to work with), *opinion conformity* (mentioning how much you agree with the opinions of that person), and *rendering favors* (indicating that you will be happy to work free extra hours or perform tacks above and beyond requirements).[15] The authors found that any kind of strategy included on a cover letter is generally better than not having any at all, and the most effective tactic was self-enhancement and the least effective was favor rendering.

Letters of Recommendation

Want to know a dirty little secret about organizational psychologists working in academics? They generally kind of dislike letters of recommendation (saying they don't have a lot of utility, which is true), but continue to use them when evaluating their own profession come tenure time. Think about it—since the applicant has complete control over who they ask to vouch for them, it's only natural that they are going to pick former bosses, coworkers, and mentors who have really great impressions of them. As such, most letters are generally glowing, which is why this is more of a "select-out" than a "select-in" part of the application process and why a bad or even mediocre letter can completely torpedo an otherwise strong package. Moreover, letters of recommendation are subject to all kinds of biases, including prestige of the letter writer's institution, attractiveness of the applicant, and—yes—gender.[16, 17, 18]

In a fascinating but disturbing study conducted by our friends and colleagues at Rice, they found that letters of recommendation for actual female applicants were more likely to contain traditionally feminine descriptors (like affectionate, helpful, kind, sympathetic, sensitive, nurturing, agreeable, tactful, interpersonal, warm, caring, and tactful) and to talk about their families, whereas letters for male applicants were more likely to have traditionally masculine words (like assertive, confident, aggressive, ambitious, dominant, forceful, independent, daring, and outspoken).[19] Why is this important? Because a follow-up study they ran found that inclusion of these feminine descriptors made reviewers less likely to want to hire an applicant.

In sum, putting together a strong application package is one of the most critical steps in getting your foot in the door of an organization's hiring process. Not only can it determine if you will be short-listed for an interview, it can influence how an employer will treat you during that interview—interviewers who have a favorable impression of you based on your résumé will spend more time in the interview trying to "woo" you and sell you on the company.[20]

5

Nail It: How to Rock Your Interview

> I'm a people person, very personable. I absolutely insist on enjoying life. Not so task-oriented. Not a workhorse. If you're looking for a Clydesdale I'm probably not your man. Like I don't live to work, it's the other way around. I work to live. Incidentally, what's your policy on Columbus Day?
>
> We work.
>
> Really? The guy discovered the new world. I'm afraid to even ask about Victory Over Japan Day.
>
> —From You, Me, and Dupree

Congrats! Someone at your dream company was wowed by your résumé and cover letter and now wants to give you an interview. In this chapter we'll discuss the psychological research on what employers are looking for during the interview processes, supplemented by quotes from real-life leaders and executives from interviews conducted by *New York Times* editor Adam Bryant as part of his weekly "Corner Office" series (http://projects.nytimes.com/corner-office).

First things first—*do your homework*. We can't emphasize this enough. But don't just take our word for it . . . listen to Maigread Eichten, the President and C.E.O. of energy drink maker FRS as she describes landing her first internship:

> I went to business school, and I decided I wanted a PepsiCo internship. They were only taking one intern, so my shot at getting this Pepsi

internship was slim to none, because I had no experience. But I decided I wanted this internship and what I did was—I think about this all the time when I interview people, sort of, why don't they do this to me?—I researched all the people coming to campus to interview. I knew everything about them. I knew everything about Pepsi-Cola and the PepsiCo company. I knew everybody in the U.C.L.A. recruiting office and I wrote the story of myself as a brand and I came up with a whole talk about why Pepsi should hire me, and the assets I could bring.

I had called up the two or three people who had been Pepsi interns from other campuses, and I found out every single thing that they had done as interns. So I had done all that work before I took this interview. I was one of the four people they took back to New York for an interview, and I got this internship. I was probably also incredibly annoying, but I certainly was superqualified. And what I would say to my kids is, to get the job you need two things. You need the functional skills, but then you also have to be superprepared, and you have to have incredible passion. You have to make that person want to hire you. They have to have a reason to hire you. There's no excuse why you can't have that.[1]

Before you pack up to head to the interview, what should you bring with you? Extra copies of your résumé, letters of recommendation, examples of past work if appropriate for that industry, pen and paper for taking notes, questions you've generated from all the homework on the position and company you've already done ... and breath mints probably wouldn't hurt. Once you've arrived (10–15 minutes early ideally), it couldn't hurt to make pleasant chit-chat with the person who initially welcomes you, regardless of their rank—in fact, the C.E.O. of the clothing group Spreadshirt, Jana Eggers, says:

I'm also going to see how they treat the receptionist. I always get feedback from them. I'll want to know if someone comes in and if they weren't polite, if they didn't say, "Hello," or ask them how they were. I'ts really important to me.[2]

What You Say May Not Be as Important as How You Say It

Are you ready? Because the next few minutes are probably going to make or break your chances of getting hired. No pressure, of course, but anyone who's read Malcolm Gladwell's popular book *Blink* is familiar with social psychologist Nalini Ambady's work on thin slices of behavior. In a nutshell, her research and a whole line of subsequent studies have found that people only need a shockingly small amount of time—measured in minutes or even seconds—to make fairly accurate judgments about you and your ability to be successful in a job.[3, 4, 5] Bobbi Brown, founder of the cosmetics line of the same name, seems to intuitively know this, saying:

> When I interview someone, I know in the first two minutes if I like them or not. I find that if it's easy to talk to someone and I see an openness and honesty and integrity, then I usually hire them.[6]

How can we make these judgments so quickly and, seemingly, so accurately? It turns out that both your *vocal* interview cues (factors like pitch, pitch variability, speech rate, and appropriate pauses) as well as your *visual* cues (physical attractiveness, smiling, gaze, hand movement, and body orientation) correlate well with interview ratings and ultimate job performance because they impact the interviewers liking of you, trust toward you, and your perceived credibility, as well as perceptions of your conscientiousness, extraversion, and emotional stability.[7, 8] The big take-aways? Eye contact (though not to the point of staring), leaning in toward the interviewers, straight posture, appropriate attire, a pleasant smile, and hand gestures matched to emphasize a point are all HUGE.

- More specifically, what's generally a little discussed but surprisingly important part of the interview that can influence evaluations of you before you've even said a word? A *handshake*. Fact: women benefit more than men from a firm handshake, probably because of gender stereotypes that female applicants will have relatively weak and passive ones, so interviewers are pleasantly surprised when we give them a solid though not crushing shake.[9] Indeed, the same study found that the quality of an interviewee's handshake as measured by strength, vigor, grip, duration, and eye contact was directly related to hiring recommendations.
- Another important nonverbal behavior that can help you out? *Smiling*. Some research has found that applicants who smile during interviews get more positive reviews than those who don't. Why? It

seems as though interviewers associate smiling with high levels of extraversion, which is generally a desired trait in a work setting.[10] Of course, don't overdo it to the point of a freaky-maniacal-Joker grin, but it turns out that old camp song was right: "Whenever you're in trouble, it will vanish like a bubble if you only take the trouble just to S-M-I-L-E."

An effective way to make sure all your vocal and visual cues are firing on all cylinders during an interview? Have *a mock interview* session before the big day—most career service centers will offer this service, but if not, have a friend videotape you answering practice questions. Not only will this help you uncover previously unknown weird facial tics ("Wow, that licking-her-lips-thing seems to really work for Kristen Stewart in *Twilight* but it just makes me look weird"), but it can also help you think about what you'll actually say during an interview . . .

OK, So the Verbal Stuff Is Important, Too

. . . which clearly matters as well. You can't show up sounding like Dupree in the opening quote and expect to get the job no matter how great your handshake, eye contact, or smile. What are some of the most common types of interviews you might experience?

Behavioral Interviews

One of the most basic tenants of psychology is that the best predictor of future behavior is past behavior—as such, an incredibly popular form of interviewing is designed to look at how you preformed in past work experience to try to understand how you would do in the job you are applying for. The founder and C.E.O. of Teach for America, Wendy Kopp, clearly believes in this method of interviewing, saying:

> We've done a lot of research on the characteristics of our teachers who are the most successful. The most predictive trait is still past demonstrated achievement, and all selection research basically points to that. But then there is a set of personal characteristics. And the No. 1 most predictive trait is perseverance, or what we would call internal locus of control.[11]

Some of these questions might sound something like this:

- Tell me about a time when you had to solve a difficult problem (to assess *problem solving*)
- Describe a situation when you had a positive influence on attitudes and behaviors of others (to assess *motivation*)
- Give an example of a situation in which you knew there were more tasks than you had time to perform (to assess *organizational skills*)
- Give me an example of a time when you had to make an important decision (to assess *decision making*)
- What has been the biggest goal you've achieved in recent years and how did you achieve it? (to assess goal setting)
- Tell me about a time when you were in conflict with a colleague or classmate because you had trouble seeing eye to eye (to assess assertiveness/interaction)
- Tell me about the most frustrating time you've had relating a concept to someone (to assess communication)
- Give an example of a time when you were disappointed in your behavior (to assess self awareness)

All of these questions are taken directly from a very thorough Interviewing Guide put together by Jennifer's undergraduate alma mater, Southwestern University (http://southwestern.edu/offices/careers/docs/Interviewing_Guide.pdf)—they report that an effective way to respond to these types of behavioral interview questions is the STAR method. Specifically, for each question, provide some context and background on the *situation* or *task*, describe the *action* you took to address the problem, and define the *results* and outcome.

Here C.E.O. of Accenture William Green describes their behavioral interviewing process and tells a fascinating story of how they ultimately used it to select an unassuming applicant named Sam:

> I was recruiting at Babson College. This was in 1991. The last recruit of the day—I get this résumé. I get the blue sheet attached to it, which is the form I'm supposed to fill out with all this stuff and his résumé attached to the top. His résumé is very light—no clubs, no sports, no

nothing. Babson, 3.2. Studied finance. Work experience: Sam's Diner, references on request. It's the last one of the day, and I've seen all these people come through strutting their stuff and they've got their portfolios and semester studying abroad. Here comes this guy. He sits. His name is Sam, and I say: "Sam, let me just ask you. What else were you doing while you were here?" He says: "Well, Sam's Diner. That's our family business, and I leave on Friday after classes, and I go and work till closing. I work all day Saturday till closing, and then I work Sunday until I close, and then I drive back to Babson." I wrote, "Hire him," on the blue sheet. He's still with us, because he had character. He faced a set of challenges. He figured out how to do both.[12]

Situational Interviews

Rather than ask you about your past job experiences, employers may ask you to respond to a series of hypothetical situations or questions (e.g., "What would you do if you became aware that a coworker was stealing from your company?" or "How would you react to a difficult customer?" or "If you found a major flaw in a product that was due in a week to your client, what would you do?") This type of interview approach—called situational judgment tests by organizational psychologists—seems to work for the founder of Watershed Asset Management, Meridee Moore, who explains:

> We give people a two-hour test. We try to simulate a real office experience by giving them an investment idea and the raw material, the annual report, some documents, and then we tell them where the securities prices are. We say, "Here's a calculator, a pencil and a sandwich. We'll be back in two hours." If an analyst comes in there and just attacks the project with relish, that's a good sign.[13]

Similarly, Teach for America follows up successful behavioral interviews with situational ones. C.E.O. Wendy Kopp explains more:

> And then if it seems like someone would be a fit here, based on that, then we'll actually try to simulate the job. I used to hire people and then realize within two days whether someone was going to thrive or not. So I said, "Let's actually find out what we're going to know two

days in, before someone starts." We just send them a bunch of stuff that they would get otherwise on their first day and say, "Here are the challenges of the day." And we ask them to write up their answers, and then actually engage with them deeply so that we understand whether they have the skills that a particular role is going to require.[14]

Companies hiring employees requiring more technical skills may also ask brain-teaser type questions such as "Why are manhole covers round?" (the interview question made infamous by Microsoft), "How many gallons of white paint are sold in the United States every year?" or "Two robots parachute on a railroad track circumventing Mars. Write a program to make them meet."[15] Some companies may ask you to verbally reason out your answer or even draw your calculations on a whiteboard. In any event, they are not necessarily looking for you to provide the correct answer but are more interested in assessing your problem-solving, logic, and reasoning abilities.

Phone Interview

Many organizations may want to interview you by phone before taking the time and expense to bring you in for a site interview in person. Some are doing this simply because it is a cheap way to screen applicants out, but others are doing it because they are aware of the psychological research about the flaws inherent in interviews (more about this in the next chapter). The same basic interview tips apply, but a few more specific tips from CNN Money come in helpful here: don't wear pajamas. Even though your interviewers can't see you, you can see yourself and you will feel cognitively sharper and more professional if you are dressed up. Put call waiting on your phone and make sure any roommates know not to disturb you. Keep your résumé and any talking points in front of you in case you need to refer to them. Work to convey your enthusiasm through your tone of voice since the interviewers won't be able to use any visual cues to infer your level of passion for the job.[16]

Meal Interview

Some companies who bring you in for a multi-day interview will probably take you to lunch or dinner to get to know you in a more informal and casual setting. Make no mistake, however—this is not a social call and you are still under evaluation. The common sense rules apply here—use proper dining etiquette, make pleasant but not overly familiar or personal conversation . . . and this is probably not the time to indulge in beer and hot wings. As the C.O.O. of Quest, Teresa Taylor, relays:

> I never hire somebody without having a meal with them. I am absolutely convinced that that's how you see what people are really like. You can tell by the way they order, you can tell by the way they treat the wait staff, you can tell by the way they drink too much or what they drink—you can pick up all these lifestyle things that you can't get out of questioning them sitting in your office. Maybe they can't make a decision on what to order, or they're very snotty to the waitress. I absolutely have changed my mind on individuals after doing that.[17]

Group Interview

For companies that utilize multiple selection steps, a common interview technique is the group interview, where the organization brings multiple candidates into a room, introduces a problem or a topic for discussion, and then lets the group interact to monitor each candidate's leadership potential, collaboration and communication style, influence techniques, and group dynamics. This type of interview might be particularly tricky for women, as some research indicates they may be less likely then men to be selected as leaders in initially leaderless, mixed-sex groups.[18, 19] However, one study by our mentor, Mikki Hebl, has shown that the type of task greatly influences gendered leadership selection—in a very task-oriented, competitive task, women are less likely to be chosen than if the task involves cooperation and coming to agreement.[20]

Regardless of the type of interview you are preparing for, there do seem to be some universal rules:

Do Not Talk Badly about Your Old Boss
Says C.E.O. of *The Onion,* Steve Hannah:

> I hate it when someone comes in and they trash their former employer. They talk about how they were held back. They talk about how they

worked for a terrible boss, and the boss did this or the boss did that. I have no idea what makes people think this, but this happens often. People think that by telling their prospective employer that their previous employer was a complete slug, that somehow this is going to make me feel, what, sorry for them? I generally figure: Well, you didn't work hard enough, and apparently you weren't smart enough to figure out the system. That's probably why you didn't advance at your last job.[21]

Do Be Thorough but Concise

Says Executive Director of City Harvest, Jilly Stephens:

I'm looking for people who can express concisely what it is that appeals to them about the job they're interviewing for. That's always quite an interesting opening question, and I'm always surprised at the number of people who can still be answering it 15 minutes later.[22]

Do Convey Your Enthusiasm and Energy

Says Home Shopping Network's Mindy Grossman:

There are a number of things that are really important to me. One— and people laugh that I have this philosophy—is that you only hire Tiggers. You don't hire Eeyores. It doesn't mean they have to be loud, but I need energy-givers and I have to get a feeling that this person is going to be able to inspire people. Are they going to be optimistic about where they're going? Are they going to attract people who are like that?[23]

Do Always Prepare Yourself for an Odd-Ball Question

One of Jennifer's former clients absolutely insisted on asking a random final question at the end of an interview ("Tell me the most outrageous thing that's ever happened to you.") because he thought it assessed how well the applicant could think on his or her feet. Depending on the culture of the organization, this type of question may actually be institutionalized into the company's interview process—for example, the C.E.O. of Zappos.com, Tony Hsieh, admitted:

One of our values is, "Create fun and a little weirdness." So one of our interview questions is, literally, on a scale of one to ten, how weird are you? If you're a one, you're probably a little bit too straitlaced for us. If you're a ten, you might be too psychotic for us. It's not so much the number; it's more seeing how candidates react to a question. Because our whole belief is that everyone is a little weird somehow, so it's really more just a fun way of saying that we really recognize and celebrate each person's individuality, and we want their true personalities to shine in the workplace environment, whether it's with coworkers or when talking with customers.[24]

Similarly, C.E.O. of Timberland Jeffrey Swartz also includes a series of unorthodox questions and scenarios to assess his company's applicants:

If we're hiring a creative person from the outside, I like to call the headhunter a few days before and have them tell the person I'm interviewing, if it's an apparel person, to please wear their favorite pair of shoes to the interview ... One guy came in wearing a navy blue Armani suit, a footwear guy, and I said: "Wow. Is this the right outdoor thing?" And he said: "I got married in this suit. This is my favorite piece of clothing on earth because it's like a wedding dress but I get to wear it again and again. I don't wear it all the time because I'm not a suit guy, but you said to wear your favorite thing and explain it. It's because I got married in this suit." I thought, "I love this guy." It's a way of asking what matters to you, and what doesn't.[25]

It's Over! Now What?

After the interview questions are over, take the opportunity to ask both broad questions about the company's goals/culture and specific questions about the job itself, but nothing that a simple Google search would uncover. The Southwestern interview guide listed earlier in the chapter has a list of potentially helpful questions. Always conclude the interview by briefly restating your qualifications and asking when you can expect to hear a decision. Last but absolutely not least, take a business card from each of your interviewers so that you can follow up that evening with a written thank you note to each person and possibly an e-mail in addition to the written note if the decision is going to be made within a day or two and you want immediate impact. If you still haven't heard anything from the company after the agreed upon time, it would be appropriate and wise to call or e-mail your contacts to reaffirm your interest in the job and ask if they've made any decisions.

6

Math Class Is Tough: Overcoming Stereotypes and Biases during the Selection Process

There's a body of research that says you should conduct first- and second-round interviews by phone, not in person. This is because when you interview in person, many variables come into play that have nothing to do with competence. So is the person good-looking or not? Is the person dressed appropriately or not? Lots of factors can sidetrack you. There should also be a checklist of questions that you ask every candidate on the phone instead. Another issue is that most people believe they are good interviewers, and that they are good judges of character. They're wrong. That's why you see clones of the boss in some companies: everybody is white, tall and from an East Coast private school.[1]

—Guy Kawasaki, the cofounder of the news aggregation site Alltop

Anyone remember Teen Talk Barbie from the early 1990s? She said a lot of obnoxious phrases like "Will we ever have enough clothes?" and "I love shopping!" Ugh. But that's not what makes her infamous in the pantheon of terrible pop culture ideas—it's this doozy: "Math class is tough!" The American Association of University Women, rightly, criticized the doll, reflecting the burgeoning body of psychological research that documents how these gender stereotypes negatively impact women's aspirations and achievement. Here we'll talk about some of the most pernicious manifestations of these stereotypes during the hiring process and what you can do to mitigate their influence . . .

Stereotype Threat

Paul Davies may be one of the funniest men we've ever met, which is somewhat ironic since he studies a decidedly unfunny topic: how women can internalize stereotypes about their gender, leading them to be less ambitious, to be more anxious, and to perform more poorly on math tests—a concept he and his colleagues Claude Steele and Steven Spencer call *stereotype threat*. For example, in one of his studies Paul had half of the female participants watch stereotypic commercials showing a female character who dreamed of becoming a homecoming queen and half watch more neutral commercials for cell phones.[2] Sadly but predictably, those women who watched the gender stereotypical commercials were less likely to report wanting to be a leader on a subsequent group task. In a similar study, he showed that exposure to these stereotypic commercials caused women to underperform on a math test and to avoid math-related items on an aptitude test administered immediately afterwards.[3]

Even the environment of a room can be enough to negatively influence and reinforce women's stereotypes about math. In a different study, Paul and his colleagues found that women who briefly sat in a room with objects that conformed to the computer science stereotype—a Star Trek poster, comics, video game boxes, soda cans, junk food, electronics, computer parts, software, and technical books and magazines—were subsequently less interested in computer science and somewhat less likely to identify with the career field than woman who sat in a more nonstereotypical room with objects like a nature poster, art, water bottles, healthy snacks, coffee mugs, general interest books and magazines. Moreover, they found that women showed much more interest in working in a company with more nonstereo-typical decorations than with stereotypic objects.[4]

How to Challenge It

As alarming as this line of research is, research by our friend and colleague Jenessa Shapiro shows that there are several ways to prevent experiencing stereotype threat.[5] For example, if you are in a job interview for a position in a male dominated industry and start to feel stereotype threat influencing your performance in an interview or on a selection test, reminding yourself of examples of successful women in math and science can make you less susceptible.[6] Using humor to help cope with the stressful situation is another way to improve your performance because it lowers your anxiety.[7]

Additionally, when women who have high efficacy (psych-speak for a strong belief in their abilities) are directly confronted with explicit gender stereotypes, not only do they *not* fall prey to them, they seek to proactively challenge them and prove the stereotype wrong.[8] For instance, here is a real-life example by Barbara Krumsiek, the chairwoman and trained mathematician of the investment firm Calvert Group:

> I remember as a young teenager, my parents lived in a neighborhood in Queens. At Christmas, we would always go next door to the couple who were Russian immigrants to say "Merry Christmas." I remember the husband asking each of us what we wanted to do—what our favorite subjects were, and what we were studying. I said I loved math. He said, "Oh, girls, women don't do math." I remember being—whatever I was—13 or something, thinking very calmly to myself, "He doesn't know what he's talking about." [9]

Implicit Associations

Alan Alda is sexist. OK, so not really—we actually adore him from his M*A*S*H days, but check out this PBS video called *Hidden Motives, Hidden Prejudice* at www.pbs.org/saf/1507/segments/1507-2.htm where he interviews two prominent social psychologists—Brian Nosek and Mahzarin Banaji—about their fascinating research on the implicit association test (IAT). Here you'll see him take the IAT and learn that he more quickly associates "female" with "family" and "male" with "career"—a finding that is typical among most participants and is, the researchers argue, a sign of his implicit attitudes towards working women, which can operate separately from any explicit, conscious beliefs he might hold about them.

Further work in this new line of research shows that women have stronger negative associations with math-related words (like algebra, formula, and geometry) and with equations than do men.[10] Furthermore, they found that the more women identified with the female gender role, the less they identified with a math identity and the more negative attitudes they had toward math. Interested in uncovering *your* implicit associations, not just regarding gender, but on race, age, weight, religion, disability, and a host of other categorizations (including U.S. Presidents)? Check out the Project Implicit Web site to take the tests: https://implicit.harvard.edu/implicit.

How to Challenge It

Because the IAT is a relatively new field of study in social psychology, there is not currently any credible research to say if and to what extent implicit associations about gender influence interviewers' decisions during an actual selection process. However, some professions have taken steps to make the selection process completely blind so that biased attitudes—either explicit or implicit—can't affect the ultimate selection decision. Consequently, economists have found that "using data on orchestra personnel, the switch to blind auditions can explain between 30% and 55% of the increase in the proportion female among new hires and between 25% and 46% of the increase in the percentage female in the orchestras since 1970."[11]

Affirmative Action Stigmas

Although almost all Americans believe in equal opportunity, one of the persistent arguments against affirmative action is that it hurts the very beneficiaries it is supposed to help—or what has been called "attributional ambiguity" since women don't know if they've been selected for a position on the basis of their gender, their merit, or both.[12] Take this exchange between *30 Rock's* Liz Lemon, the head writer of a Saturday Night Live-esque show, and her coworker Pete as they discuss the role of affirmative action in her career:

> **Pete:** Well, well, well, never got a hand-up, huh Liz Lemon? . . . You attended the University of Maryland on a partial competitive jazz dance scholarship.
>
> **Lemon:** So?
>
> **Pete:** So, NCAA competitive jazz dance was created as part of Title IX—because of a program that favored women.

Lemon: Favored women to correct an imbalance.

Pete: You were only hired by the Second City because they needed someone who could remember to feed the theater cat.

Lemon: Oh no, Otis!

Pete: You're gonna hate this one: The only reason NBC picked up The Girly Show (Liz's first show as head writer) is because of flack they got from women's groups after airing the action-drama "Bitch Hunter."

Lemon: Oh my God! I'm no better than Toofer. Or Lutz with his B.S. Inuit ancestry. Or you, whose dad was in the Masons with Dave Garraway. I shouldn't be here!

Pete: This is America. None of us are supposed to be here.

Lemon: I need to dance this out.

The bad news is that a line of research by Madeline Heilman suggests that Liz's reaction to learning she was the recipient of affirmative action is not unique—she and her colleagues found that if women think they have been selected for a leadership role based solely on their gender and not merit, they are less likely to choose demanding assignments at work and they tend to devalue their abilities and contributions.[13]

How to Challenge It

The good news is that this same line of research shows that when women are provided with positive assessments of their abilities, they do not experience these same negative outcomes after being preferentially selected based on their gender.[14] Research that Jennifer and her mentor Mikki Hebl have conducted has also shown that to get more people onboard with the use of affirmative action, it is important to show not only how it will help those it targets but, importantly, those who are not the intended beneficiaries.[15]

Résumé Name Biases

Although overt discrimination is, of course, illegal, some folks might knowingly or unknowingly use gender, age, and racial cues after initially reading your name on a résumé to make initial judgments about your competency and qualification for a job. There is a long history of so-called "audit" studies that send out equally qualified résumés to employers with only the name on the résumé changed to evoke different gender and racial associations in order to see who gets more callbacks. One provocative study by economists found that "Brad" got called back almost 16 percent of the time (the highest rate), but "Aisha" only got called back about 2 percent of the time (the lowest rate).[16]

How to Challenge It

Well . . . short of legally changing your name for a résumé, there's not too much you can do about this one, unfortunately. However, if you do get your foot in the company door and are able to get an interview, our colleagues at Rice have found that there are some ways for stigmatized individuals to increase the likelihood of a positive interaction with their would-be employer.[17] For example, when you provide individuating information about yourself, the interviewer can see you and all your knowledge, skills, and abilities for who you really are and perhaps get over that initial stereotype. They also found that displaying increased positivity through nonverbal behaviors like increased smiling and an upbeat tone of voice and through verbal communication ("I'm excited about the possibility of working here") was also helpful in improving interpersonal interactions with potential employers during the selection process.

7

Compensation and Negotiation: Getting What You Are Entitled To

Don't tell Eden's boss, but when she got the phone call with her dream job offer she was so excited she didn't actually hear the salary that was offered. It wasn't until a few minutes after she hung up that she realized that although she had a job, she had no idea how much she would be paid. After a symbolic slap on the head, she recovered by sending an e-mail to request the offer in writing. Sigh of relief. And here's hoping he doesn't read this book. 'Cause that would be embarrassing.

Compensation is an incredibly important—and crazy-sensitive—aspect of work. Even though it was Eden's dream job, she may not have accepted the offer or stayed in the job if the compensation had been inadequate. We may choose a job because we want to make a difference, help people, or care for lost puppies, but at the end of the day, the vast majority of us are also looking to get paid. Insert pop music "It's all about the Benjamins, Baby!" here.

And here is one of the most important pieces of information we could share with you: women *still* get paid *less* than men for doing the *same* jobs. This is so important we need to say it again so you don't accidentally skim over it. **WOMEN GET PAID LESS THAN MEN.**

How Much Less?

The discrepancy amount depends on what types of job you look at, whether you control for differences in career interruptions, and at what level of company hierarchies. One statistic from the Department of Labor suggests that women in the United States earn about $.77 for every $1 earned by men in full-time year-round positions.[1] Some might argue that this gap is explained by the job and family choices of women. Nevertheless, in a study of nearly 10,000 graduates of MBA programs, women were paid $4,600 less per year than men in their first job.[2] This pay difference persisted even after controlling for prior experience, career aspirations, region, industry, and parental status. Importantly, the pay gap increases over the course of a career because women are less likely than men to be promoted into higher-paying jobs.

What's Driving the Pay Gap If Not the Job and Family Choices of Men and Women?

A lot of factors contribute to gender differences in salary, but two seem particularly critical. The first involves stereotypes of women and men. Women are stereotyped as communal in orientation, which means people-oriented, nice, and caring. Think Bree on *Desperate Housewives* or Emma from *Glee*. Men are stereotyped as agentic in orientation, which means decisive, authoritative, and assertive. Think a subdued Jack Bauer (from *24*) or Jack Shephard in his leader-of-the-island days (on *Lost*). Which of these stereotypes seems more like the ideal employee or leader in most jobs? Yup, you got it—the agentic, masculine ones.[3] So stereotypes of men are closer to expectations of good employees than are stereotypes of women, which means that women have to work harder to prove their competence. Given exactly the same qualifications (e.g., an identical résumé), the stereotypes of men will help them to get a higher salary than women.

In addition, the stereotype-based expectations of men and women ultimately shape men and women's behavior. Because people generally expect women to be communal and men to be agentic, men and women tend to fulfill these roles. For example, women tend to behave in ways that emphasize cooperation, whereas men are more likely to emphasize competition. These behavioral tendencies, together with the stereotypic expectations, shape the behaviors that are socially acceptable and those that are punished.

Women who behave in agentic or assertive ways, and to some extent men who engage in communal or nurturing ways, receive social punishments. Just look at some of the political figures of the past few years! Sonia Sottomayor was grilled and rebuked for her powerful and authoritative statements about the judicial system in her confirmation hearings for becoming a Supreme Court Justice. And remember the moment of the 2008 presidential primary season when Hillary Clinton got teary-eyed when talking about the state of the nation under the previous president? The response to this singular moment—which included debate about whether her "outburst" diminishes perceptions that she was too forceful or "shrill" or if it instead reflected the fact that she was "too emotional, too sensitive, or too weak" to be commander in chief—reflects the delicate balance women encounter between communality and agency.

These same gendered expectations lead to the emergence of a second factor that influences the gender pay gap: how men and women experience the negotiation process.

Women Don't *Ask* as Much

Most of the research evidence suggests that women share part of the blame for—and by implication, part of the responsibility for changing (!)—their lower salaries. Women are less likely than men to initiate negotiations. Because asking for money is perceived to be a selfish endeavor, it is also inconsistent with stereotypes of women as communal. Women who bargain on behalf of themselves worry about backlash that might result from being seen as too assertive.[4]

In addition, men think they are entitled to more money than women feel entitled to! A famous social psychologist named Brenda Major and her colleagues studied gender differences in entitlement, which refers to what people think they deserve.[5] In the first experiment, undergraduate students were told to indicate what they should be paid for a fixed amount of work. Men paid themselves more money than did women. In the second experiment, a different group of students was told to do as much work as they thought was fair given a particular amount of money. Women worked longer and produced more correct work than did men. These findings suggest that women feel less entitled to pay than men, which may be one of the reasons why women have a harder time beginning the negotiation process.

Unfortunately, Women Don't *Get* as Much

Across 21 studies of nearly 3,500 participants, men negotiated better salary-related outcomes than women.[6] This may be partly because women tend to be penalized more than men for asking. A series of experiments suggests that, compared to women who accept compensation offers without argument, women who initiate negotiations are perceived as less nice and more demanding and receive less positive outcomes as a result.[7] In other words, women's concerns about backlash are well-founded. But don't let this stop you from fighting the good fight!

Don't Give up the Fight!

Research also points to situations in which women feel more comfortable and are more successful in salary negotiations. For example, women reported feeling more comfortable initiating negotiations when the situations were framed as "opportunities for negotiation" as opposed to "opportunities to ask."[8] This may be because women felt it was more appropriate and polite to negotiate than to explicitly ask for a particular outcome. Women also felt more comfortable in general (and relative to men) when the negotiation situation was more clearly structured as opposed to ambiguous.[9] Finally, women performed better in negotiations when they were arguing on behalf of someone else than when they were arguing on their own behalf; women were better advocates for others than for themselves.

Based on a review of the research literature like that described here, Catherine Tinsley and her colleagues offered several strategies that women might take to ensure more effective negotiations. These suggestions are based primarily on the premise that, to maximize positive outcomes of negotiation and minimize potential backlash, women might work toward emphasizing both communality and agency—if women can communicate assertive competence at the same time as a caring demeanor, they may be able to garner the best outcome.

1. **Reaffirm aspects of yourself or your personality that are feminine in nature.** The basic idea here is to remind your negotiation partner that just because you are engaging in the assertive behavior of bargaining doesn't mean you aren't being "womanly" enough. If you approach a negotiation by focusing your request on the context of your team, for example, it may be more consistent with your and your

negotiation partner's gender stereotypes of women as nurturing and looking out for your teammates (i.e., it might be easier!). You can state that you need a raise to ensure that you can be better equipped for continuing to be a critical contributor to your unit/organization. Alternatively, you could engage in role-switching with a trusted colleague; you can each ask for raises on the other person's behalf. Since women are better advocates for others, this may result in a good outcome for everyone. Finally, it may help to do some mental reframing; convince yourself that your request is not selfish (*not* that there is anything wrong with asking for money you deserve!) and instead serves the larger goal of your family, workgroup, or organization.

2. **Deflect assertive behaviors away from your gender identity.** Women's negotiation sessions may also be improved by putting distance between yourself and the more assertive or dominating behaviors that are required in negotiations. To the extent that it is feasible, plan your negotiation discussion at a time when it will be perceived as less threatening, like when there is a budget surplus rather than in the middle of layoffs. It can also help to emphasize shared goals and interests; by using "we" statements rather than "I" statements (e.g., "We both want our team to excel. One way to accomplish this goal is to compensate team members according to the strength of their contributions."), you might actually deflect some of the potential negative reactions. If you can find ways to focus on the position rather than your gender, this could also be helpful in minimizing backlash (e.g., "In my role as a leader, it is critical that I ensure resources are allocated appropriately.")

3. **Change the gendered expectations.** In an ideal world, you wouldn't have to worry about gendered perceptions or your own beliefs about entitlement, and you certainly wouldn't have to compensate for other people's biases. So create that ideal world! Over time, you have the opportunity to modify—in small and not-so-small ways—the expectations of men and women in your organization. If you build strong social networks with powerful allies, you can build an organizational climate that supports gender equality in all decisions, including compensation.

General Negotiation Strategies: What Else Might Work?

In addition to the specific strategies for women, it might be helpful to consider some general suggestions for effective negotiations. Keep in mind that successful negotiations require that both parties feel that the deal is fair—you'll still have to work together, so make sure you preserve the relationship!

- **Identify your goals.** Know your ideal goals, as well would be acceptable. Also get some idea of your negotiation partner's preferred outcomes. Come with a written list and potential responses to denials if that will help.

- **Make a strong case.** Find relevant comparisons, both internal and external to the company, that help to justify the compensation you are requesting. Review objective markers of your own success and value to the company.

- **Use integrative framing.** Think win-win. Avoid ultimatums. And try to create a bigger pie rather than aiming for a bigger piece of a shrinking pie. ("Mmmm . . . Pie . . . "—Homer Simpson)

- **Consider multiple objectives.** Don't get stuck on salary if you are also interested in other aspects of compensation like retirement plans, company buy-ins, or other potential benefits (e.g., telecommuting or compressed work weeks). There may be more flexibility on some aspects than others. If changes are impossible at the particular moment, ask for a formally scheduled review of the request in a few months.

- **Follow up.** Maintain the relationship by expressing gratitude for anything you do get, even if it is just the time devoted to the discussion.

The pay gap is a persistent, persnickety problem that young women encounter in the working world every day. But being forewarned is being forearmed—understanding our own biases and those of the people with whom we work and negotiate is a first step toward pay equity.

8

It Was the Best of Times, It Was the Worst of Times: How Female Workers and Entrepreneurs Can Survive and Thrive in Tough Times

> This loss of a man's paycheck means that millions of families now rely on a woman's job to make ends meet. The persistent gender pay gap is adding insult to injury for families already hit hard by unemployment.
>
> —Center for American Progress[1]

Do you remember anything particularly notable about February 2010? If you were like us, you were living through the Soviet-area bare grocery store shelves and organized snowball fights that came to symbolize the SnowMG/Snowpocalypse/Snowmageddon madness here in the D.C. area. But an event more impactful actually occurred that month as well—it was announced that for the first time in American history, more women than men were nonfarm employees (64.2 million vs. 63.4 million).[2]

Hooray! Woohoo! We are women, hear us roar! . . . Right? For many women, of course, this is a bittersweet pill to swallow—although women's unemployment numbers also look better than men's during this recession and we are coming close to comprising more than 50 percent of the work-force,[3] these milestones are occurring while untold numbers of families are struggling to pay their bills. This best of times/worst of times paradox isn't terribly empowering as so many other women and men are suffering.

In addition to this painful reality, what are some of the less obvious downsides of the faltering economy?

Is Diversity Less Valued in Tough Economic Climates?

Most people don't get ideas for their dissertations while waiting at the dentist's office. But there Jennifer was in the fall of 2002, sitting in the reception area of her dentist and longtime family friend Dr. Lewright reading *Time* magazine when a quote from an unemployed Asian-American woman caught her eye: "Diversity in hiring has fallen away as a priority."[4]

Spurred by the idea that changes in an organization's economic situation could influence diversity dynamics, she set up an experiment to see how economics and diversity might intersect.[5] Specifically, half of the participants in the study were asked to imagine that they were applying for an HR manager position in a company whose financial outlook was promising whereas the other half was led to believe the company was faltering. They were then asked to conduct a series of "in-basket" exercises that were ostensibly in place to test how well they would do in the position but were really intended to measure how the economic climate influenced their attitudes toward diversity in the company.

What did we find? As expected, a negative economic outlook caused participants to rank diversity lower as an organizational priority than if the company was doing well financially. Additionally, we found that female participants and older participants in the study were more likely than the male and younger participants to believe that working mothers in the company shouldn't be penalized for being unable to perform after-work tasks such as picking up a client from the airport at night because of family commitments.

In perhaps our most provocative finding, we also discovered that economic climate influenced our participants' recommendations for hiring a marketing assistant—we had participants evaluate four applicants' résumés (pretested to ensure they were of equal quality) with names that we had also pretested to match preexisting gender and race categories ("Roydell Jenkins" for the black male, "Mary Catherine Pierce" for the white woman, "Celina Rodriguez" for the Hispanic woman, and "James O'Sullivan" for the white man). What did we find? When participants thought the organization was doing badly, they were more likely to recommend the white man, and when they thought the organization was doing well, they were more likely to recommend the minority woman. As such, it seemed to our participants that employee diversity was a "luxury" they could support when the economic outlook was bright, but when times were tough they fell back on the same gender and racial stereotypes.

What Are the Unique Stresses of Females as Breadwinners?

One advice columnist was upbraided by a reader for allegedly not recognizing the psychological toll of job loss on women:

> Dear Amy: You have expressed sympathy in your column to men who have recently been forced out of the workplace by the current economy. Yes, support groups for men who have lost their jobs abound, while those for women in the same situation are nonexistent. Frankly, this smacks of the old double standard: Men's jobs are important, women's are not. I am 57. On top of being dismissed by employers to whom I am now invisible, on top of being unable to continue to do work at which I am very, very good, I have to bear society implying that a man losing his job is a crisis; a woman losing hers is not. If men and women are equal in the workplace, then the effects of being thrown out of the workplace must also be seen as equal. Dismissing the psychological impact of job loss for women like me only adds to all the many other negative aspects of our situation.[6]

The reasons why the last year has been frequently dubbed a "he-session" or "man-session" aren't terribly surprising—during economic downturns, many of the industries hit most quickly are in male dominated professions such as construction and manufacturing whereas female dominated industries like health-care and education have been more stable.[7] But is this focus on male employment warranted? To some extent, the psychological research supports this concern about unemployed men's well-being, as men who perceive themselves as inadequate breadwinners report more depression and marital conflict and feel more time conflicts between work and family responsibilities.[8] But there is a growing body of social science literature examining the stresses and some surprising benefits of women who are the primary breadwinners in their family. This line of research focuses on six aspects of this unique role[9]:

(a) **Having Control**—Although most female primary breadwinners in the study reported feelings of appreciation and empowerment through being able to support their family and having greater say in family financial decisions, many also admitted that the gender stereotype role-reversal caused tensions in their marriages, particularly over control of the family purse strings and over housework, where despite their full-time work schedule, the women were still doing most of the "second shift" work back at home.

(b) **Valuing Independence**—Almost all of the study participants mentioned being independent and self-supporting as an integral part of their self-identity, and they valued knowing that they had skills that they could utilize to support themselves and their children if anything happened to their partners.

(c) **Feeling Pressure and Worry**—The women in the study almost uniformly mentioned the pressure of being the primary breadwinner as one of the greatest stressors they faced. Several women also noted that the "mommy guilt complex" they face is probably unique to women, as they feel financial pressure to work but societal pressure to stay home.

(d) **Valuing Partner's Contributions**—Many primary female breadwinners mentioned spending an inordinate amount of time making sure that their partners felt their contributions were important, even though their husbands continued to struggle with self-identity and esteem issues. Interestingly, for several of the women, this renegotiation of traditional gender roles meant redefining or outright rejecting the idea of "breadwinner" so that both individuals feel good about their roles.

(e) **Feeling Guilt and Resentment**—A smaller subset of the women in the study reported feeling immense guilt over feeling that they needed to be at home more to be better wives and mothers but still wanting to pursue careers. Other primary female breadwinners indicated feeling occasional resentment toward their partners who didn't contribute enough to family chores and household needs, who didn't seem to value their wife's contributions, or who weren't attuned enough to the family's financial situation and accumulated large amounts of debt.

(f) **Valuing Career Progress**—Most of the women in the study described themselves as ambitious, goal-oriented, and internally driven, and found it rewarding that they were making use of their advanced degrees and intellect. However, some of the female breadwinners noted that the discrepancy between their high levels of career achievement and ambition and their partner's lower levels contributed to frustration and struggles to understand the difference.

The Upside of a Down Economy

Whew. So given the bleak outlook of the economy and the many negative outcomes associated with it, are there any silver linings to be had?

Gender Equality at Home

Can the increasingly prevalent house-husband phenomenon produce a more equitable home situation where women and men equally share in the second-shift duties of childcare and housework? Recent sociological research indicates this might be a possibility, finding that men who aren't the sole breadwinners in their families are more likely to have gender egalitarian beliefs.[10] Unfortunately, it will take persistent work within our generation for this equality to be achieved, as other sociological research confirms that "gender trumps money," as women—regardless of the value of their paycheck—continue to do most of the household work.[11] However, given the dramatic rise of female breadwinners over the last few decades—they accounted for only 4 percent of married couples in 1970 but 22 percent in 2007, according to the Pew Research Center[12]—we are hopeful that women will continue to make strides toward equality and equity both in the office and the home.

More Female Entrepreneurs?

Will women who have been laid off or have seen their hours cut back start to consider the self-employed route to gain more control over and stability in their employment and working hours? For example, Jennifer's lifelong (almost literally—they are coming up on three decades of friendship) friend Laura has taken several effective steps to "recession-proof her life" by taking jobs in several different interesting sectors, including working in an art gallery, working with Whole Foods to give chair massages to harried customers, serving as a contract bookkeeper, and expanding her massage therapy business in two different Texas cities.

So is the current economic climate enough to prompt the next Debbie Fields or Mary Kay to start her own successful company? It is certainly possible, but research suggests this could be an uphill battle—psychologists have found that women tend to have lower entrepreneurial career intentions than men of similar backgrounds and educational levels.[13] The reasons for this are multifaceted, but some social scientists have pointed to the stereotype of entrepreneurship as a primarily male occupation as being one of the obstacles to more female involvement.[14]

- Promisingly, however, they found that when entrepreneurship was explicitly framed as requiring both masculine characteristics (being aggressive, risk taking, and autonomous) *and* feminine characteristics (being caring, enjoying networking, and humble), women were more likely to report having entrepreneurial intentions than if the career path was framed as masculine only. Focusing on the aspects that research has found that draw women to entrepreneurship—having an encouraging business partner, focusing on building professional networks, and focusing on protecting intellectual capital[15]—might help increase our ranks in this career path, too.

- Luckily, for those impressive and ambitious women who are looking to start or grow their own business, the resources and networks available to them have expanded tremendously. For example, one sassy Web site we love is by Carla Thompson, a former Silicon Valley marketing exec, and is called SharpSkirts.com, run out of her new hometown of Austin, Texas. Thompson says in an interview with *New York Times* writer Adriana Gardella (who writes the informative blog called "She Owns It" as part of the *Times'* "You're the Boss: The Art of Running a Small Business" series), "I got tired of reading articles that asked where the women entrepreneurs were . . . I was surrounded by them and knew they had an abundance of skills to share."[16]

Section Two

How to Make It Work When Navigating Interpersonal Relationships: Why the People Make the Place

Your fearless authors first met in the windowless basement of Sewall Hall at Rice University in Houston, Texas. Here we as poor but motivated graduate students forged enduring, supportive, rewarding relationships with each other and with supervisors and coworkers that helped us survive graduate school. Our experiences confirm recent findings from Gallup: the quality of these relationships helped us to be sane, happy, and productive.

Many organizations use Gallup's popular job satisfaction survey to assess the state of their workforce and one item in particular seems to make test takers snicker: "I have a best friend at work." It's easy to read this question and dismiss it outright—what is this BFF business? Are we in sixth grade recess again? Though on its surface the question might seem frivolous, Gallup has found that it is a powerful predictor of team success, desire to stay with the organization, productivity, and successful stress management.[1]

This best friend effect mirrors a robust body of psychological literature that confirms we humans are social creatures. One of the most fundamental human motives is a need to form strong and enduring relationships with other people. A task for any doubters: add up the number of hours a week you waste on Facebook learning that an acquaintance from elementary school had a cheese sandwich for lunch. And given that we are increasingly spending a majority of our waking hours at work, successfully managing interpersonal relationships on the job is key to achieving our individual and collective happiness and sanity. In fact, these work relationships are so important, they form a central tenant of organizational psychology: "the people make the place."[2]

Since leaving Rice, we've learned that positive work relationships with both men and women are crucial to our happiness. Because men tend to have access to more resources and more "ins" with power-holders than women, they can be particularly good mentors. Indeed, research suggests that male mentors can provide more instrumental (i.e., tangible) forms of support than female mentors.[3] Eden feels lucky to work with Dr. Jose Cortina, a formidable organizational psychologist who has given her feedback about classroom teaching, commented on drafts of manuscripts, and introduced her to movers and shakers in the field. Female coworkers can be particularly good sources of psychosocial support; some of the best informal and unpaid counseling out there may come from gal pals at work.

And although some of Jennifer's favorite people at work are women, she equally appreciates her male coworkers—in fact, she had gloomily resigned herself to the belief that one particularly charming male colleague, Phil, would only ever be a good friend until one day several years ago when she was surprised but delighted to learn that he felt the same way. Now one joyful October wedding later, she can personally testify that you never know what unexpected professional *and* personal developments might be in store for you when you take a job.

Relationships at work also include more structured forms. One of the most important relationships we have is with our direct supervisor. Research has demonstrated that the quality of our relationships with supervisors (sometimes called "leader-member exchange") affects a range of critical outcomes, from stress on the job to work-life conflict. We felt these effects very personally under the tutelage of our grad school supervisor, Dr. Mikki Hebl, who embodies the label of "wonder woman." She balances a strong, impactful research program on discrimination in the workplace with motherhood (three kids under the age of six), but always makes time to host pizza parties and goal-setting lunches. This supervisor has formed high quality relationships with supervisees that pay off in their happiness and productivity.

Alas, we are aware that not all interpersonal relationships at work go as smoothly as the ones we've described above. What if Mikki hadn't been the supportive, encouraging mentor she was and instead was threatened by having two young women working under her? What if instead of being a thoughtful colleague, Jose was blatantly dismissive of women? And what if instead of welcoming a dating relationship, Jennifer's coworker's advances were perceived as harassing?

To help young women harness the power of positive interpersonal relationships at work while mitigating the negative ones, this section of the book will describe challenges that occur when young women work with men, other women, and older workers, including topics such as:

- Working with queen bees (that rare but unfortunate breed of more powerful women who may try to undermine their younger counterparts)
- The mentor-mentee relationship (how can different types, and genders, of mentors support you professionally and personally)
- Balancing dating and work (when is it appropriate to date on the job and recognizing some of the common pitfalls)
- The gray to green shift (understanding older workers and helping them understand you beyond the slacker, over caffeinated, wired-in millennial and Gen X stereotypes)
- Interpersonal vs. formal discrimination (the difference between blatant, illegal discrimination and the more subtle, nonverbal variety)
- Sexual harassment (both the legal definition and the psychological and organizational impacts of experiencing it on the job)
- Meta-perceptions (or how what-I-think-you-think-of-me can dramatically influence how coworkers interact and understand each other).

Let's go see why it is that the people really *do* make the place on the job . . .

9

Dipping Your Pen in the Company Ink: The Pleasures and Perils of Dating on the Job

As fans of the American sitcom *The Office* are aware, the workplace can be an ideal setting for meeting a romantic partner, best evidenced by the will-they-or-won't-they Pam and Jim relationship finally culminating in marriage. However, viewers also witnessed the train wreck of the Dwight-Angela-Andy triangle as it brutally unraveled in front of their shocked but amused coworkers. Though fictional, do the intra-office shenanigans of the Dunder Mifflin Paper Company employees reflect emerging patterns in real-life workplaces?

National data suggest that they do. A survey by the Society for Human Resource Management showed that over a third of employees (37%) admitted being romantically involved with someone at work.[1] With the confluence of women entering the workplace at unprecedented rates, longer hours spent at work, a recruitment and selection process that nets employees with similar interests, personalities, and educational backgrounds, and Americans waiting later in life to get married, intra-office romances are on the rise.

We've witnessed the pleasures and perils of workplace romance with our own eyes. One of our college friends, Shannon, is a doctor who took a trip with several of her colleagues to rural Guatemala to help staff a clinic. She had seen these guys every day for months in their white coats and ties and barely noticed them, but the game changed the moment they matched their stethoscopes with rugged hiking boots. In the midst of the intense working conditions in the mountains of Guatemala, she fell hard and fast for one of her supervisors. Research confirms that workplace couplings are particularly likely to emerge in situations and professions where the stress is high, demands intense, and work environments physically close. This might all be fine and dandy, if not for one major problem: Shannon was married. As you might guess, their colleagues were less than thrilled by the romance.

There are two main reasons why this workplace romance was particularly problematic. First, studies suggest that coworkers and supervisors look down on intra-office dating when it involves infidelity. In one experiment, survey respondents evaluated 50+ different workplace romance scenarios. Across every scenario, the marital status of the people involved in the romance was the strongest predictor of observers' negative reactions.[2]

Second, supervisor-subordinate romances are particularly tricky. One partner may have influence on make or break decisions for the other partner, potentially leading to either preferential treatment (of course we think our romantic partners deserve a promotion!) or quid pro quo harassment (sex gets close to sexual harassment when it involves a supervisor and their subordinate). Even if the couple is able to avoid these outcomes, other people in their workgroup may feel inequity exists. In line with this, research shows that supervisor-subordinate relationships are more disruptive and less tolerated by coworkers than relationships between peers.[3]

Unfortunately, Shannon's workplace romance ultimately created personal angst, tears, and hostility that affected her patients and caught the attention of her direct supervisors, who put her on probation. The potential for workplace romance to have detrimental effects on performance perceptions was demonstrated convincingly in a recent series of experiments. Participants completed a "performance review" of a manager who was described as generally competent in several feedback forms. An e-mail was also provided that either gave general information about the manager or implied that she or he had engaged in sex-related behavior (e.g., flirting, dating, sex) at work. In the "sexy" condition, the manager was described as likely to "get along with everyone, especially employees of the opposite sex . . . if you know what I mean." Things should get more interesting once she or he settles in at this company. A manager who "makes things interesting" was perceived as less effective, productive, and promotable than a person with identical qualifications.

Then again . . . Eden's brother Ben fell for his future wife and mother of two cheek-pinching cute boys at a company party. He'd been communicating with her about a project via e-mail for months, all that time assuming incorrectly that "Sam" was a man. He was blissfully surprised when they finally met in person. Ben and Sam dated, married, and had their first child while working together for a small start-up company that was later sold for a big profit.

So how can you avoid the pitfalls of workplace romance without missing out on a great love? Given the increasing likelihood that such relationships might develop on company time, smart gals should consider several issues before jumping in to such a relationship:

1. **What is your company's policy, if any, regarding intra-office dating?** Some organizations outright forbid it, especially if one party is in a supervisory role, while others actively encourage it; some require the couple to sign a legal document protecting the company from potential litigation while others rely on the maturity of their employees to navigate potential landmines.

2. **What will your coworkers and managers think?** Psychological research suggests that most coworkers and managers will be encouraging of an intra-office romance if they think the couple is in it for the right reasons—love, commitment, and monogamy.[4] However, they are likely to be unsupportive if they believe one party is using the relationship to gain an unfair advantage in promotions or work assignments, if the partners have unequal organizational status (that is, if there is a perceived conflict of interest), if the romance negatively impacts the work environment, or if one or both parties are married.[5, 6] The negative reactions of Shannon's coworkers' to her infidelity can be contrasted with the fact that Ben and Samskriti's coworkers were members of their wedding party.

3. **Are you willing to leave workplace drama out of the romance?** Even the most supportive coworkers will be annoyed by workplace couples who are indiscreet in their PDA, who allow arguments outside of work to interfere with workgroup dynamics, or who abuse intra-office communication systems for cutesy or racy exchanges—another downside: your bosses and IT folks also likely have access to such transcripts.

4.   **Are you prepared for the consequences if things go awry?** In such a case, you may have to have face daily awkward or painful interactions with your former partner, particularly if they go on to date someone else in the company. In other scenarios, the organization may ask one of the parties to transfer teams, departments, or even offices. In the most severe outcome, one or both employees could be fired if they violated the company's stated policy on dating.

Given the potential negative outcomes—sexual harassment lawsuits, litigation from coworkers who feel one of the parties received an unfair work advantage, or the potential for an unprofessional office environment—why would a company actually encourage such workplace coupling? Research indicates there are several positive professional outcomes to be had from a romance between office peers: increased performance, creativity, and productivity (you want to look good in front of your partner, after all), enhanced commitment to the organization, and reduced absenteeism.[7] Ben and Samskriti commuted to work together—thus providing guaranteed QT in the mornings and evenings and qualifying them for carpooling benefits.

As with most areas of life, the best advice before pursuing such a relationship in the workplace is simple: just be smart about things. *The Office*'s long-suffering Michael should have taken such advice to heart before entering into an ill-fated affair with his boss Jan, who subsequently gave him a poor performance review. Only later does the realization hit him: "You expect to get screwed by your company. You never expect to get screwed by your girlfriend."

Cubical Cupids in Context[8]

- 75 percent agree that romantic relationships between peer coworkers are a-ok.

- 66 percent of men report being flirtatious at work compared to 52 percent of women.

- 35 percent of women report having had an office romance compared to 45 percent of men.

10

Mean Girls at Work: Coping with "Queen Bees"

The two women exchanged the kind of glance women use when no knife is handy.

—Ellery Queen

There is a special place in hell for women who do not help other women.

—Madeleine K. Albright

Women can be each other's strongest champions or harshest critics. We hope you find true friends and mentors among the women with whom you work, but the sad truth is that you'll probably also find some back-stabbing b**ches. Knowing how to spot these "queen bees" and what sets them off might help you cope.

How to Spot a Queen Bee

A "queen bee" is a woman who has power but does not share it with other women, who undermines rather than nurtures female subordinates, or who tries so hard to act like one of the guys that she isolates herself from other women. Queen bee behaviors may include taking credit for your work (think Sigourney Weaver in *Working Girl*) or criticizing your every move (think Meryl Streep in *The Devil Wears Prada*). These are the kinds of things that can make your blood boil and can ultimately make it impossible for you to advance in your company.

What Sets Them Off

It's not you, it's them. For real.

We wanted to understand why women might undermine each other, and thought a lot about what might set queen bees off. Our guess was that it probably had something to do with feeling threatened. Yes, this really goes back to the basic idea that we put other people down to make ourselves feel better. Women may feel a threat to their "special" position as the token woman among a male leadership team, or a threat to their self-confidence when they see other women as competition at work. If you are young, confident, attractive, and/or capable, your presence may be enough to set off a queen bee.

To study this, we brought undergraduate students into our research lab. We asked women to act as a "supervisor" for a fake "subordinate" who was supposedly named either Katherine or Kenneth. That "subordinate" was described as being either really great or not-so-great. You might think that people would complain about lousy subordinates, but guess again— women actually gossiped more about female (but not male) subordinates when those women were described in a positive manner than when they were described negatively.[1] We interpreted the finding that women gossiped about strong female subordinates to be evidence that the queen bee is set off by feelings of competition and inadequacy.

In another study, we told women that either only one person or multiple people could advance to a "leadership" position. When women felt it would be difficult to advance, they indicated that they would help out a man more than another woman.[2] To make sure our findings were not unique to undergraduates, we also analyzed data from the National Study on the Changing Workforce, which is a nationally representative survey of adults. In line with our expectations, we found that when women are tokens in their organizations, they receive less support from female supervisors than male supervisors.

Our findings suggest that in the very situations where women might need each other the most, they may be the least likely to help. This sad but true phenomenon is captured well by Vicki Ho, the general manager of Asia services for GE Healthcare Clinical Services, who lamented, "Women will not necessarily pull other women up with them when they get promoted. Someone who's broken open the doors to the senior level may still feel threatened by other women . . . the higher up you go, the more qualified people there are with like skills to your own. Some people react by cutting others down." (p. 4)[3] (For additional quotes and insights by Ms. Ho and 29 other successful female business leaders, be sure to read "The Next Generation of Women Leaders: What You Need to Lead but Won't Learn in Business School" by Selena Rezvani).

How to Cope

If women are most likely to transform into queen bees when they feel threatened, then we have the opportunity to reduce or redress that threat. This isn't about "playing dumb," but rather about managing interpersonal dynamics proactively.

1. **Respect hierarchy.** If she's your boss, she's your boss. If you are respectful of her position of authority, it is more likely that she will be respectful of your position as an actual person. This means you need to ask her opinion before charging down a new path on a project, and that you should defer to her in meetings with higher-ups or clients, listen attentively to her ideas, and laugh at her jokes.

2. **Don't be a doormat.** Being respectful doesn't mean you should forget that you have an opinion. Voice your suggestions and concerns in contexts in which they are least threatening: one-on-one with your boss or in team brainstorming sessions. If possible, frame your comments in such a way that they build from or strengthen the queen bee's ideas so she can save face. If you absolutely and fundamentally disagree with her, you should say so as kindly and deferentially as possible. Saying "with all due respect" doesn't work (it can actually convey the opposite), so instead you might try something such as "I see a lot of positives in that idea. One concern that the clients/customers/project lead might have is X."

3. **Gently renegotiate the relationship.** Once you have conveyed respect and competence by following steps 1 and 2, you'll be in a good position to push for a more positive working relationship. One way to do this is to ask her advice on a work-related task or invite her to coffee to talk shop. When all else fails, it may be time to be direct. Sometimes the fastest way to break down an interpersonal

barrier is to express concern or hurt. Yep, think "I" statements. You might try something like, "I've been feeling like I might have done something to upset you. It's really important to me that we have a good working relationship. Can we talk about what is going on?" Keep in mind that, despite this person's behavior, she could become an advocate in the long-term. She worked hard to achieve her position and may be simply protecting her turf. Take away the threat, and the "queen bee" may actually be a powerful champion.

Let this also be a warning to all you future power-holders. Let's reject our own fears and insecurities. Let's help each other rather than holding each other down! And no, we are not professional cheerleaders. Remember what Lindsay Lohan said in the movie *Mean Girls*: "Calling somebody else fat won't make you any skinnier. Calling someone stupid doesn't make you any smarter. And ruining Regina George's life definitely didn't make me any happier. All you can do in life is try to solve the problem in front of you."

The Worst Kind of Bully[4]

- 37 percent of workers have been bullied
- 72 percent of bullies are bosses
- 57 percent of targets are women
- 40 percent of bullies are WOMEN

11

The Gray to Green Shift: Understanding Older Workers and Helping Them to Understand You

In her starring guest role on *Saturday Night Live* in 2010, the 88-year-old Betty White reminded millions of young fans everywhere that just because they qualify for senior citizen discounts doesn't mean old people can't perform their jobs under pressure. Just as convincingly, 28-year old Hope Solo blew fans and competition away as a goalkeeper on the gold-medal-winning U.S. Women's Soccer team for the 2008 Beijing Olympics before returning to the United States and advocating for better childhood nutrition in public schools, proving that young people can be strong role models. Despite these remarkable members of different generations, research suggests that older and younger workers do not always get along; if Betty and Hope had to work together, it could get ugly.

As unique as it may seem to work with someone like Betty White, the likelihood that 28-year-olds will work with 80-year-olds is increasing. The U.S. Census Bureau has projected that the population of individuals 65 or older will more than double in the next 50 years. Moreover, shrinking retirement plans and increasing life spans mean that you could very well be working with people from your parents' AND your grandparents' generations. Unfortunately, research suggests that interactions between people from different age groups can be strained or even contentious. Age dissimilarity in the workplace has been associated with negative outcomes such as bad moods,[1] poor communication,[2] and intentions to leave the organization.[3] Sadly, it has been stated that generational diversity in the workplace has created a "psychological battlefield."[4]

What Makes Interactions between Older and Younger People So Difficult?

Like gender, age is a readily observable characteristic that comes with baggage. This baggage is based to some extent on genuine differences in values, perspectives, and personalities for people of different ages and generations. In addition to these actual differences, we have expectations about people based on their age and expectations about what they think about people of our own age group. These stereotypes and metastereotypes can affect how we treat people in different generations and how they treat us.

Who Are "Young People," Anyway? A Generational Primer

> Traditionalists believe in the chain of command. Baby boomers operate with their own command. Gen Xers are working towards a change of command and Millennials don't command, they collaborate.
>
> —Lancaster and Stillman, 2002 p. 17

When people talk about a "generation," they are usually referring to a group of people who were born around the same period of time in the United States and thus have in a common historical/cultural experience. Many kids born in 2010 are likely to have a cell phone and laptop before they finish elementary school. It stands to reason that these kids could feel differently about technology and communication than people who didn't grow up attached to electric outlets. Some of the generations and shaping experiences that may be most relevant to you in your workplace are described in Table 11.1.

Keep in mind that just because your grandma gets her kicks by playing Yahtzee and watching TV doesn't mean that everyone her age would prefer to do so. Importantly, statistics about groups of people are typically averages that do not apply to all the members of that group. Nevertheless,

TABLE 11.1
Characterizing Members of Different Generations

Approx. Year of Birth	Labels	Shaping Experiences
1926–1938	The Silent Generation, Traditionalists	Fathers Were in World War I, Childhood in Great Depression
1939–1960	Baby Boomers	World War II, The Civil Rights Era, Time of Opportunities
1961–1981	GenX, Baby Busters	Dual-income Families, MTV, Faltering Economy
1980–2000	GenY, Generation Me, Millennials	September 11, Reality TV, the Internet
2001–2011	Gen Z, Gen Tech, Digital Natives	Social Media, Higher Education, Global Recession

some research suggests that there may be some overall, average-level differences between individuals from younger and older generations that can help us to understand each other.

How Can Young People Better Understand Older People?

Challenge Your Own Stereotypes

You may believe, as most Americans do, that older workers are resistant to change, lack energy, and are technologically stunted.[5] We call out "stereotypes" on this one! These beliefs do not accurately characterize all older workers. Instead, although research suggests that as people age they may lose some cognitive abilities related to memory and processing speed, they actually *gain* important knowledge that is relevant to performance on the job.[6] And you may be interested to know that small changes begin around 20 years of age, so you can stop being so impatient.[7]

Remember That Age Is Just a Number

Chronological age and subjective age mean different things. Someone could be 65 but act and feel like a 50-year-old, so avoid making assumptions about people based on numbers.

Try to Consider Where They May Be Coming From

One of the biggest potential sources of conflict between Boomers and Millennials may be from differences in values about work. For example, survey research suggests that work is more central to the lives of Boomers than Millennials.[8] Boomers are more likely to stay with the same company over the course of their career and so may be critical of what they perceive to be behavior that reflects a lack of commitment to the company, like flexwork or job-hopping.

How Can Young People Get Older People to Understand Them?

Be Aware of Stereotypes

An episode of the popular show *60 Minutes* portrayed young people as "narcissistic praise hounds now taking over the office." Moreover, some empirical research is fueling the battle. Based on surveys of 1.4 million people between the 1930s and the twenty-first century, one set of prominent scholars concluded that "Managers should expect to see more employees with unrealistically high expectations, a high need for praise, difficulty with criticism, an increase in creativity demands, job-hopping, ethics scandals, casual dress, and shifting workplace norms for women."[9] Using a sample of over 100 studies with the same measure of positive self-views, the self-esteem of college students in 1994 was significantly higher than the self-esteem of college students in 1968. These findings have been extended to the millennial generation: people in their 20s and 30s are described as having an inflated sense of themselves.[10] Yup, the picture of young people isn't exactly pretty. You can combat many of the negative stereotypes proactively by demonstrating concern for others or receptivity to feedback.

Make the First Move

One of the easiest ways to reduce stereotyping is to get to know people for who they actually *are* beyond whatever category they happen to belong to. If you feel your age or the age of your coworkers is getting in the way of your working relationship, invite them to coffee or lunch or happy hour. Find out what their interests and hobbies are and what they like/don't like about the job, and share your own preferences. Psychologists call these kinds of details "individuating information" that can set people apart from stereotypes about their group and reduce biased behaviors. Moreover, any points of commonality that arise in this kind of conversation can help to break down barriers that emerge when you have to work together again.

Unique Considerations for Young Women

Being young is one thing, but being a young woman may be something else altogether. Somewhat differently from our mothers and grandmothers, we tend to expect to be treated the same way as our male colleagues—we grew up after the feminist movement and have benefited from the efforts of our foremothers on many fronts, including the workplace. We think we can be superwomen who balance jobs, families, work out sessions, and friends with ease! And damnitalltohell, we're going to make it work!

Older people, however, may have been born during a time when breadwinner-homemaker roles were definitively and inextricably gendered. Popular TV shows, which both reflect and influence culture, in the 1950s were *Father Knows Best* and *The Donna Reed Show*. Take a second and compare the images of women in these shows to women in your favorite shows—in our case, *Buffy, Alias,* and *Grey's Anatomy*. The differences in the lives of women illustrated in television are remarkable.

Many of your older colleagues probably helped to fight for women's rights, or at least joined the "equality" train a long time ago. But some of your older colleagues are probably still influenced by the world in which they were raised. They may find it somewhat unsettling, perhaps at an unconscious level, to see you leading projects, foregoing motherhood, taking work by the balls, or doing other not-so-traditional things. This means you might want to handle your relationships with older coworkers with care: help them to see that you are a worthy coworker, supervisor, or subordinate by demonstrating your competence respectfully. Respect goes a long way with any generation, and should be used liberally.

12

Networking: It's More Than an Internet Connection

Have you ever played the "Six Degrees of Kevin Bacon" game? You start with the name of a movie star—say Salma Hayek—and find a way to connect her, through the appearances she's made in their career, to a movie with Kevin Bacon. So you might say that Salma was in *Fools Rush In* with Matthew Perry, who was in *Friends* on which David Arquette once guest-starred, and David Arquette was in *Scream* with Neve Campbell who was in *Wild Things* with Kevin Bacon. Whew! It only took three actors to connect Salma to Kevin (and yes, we are on a first name basis in our minds).

These kinds of connections extend way beyond the bounds of the silver screen. A classic social experiment tested the "Six Degrees of Separation" theory which serves as the empirical basis supporting our silly game.[1] Experimenters asked a sample of men and women from the population to send a message to a random target person using only friends or acquaintances who really are on a first-name basis who would be the most likely to know the target person. This process started in Wichita, Kansas, and Omaha, Nebraska, and ended in Sharon, Massachusetts. The number of stops between strangers in Nebraska and Massachusetts ranged from 2 to 10 with a median of 5. When we first learned of this experiment we were blown away! Sure, movie stars are connected, but how on earth could a midwesterner in the 1960s be connected to a stranger on the East Coast by only a few people?

Part of the answer is simply a matter of math and probability deemed "the small world problem." The average person comes into contact with hundreds of people over the course of a few months (not to mention all of our Facebook friends), and there is a small chance of overlapping connections. Facebook and LinkedIn do this sort of connecting for us. By considering the people to whom we already have ties, Facebook performs the freakily-psychic feat of "recommending" new "friends" for us. An additional part of the explanation for the "small world" phenomenon is the fundamental human motivation for social connection—as social beings, we crave genuine connections with others. This could be because modern forms of happiness involve meaningful relationships, or because our evolutionary ancestors relied on each other for physical survival.[2] Our lives are clearly embedded in interconnected social networks. But how do social networks emerge at work, and how can we network our way to our personal/professional goals?

Networks at Work

> Position yourself as a center of influence—the one who knows the movers and shakers. People will respond to that, and you'll soon become what you project.
>
> —Bob Burg

In the world of work, networks—whether within a department, division, organization, or industry—take on important meaning. Social network researchers study these webs by asking employees within a particular unit to list the names of people that fulfill particular criteria like:

- Who provides you with the inputs you need to do your job?
- To whom do you distribute the outputs of your work?
- With whom do you talk frequently about work-related topics?
- From whom do you ask advice?
- Who do you consider to be close friends?

These questions get at different kinds of networks, each which reflects a particular type of relationship between people. The first two items reflect workflow, the third communication, the fourth advice, and the fifth a friendship network. Your position in these kinds of networks can have huge implications for your experience and success at work. Major social network position attributes include:

Centrality: In a given network like your company or work unit, how connected are you to all the other members? Being in a central position (i.e., a "hub") in a network can be useful in and of itself because it means you're in the know.

Criticality: In a given network, is your position interchangeable with someone else's or are there few alternatives? In other words, if you were to be taken out of the network, would people still be able to do their jobs or communicate with each other? Being critical in a work network is a unique kind of power.

Boundary Spanning: Are you connected to more than one network? If you have strong connections to people in different networks, you can rule the world! Okay, maybe not the entire world, but your position can help you to get work done in new ways, innovate new ideas, or even find a new job.

What Do the Networks of Women Look Like?

It has been argued that one of the reasons women have a harder time than men reaching the highest levels of organizations is because they are excluded from social networks that give them access to promotions. The whole idea of "the good ole boy network" was based on anecdotes about men being hired or promoted simply because they played golf with the male boss. Indeed, research suggests that men and women's networks differ in ways that can affect their advancement.

A network study in an advertising company showed that men tend to have stronger relationship ties with men than women do with women.[3] In addition, a survey of 140 employees of a newspaper publishing company suggested that with regard to interaction networks, overall, women were less central in the overall organization network, in networks dominated by men, and in the network of power-holders. That is, women were less central in some networks than men. Importantly, centrality in these networks predicted promotions over the next three years—women were less likely than men to be promoted.[4] It seems clear that networks can provide information and relationships that support careers.[5] If you're interested in moving up, you might want to think about improving your own social networks.

Network It, Girl!

> More business decisions occur over lunch and dinner than at any other time, yet no MBA courses are given on the subject.
>
> —Peter Drucker

The term "networking" generally refers to efforts intended to establish effective relationships with key people internal or external to your company. A survey of alumni from an MBA program over a 35-year period suggests that men and women report engaging in a similar amount of networking behavior, but these behaviors have different consequences for their career success.[6] For example, whereas engaging in professional activities seemed to improve compensation for men, it actually reduced women's compensation. So what kinds of networking strategies might work for women?

Develop Different Kinds of Networks

Friendship networks and workflow networks are not necessarily aligned; networks can be social (i.e., who do you go to for talking about your life?) or task-oriented (i.e., who do you go to for the things you need to do your job?). If you have a diverse set of relations, you may have more resources to draw on in relevant situations. One set of connections might be useful when you need advice about how to deal with an unethical boss, and another set of connections might be useful when you want to put your name in the hat for a developmental opportunity.

Make Yourself Central

We told you about the power of network centrality—take advantage of it! Networking involves working toward increasing your visibility within the network. You can accomplish this by socializing at company events, taking on high-profile assignments, or volunteering for committees that do work that will appeal to most members of the network.

Reduce Distance to Powerful Others

Location within company is related to influence—being in the right place in a company increases knowing how to get things done. If there are currently two connections between you and the boss, try to make a direct connection. It may be appropriate to share a particularly good example of your work with the boss, or to communicate with him/her more frequently to reduce the distance between you. But keep in mind that upward ties should be balanced with relationships with peers and subordinates. They may not be the "movers and shakers" but many of these individuals are the "doers" who are essential for your own performance on the job.

Become a Boundary Spanner

Maintain external contacts and participate in the community to keep your options for innovation, collaboration, and job opportunities as open as possible. In our chapter on job searches, we mentioned that weak ties are particularly powerful ways to optimize the benefits of networking.

The way of the world is meeting people through other people.

—Robert Kerrigan

Whether you are looking for a new job, seeking advice, looking for social support, or needing information to do your job, the interpersonal networks in which you are embedded can determine your effectiveness. Attending to these social networks may help you get exactly what you need.

13

Subtle, Yet Significant: Contemporary Forms of Sexism in Interpersonal Interactions

When you think about gender discrimination, you may picture a sign that says, "Men only" or a judge telling a female attorney that, "women belong in the kitchen, not in the courtroom." We flash on the 1980 movie starring comedy giants Dolly Parton, Lily Tomlin, and Jane Fonda called *9 to 5*. Three women band together to overthrow their boss who has demeaned, criticized, and ultimately underestimated each of them. It may feel dated, but it's a classic.

This type of overt sexism is also dated, but classic. For better and for worse, this traditional form of sexism has morphed into a much more subtle form. On the "better" side, women really are much less likely to encounter directly sexist statements than we were 30 years ago. On the "worse" side, the contemporary kind of sexism is problematic because it is difficult to identify, assess, prosecute, and eradicate. It is easy for us to point to statements like "women don't belong in the courtroom" and say that *this* is sexism. It is much harder for us to know whether being left out of happy hour invitations, passed over for promotions in favor of equally qualified male colleagues, or ignored in team meetings can be attributed to our gender.

What *Does* Sexism Look Like in the Twenty-first Century?

Traditional beliefs about women reflect ideologies that women are best suited for household and childcare labor. In other words, a traditional widespread belief about women is that they should be homemakers. Researchers studying this kind of "old-fashioned sexism" ask participants to indicate how much they agree with statements like, "women are generally not as smart as men" and, "when both parents are employed and their child gets sick at school the school should call the mother rather than the father."[1]

Since the feminist movement, there has been a substantial increase in the proportion of women who work for pay outside the home and corresponding increases in social norms to appear to be nonsexist. These changes have lead to shifts in beliefs about women. People now generally want to appear nonsexist, but may secretly or unconsciously hold negative feelings or beliefs about women. Some of the major aspects of these beliefs include denial of continuing sexism, negative reactions toward women's demands for equality, and resentment about "special favors" for women. Researchers who study "modern sexism" ask people to indicate how much they agree with statements like, "discrimination against women is no longer a problem in the United States" and, "it is rare to see women treated in a sexist manner on television."

To understand how these contemporary sexist beliefs translated into sexist behaviors, a social psychologist from Penn State named Janet Swim and her colleagues asked male and female undergraduate students to write brief entries about any "gender-related incidents" they experienced in a diary at the end of each day over a three-week period.[2] Women reported between one and three incidents each week, whereas men reported about one incident in the same time period. Some of these gender incidents were traditional in nature; for example, one student reported that a male friend said, "You're a woman, so fold my laundry." In addition, women reported being exposed to demeaning language, such as a comment that an action was "stupid women's lib shit." Finally, women reported feeling sexually objectified by references to their body parts, sexual acts, and threats of sexual contact. For example, one woman was complimented on the belt she was wearing and a man said, "Forget the belt, look at the rack."

Sexist beliefs are clearly communicated to women in a variety of negative interpersonal comments. Nonverbal behavior can also communicate the same demeaning or sexually objectifying beliefs. T-shirts made for women exemplify one such behavior by depicting an arrow pointed upwards and stating, "My eyes are up here." More subtle kinds of negative interpersonal communication, such as decreased eye contact, increased interpersonal distance, and attempts to end interactions prematurely can also demean women.[3]

Importantly, research also shows that sexism can manifest in ways that *seem* to be positive. A form of bias toward women called "benevolent sexism" reflects beliefs that, as the mothers of our children and as our own mothers, women should be protected, cherished, and revered. People who are high in benevolent sexism might agree strongly with statements like, "Many women have a quality of purity that few men possess" and, "In a disaster, women should be rescued before men."[4] Generally, this looks a lot like paternalistic or patronizing behavior—like a how a parent talks to a child and might manifest in sexist behaviors like calling women diminutive names (e.g., "sweetheart" or "honey"), protecting women from dangerous or challenging tasks, or implying that women might be overwhelmed by stating, "don't worry your pretty little head." But even these subtle, potentially positive behaviors can have negative consequences for women at work.

If Discrimination Is Subtler, Does That Mean Its Consequences Are Better?

The change in discrimination from overt to subtle in form has, unfortunately, not yielded better outcomes for women. A friend of ours, Sarah, designed her dissertation to answer the question of whether traditional/ formal types of discrimination have worse outcomes than the modern/ subtle types of discrimination. Undergraduate women came into the lab to participate in what they thought was a study about assessment in hiring decisions. In the "formal discrimination" conditions, participants "accidentally" overheard the assessor say that there was (or was not) sexism in the study. (Specifically, the assessor said, "I don't know why we are getting so many women in here as participants. I don't know why we keep collecting their data because we aren't gonna hire one. I don't like the thought of having a woman consultant.") In the "interpersonal discrimination" conditions, the assessor behaved in subtly negative ways toward the participant by using: decreased amounts of eye contact and smiling, and increased amounts of rudeness, frowning, and hostile tones compared to individuals that were not in this condition. The results showed that women performed worse on the task when the assessor treated them negatively than when the assessor was sexist.[5] In Sarah's study, the outcomes were actually worse for women who experience subtle discrimination than when they encountered more obvious forms of sexism.

Such outcomes seem to extend to the benevolent forms of sexism, too. We did two studies to assess the job-related outcomes of benevolent sexism.[6] In the first experiment, men and women worked on a task while ostensibly communicating with another person via video Skype. Their partners were actually experimenters posing as participants in the study. These "partners" treated the actual participants in a manner consistent with traditional (hostile) sexism or benevolent sexism. In the hostile sexism condition, the "partner" told the participant that "Just let me do it. I know this is hard for girls (guys). I don't want you to screw this up." In the benevolent sexism condition, the "partner" told the participant, "Let me help you with this. I know this kind of thing can be hard for some girls (guys). I don't want you to struggle too much." In a third condition, the "partner" didn't say anything. The results suggested that both types of sexism lead the participant to feel that they were less competent than they did in the no communication condition. In this study, benevolent and hostile sexism lead participants to question their own abilities.

We also wanted to understand whether these experiences affect how women see themselves in the real world outside of the laboratory. We asked working women to complete questionnaires that asked them to evaluate their self confidence. In addition, we asked them to indicate how often their supervisor does the following things: (1) "protects me from unpleasant news, independently of my wishes," (2) "assigns me easy tasks so that I don't have to struggle," (3) "insists on helping me even when I don't need it," (4) "lightens my workload when it is not necessary," (5) "gives me less work so that I don't get overwhelmed", and (6) "calls me 'sweetie', 'honey', or other diminutive terms." There was a strong, negative relationship between the amount of benevolent sexism that women reported and their self-confidence; benevolent sexism undermined how women evaluated themselves.

The point is this: just because it is subtle doesn't mean you should dismiss it.

How Should I Handle It?

The subtlety of sexism can make handling it particularly problematic. It may seem easier to brush it off and keep on truckin'. We agree with the keep on keeping on part, but we worry about the pernicious effects that unchecked subtle sexism might yield.

The First Step Is Admitting They Have a Problem

Despite stereotypes that women are "oversensitive," most women question their judgments when they encounter ambiguous sexism. In one study,[7] pairs of undergraduate women worked together on a series of tests. One of the women got feedback that they had performed poorly and that, "Like most women, you exhibit traditional thinking when creative thinking is more appropriate." Neither the woman who got this feedback, nor her partner on the task, indicated that sexism took place when experimenters asked aloud. In other words, women minimized the sexism that was possible. However, when their statements were private on a written, anonymous form, both the woman and her partner indicated that sexism took place. This suggests that women minimize sexism so they don't look like complainers. Importantly, however, women who minimized discrimination blamed themselves for failure and rated themselves as less creative—in other words, they took the negative feedback to heart.

Take a Direct Approach

Confronting prejudiced statements by expressing dissatisfaction to the person who made the remark may be an effective way of making change. In a series of experiments involving racial discrimination, confrontations reduced the likelihood of discrimination in a subsequent task.[8] You might try something simple like, "It made me uncomfortable when you said. . . ." However, be aware that this kind of confrontation can be a little dicey, since people who make such statements may be disliked.[9] The double-edged sword—you may be successful in reducing sexism, but you may have to deal with some backlash.

Take an Indirect Approach

An alternative route would involve a less direct type of confrontation. One option would be to enlist the help of an ally who (a) has more power than you and/or (b) doesn't care if the sexist person likes them (e.g., doesn't have to work with them or depend on them for the job). Confrontations by majority group members (such as white people and men) can be just as effective in reducing prejudice as confrontations by targets themselves. Another indirect option would be to address subtle sexism with subtle signs of displeasure. For example, you might refrain from laughing at jokes that are somewhat sexist (even if they seem a little funny).

As another example, if someone asks you to clean up after a meeting or bake cookies for an event (or other gender-related stereotypic behaviors that are not your responsibility), you could respond by saying you're busy working on your job. This is an indirect kind of response that may nonetheless convey the point that gender stereotypes do not apply and are not welcome. If you feel the sexism is escalating, or getting in the way of your ability to do your job or in the way of your psychological health and well-being, you may want to seek the help of folks in human resources or a trusted mentor to help you manage the problem in a more formal way.

Warning: Don't Fight Fire with Fire

Our first instinct when hearing offensive comments or jokes about women is to come up with equally offensive zingers about men. We speak from experience when we say it really is better to take the high road. She's not proud to admit it, but Eden gave into her dark side and let the zingers fly fairly recently. A colleague made a (possibly benign?) statement about how women might have a harder time getting work done when they became mothers. Angry about the stereotypic assumption implied by this comment, Eden (embarrassingly) responded by saying, "I guess that's men's excuse during football season." Her colleague stammered and blushed and felt horrible. And of course, so did Eden. Like Meg Ryan concluded in *You've Got Mail*—it wasn't worth it, no matter how good the zinger felt at the moment it zinged. Fighting sexism with sexism simply promotes sexism.

Sticks and Stones

Not all nursery rhymes are based in reality. This should actually be somewhat comforting given the weird things we tell our children about getting baked in ovens and cradles falling from trees. Words and even nonverbal behaviors really can hurt you. Over time, hearing negative things about women can affect how we see each other and ourselves. Find a way, for yourself and all the other women who may be affected, to make change in your workplace.

14

Let's Talk about Sex . . . ual Harassment: Your Rights and How to Use Them

It could start as an icky feeling in the pit of your stomach or a few goose-bumps on your arm. Something just feels *wrong*. The imaginary, yet incredibly important, boundary between your comfortable and uncomfortable zones has been crossed. When these physical and psychological reactions follow interpersonal experiences at work, they could be signs that you are encountering sexual harassment.

According to the Equal Employment Opportunity Commission (EEOC), a government agency that enforces civil rights laws in the workplace, sexual harassment is form of gender discrimination that violates the Civil Rights Act of 1964.[1] Specifically, sexual harassment involves, "Unwelcome sexual advances, requests for sexual favors, and other verbal or physical conduct of a sexual nature constitute sexual harassment when this conduct explicitly or implicitly affects an individual's employment, unreasonably interferes with an individual's work performance, or creates an intimidating, hostile, or offensive work environment."

If you haven't personally experienced sexual harassment, you might be thinking something like "How dumb would someone have to be to request sexual favors from someone they work with? Even the clueless boss on *The Office* knows he can't do that." (Just check out season 2's episode on the topic.) Unfortunately, this stuff happens way more often than we'd like to think. In the year 2009 alone, nearly 13,000 sexual harassment claims were filed with the EEOC. And despite Demi Moore's convincing portrayal of a female harasser in *Disclosure*, the vast majority (84%) of claims are filed by women. It follows that sexual harassment is a real problem that many women face in the workplace.

What's the Difference between Sex and Sexual Harassment?

It wasn't many pages ago that we discussed some of the potential benefits of intra-office romance. How do we know when our colleagues' behavior should be classified as "harassment" as opposed to "romance"? One of the reasons that sexual harassment may be happening is that the same behavior can be interpreted very differently by different people. It could be argued that not all sexual behavior at work is harassing.

In a series of surveys of employees in manufacturing, social services, and university settings, researchers asked participants to indicate how often someone they work with: (1) displayed, used, or distributed sexual materials; (2) told sexual stories or jokes; (3) tried to draw them into a discussion of sexual matters; (4) gave them sexual attention; (5) touched their face, butt, thigh, or another "private" part of their body; and (6) exposed a private part of their body to them.

The researchers found that about half of the employees in these organizations had been exposed to some or all of these sexual behaviors in the course of the previous year. For us, encountering any one of these things would get our internal "harassment-o-meter" buzzing. Some people, both men and women, actually reported that they "enjoyed" these behaviors. Importantly, however, exposure to sexual behavior was associated with lower psychological well-being *even* for people who said they enjoyed it.[2]

When does sexual behavior at work become sexual harassment? The difference can be as simple as this: when it is unwelcome. There are two primary types of harassment: quid pro quo and hostile work environment.

Quid Pro Quo

When aspects of employment are contingent on sexual acts, this almost certainly constitutes sexual harassment. This could involve punitive actions (e.g., "If you don't have sex with me, I'll fire you.") or rewards (e.g., "If you have sex with me, I'll promote you."). This type of harassment can be explicit, but it can also manifest in more subtle ways. For example, you may graciously turn down a colleague who asks you out and find out a few weeks later that this colleague told your boss that you aren't ready for a promotion. It sucks, right?

Hostile Work Environment

The environment in which you work can also be harassing. If pornographic pictures or sexual jokes are common, you may be exposed to a hostile work environment. As an example—if one of us worked for Howard Stern, we think we might feel like we were in a hostile work environment. If the people you work with make you feel self-conscious about your body or clothes, you may be in a hostile environment. If you witness other women being subject to harassment, this can create a hostile environment.

Outcomes of Harassment

Both types of sexual harassment are problematic. Results of more than 40 studies on outcomes of sexual harassment suggest that people who experience harassment feel less satisfied with their jobs, less committed to their organizations, and are more likely to have physical and mental health symptoms.[3] Harassment also leads women to feel like they need to overcompensate, or to work harder to be accepted and recognized as good workers.[4] Moreover, a study of employees at a public university suggests that even controlling for personal experiences of mistreatment, observing others subject to harassment has negative outcomes for men and women.[5] In other words, you don't have to be personally targeted by harassment to be affected by it.

So What Can I Do about It?

You're getting that icky feeling when a coworker makes demeaning comments about women's body parts or you're wondering whether your wimpy annual bonus was because you turned down the boss. A lot of people in these kinds of situations choose not to label their experiences as harassment. To tell yourself (or worse—to tell someone else) that you have been a victim of harassment might make you feel that the world is not a just place, that you have done something wrong, or that you have to now engage in some sort of action that you don't really want to do. As a result, common reactions to harassment[6] include denial ("I tried to forget it") and avoidance ("I just stayed out of his way").[7]

But there are other ways to cope. For example, you could engage in direct communication with the perpetrator ("I don't like it" or "Stop"). You could also engage in social forms of coping ("I talked to someone I trust"). Finally, you could advocate for change by filing a formal complaint or talking to authorities internal or external to the company.

A lot of targets of harassment might not advocate for change because of concerns about the potential backlash or retaliation they may encounter if they file formal complaints. Retaliation is absolutely and definitively illegal and prosecutable. Nonetheless, it is unfortunately a possibility that can occur when a complaint is filed. It is also possible that organizational representatives would encourage targets of harassment to drop complaints. A more positive, and we hope, more common, response might be to discipline the perpetrator/harasser.

Which Strategy Is Most Effective?

The honest answer is the research isn't clear: we don't know. One survey of staff members at a university who reported unwanted sexual attention examined responses to whether or not "the situation involving unwanted sexual communication got resolved to your satisfaction." The results suggest that in this particular company, making a formal complaint was not associated with greater satisfaction with the outcome of sexual harassment. However, talking to the harasser using nonaggressive strategies increased satisfaction with the outcome.[8] For some women in some situations, it may be effective to confront the perpetrator directly by naming the behavior that was offensive, holding them accountable for their actions, and demanding that it stop.[9] Another option would be to enlist the support of someone else in your company to go with you and stand by you in your talk with the harasser. Our best advice is to do what feels right to you—you are the one who is going to have to live with the good and not-so-good outcomes of your decision.

If You Decide to Respond Formally . . .

You can choose whether to make a complaint about the harassment to representatives within your organization (e.g., the EEO or HR office at your company) or to pursue external alternatives (e.g., state Fair Employment Practice agencies or EEO office). You should be aware that claims with the EEOC must be filed within 180 days of the last instance of harassment. The process of investigation of the claim can take a year, and most cases do not go to federal court. Internal investigations may happen more quickly but are unlikely to result in compensatory or punitive damages. In either case, you may want to consult an attorney. In addition, you should document all evidence related to your complaint, including journals of times/dates/content of harassment, making copies of offensive material, and discussions with other people about the situation.

We would be irresponsible authors if we did not also mention here that rape is a criminal offense that is separate from sexual harassment. No means no everywhere, including the workplace. If you have been sexually assaulted at work, this is a criminal manner and you should call the police.

> Sexual Harassment on the Job is Not a Problem for Virtuous Women
> —Phyllis Schlafly

Due respect to Phyllis, we could not disagree more with this statement. Sexual harassment is about the perpetrator and their desire to gain or maintain power. If you have been exposed to harassment, let us be the first to assure you that *you do not deserve it and it is not your fault.* You can regain your power by making choices about how to handle the experience in the way that is best for *you.*

For Women with Power: What Can Companies Do about Harassment?[10]

Preventative Organizational Actions: Best Practices

- ***Top management commitment.*** Visible support for all harassment policies, including participation in training and inclusion in vision/ mission statements.
- ***Zero tolerance sexual harassment policy.*** This should include multiple safe reporting channels without fear of retaliation and specific processes associated with claims.

- *Harassment-free notification to applicants and new hires.* This sets clear norms about appropriate and inappropriate behavior.
- *Regular organizational assessments.* Conduct attitude surveys to assess experience with or perceptions of harassment.
- *Regular, directed training.* Use training to maintain culture in the organization.

15

Heroes and She-roes: The Powerful Role of Mentoring in Organizations

How important it is for us to recognize and celebrate our heroes and she-roes!

—Maya Angelou

As mentioned in the introduction to this section, we are extremely fortunate to be the products of two kick-ass female mentors—Dr. Mikki Hebl from our days at Rice University and Dr. Traci Giuliano from Jennifer's undergrad career at Southwestern University. Both women share a passion for playing and watching sports (Mik's beloved Packers vs. Trace's adored Steelers), for spending time with their beautiful children and respective partners, and for teaching and mentoring students. In fact, when they met each other many years ago at a conference dedicated to the teaching of psychology, they felt an instant friendship that has resulted in years of research and collaboration between themselves and their students. Given our phenomenal experiences with mentoring, we are excited to share some of the research on the topic—as well as some of the choices and trade-offs you may encounter—to help guide you as you seek out your own heroes and she-roes:

Why Be a Mentee?

Given all of your competing professional and personal demands, it is perfectly reasonable to ask whether mentoring is really worth the time. One overarching research project that looked at over 43 individual studies about mentoring found small but consistent positive effects,[1] showing that:

- Employees who have been mentored report being more satisfied with their careers, think they are more likely to advance in their career, are more committed to their careers, and are more satisfied with their jobs than employees without mentors.
- Moreover, specific career-related mentoring was related to greater compensation, salary growth, and more promotions.
- These benefits are particularly enhanced if both you and your mentor feel like the managers in your organization support the relationship.[2]
- Mentors can also help expose you to new and different parts of the organization, can give you challenging work assignments that develop your breadth of skills, can provide specialized and personalized coaching feedback, and can make you more visible to senior organizational managers.[3]

Why Be a Mentor?

As you progress in your career, you may want to think about giving back by becoming a mentor yourself—though there are obvious benefits to being a protégé, do mentors actually get anything other than the feeling of altruism from "paying it forward?" Research suggests that they do:

- Mentors can gain career-based benefits through being recognized by others and they can gain relational benefits through having a rewarding experience and through building a loyal base of support for themselves in the organization.[4] They can also feel like they are contributing to their legacy and positively guiding the next generation.
- Additionally, mentors often report feeling personally gratified by the experience and learning new skills from it that benefit their managerial abilities.[5]
- Think you are too young to be a mentor? Think again—many organizations are now looking at "reverse mentoring" where they have younger and newer employees work with older and more tenured workers to share tips about social networking media and technology.

Formal vs. Informal Mentoring

You are probably most familiar with the concept of informal or spontaneous mentoring—you see someone whose career trajectory, technical skill set, or myriad other desired qualities you are impressed with and so decide to strike up a relationship with him or her to learn more about their style, techniques, and philosophies. Research by Herminia Ibarra has indicated that you should think about these three factors when selecting professional role models:[6]

- **Effectiveness**—How successful is this individual?
- **Feasibility**—Will this individual's style work for me?
- **Attractiveness**—Do I like this individual and want to be like him or her?

Importantly, her research suggests that role models don't have to be all or nothing—that is, you can and should pick and choose qualities you'd like to emulate from a number of different exemplars.

In contrast to the spontaneous mentoring relationships you might develop on your own, some larger organizations have been put into place formal mentoring programs to help onboard new employees or to guide midcareerists—some of these are strictly voluntary whereas in others you may be volun-told to participate. If the latter is the case and you're not terribly enthused about being assigned the professional equivalent of a blind date, there are, fortunately, several things you can do to help make the formal mentoring experience even better[7]:

- **Have a say in selection.** The more input that both protégés and mentors have in the matching process, the more satisfied both parties are going to be with the quality and outcomes of the relationship. Why? It is possible that because the parties feel they have a voice in the match-up, they start to psychologically invest more in the relationship.
- **Ensure high quality training.** Providing training to mentors unfortunately isn't enough; the training has to be of high quality before it positively influences the mentoring relationship, possibly because these type of training programs not only focus on the nuts-and-bolts of mentoring but the emotional component as well. Interestingly, too much training can actually make mentors frustrated

and annoyed with the formal program requirements and sour them from participating.

- **Proximity doesn't matter as much as you might think.** Although mentors and protégés that are physically located close to each other end up interacting more, proximity didn't seem to affect the quality or outcomes of the mentoring process. As such, don't be afraid to seek out a great mentor who happens to be in a different building or even a different city if there are useful ways to connect with him or her.

- **Picking someone inside or outside of your department brings different outcomes.** Some research suggests that you should seek formal mentors within your own department because you will naturally interact with them more because of your shared proximity and because they can give you the inside scoop on navigating internal office politics; however, separate research suggests that formal mentors outside your department can be useful because they can give you alternative perspectives on the organization that you wouldn't ordinarily have and because they can help you expand your network. Our suggestion—why not seek both kinds?

Female vs. Male Mentors

The founder of Watershed Asset Management, Meridee Moore, has some stellar advice for those seeking professional role models:

> Find a mentor. And it doesn't have to be a mentor who looks like you. They can be older, a different gender, younger, in a different business, but someone you admire and respect, and just attach yourself to that person and learn everything you can. I've done this my whole career. It is so valuable, especially if you choose a good one and they end up teaching you everything and then rejoicing in your success.[8]

Her advice to seek many types of mentors that fit different demographic profiles is astute, as the research shows that you can probably expect different types of relationships with different genders. For example, as much as we women may hate to think it, there is real value in tapping into the old boys' network. In fact, one slightly depressing study found that (1) MBA graduates who formed relationships with White male mentors on average made almost $17k more than those graduates who only worked with female or minority male mentors and (2) women are less likely to have these lucrative mentoring relationships with older white men.[9] This discrepancy in outcomes extends to promotions as well—male mentees are often able to utilize their informal connections with powerful male mentors, whereas women more often tend to rely on formal bureaucratic procedures to advance.[10]

There are a number of compelling and probably mutually reinforcing theories to explain why female employees have fewer male mentors[11, 12]:

- Younger women have a harder time gaining access to these informal male networks where potential mentoring relationships develop, such as on sports teams, locker rooms, or even in bathrooms.
- Younger women may be reluctant to pursue a mentoring relationship with an older male, lest he or their coworkers misinterpret the relationship.
- Mentors and mentees are naturally attracted to those who look and act like them, so these relationships last longer and are of higher quality than dissimilar matches.

If white male mentors offer such great financial benefits, why would any bright young woman still look for a female mentor? Obviously, most of us don't just care about salary and compensation—so while well-placed male mentors can help us with this side of organizational advancement (also called *instrumental* benefits by organizational psychologists), research shows that it is often female mentors who are best equipped to provide emotional, friendship, support, affirmation, and counseling (or so-called *psychosocial*) benefits to us.[13]

We certainly don't mean to broadly stereotype and imply that only men can provide career mentoring and only women can provide psychosocial mentoring—in fact in the movie *Up in the Air*, it ends up being George Clooney's character who—by the end—provides emotional support to his young protégé played by Anna Kendrick and the older woman played by Vera Farmiga who ends up being kind of a ballbuster despite earlier indications that she was more empathetic.

Case in point, take this example provided by the C.E.O. of Prescription Solutions, Jacqueline Kosecoff, talking about savvy, analytically inclined women teaching other working women about financial issues:

Q. You run mentoring programs for women executives. Tell me about those.

A. I started out without mentors, so I'm acutely aware of the value of a good mentor. Often in a company, the people who are high-maintenance get all the attention, rather than the people who are high-performing and high-potential. So I try to make the mentoring program about the high-performing, high-potential people.

One of the things I've found is that women often don't speak financial language as well as they need to in order to go to the next level. So, for example, a lot of our women executives never went on to get an M.B.A., and yet they're in a big corporation where they need to understand financial matters. They're a little bit reluctant to go to the guys, as it were, and say: "Excuse me, I don't know how to read a balance sheet. Could you teach me how?"[14]

We love this example because it shows that it is certainly possible that female mentors can provide both the career-enhancing (financial and analytic skills) AND the relational benefits (advice on work-life balance and dealing with stress) to receptive younger women.

What to Look for and What to Avoid

A body of research thankfully provides tips that can enhance your mentorship experience:

- **Do avoid mentors in formal programs who feel forced to participate.** As one senior partner in a professional service firm said, "Please, not another Mickey Mouse mentoring system. Do I really have to waste my time taking subordinates from some other department out to lunch? You have to be kidding."[15] If you are unfortunately randomly matched up with some negative jerk like this—RUN. You don't need that toxicity.

- **Do seek out opportunities to meet female mentors in a more social setting.** Not only can this be a fun and informal way to get to know each other better, it can be helpful in building trust, emotional bonds, feelings of identification, and common values, which are all key in creating successful mentoring relationships.[16]

- **Don't only pick high-performing peers to be your mentors.** While you could definitely learn from these high-flyers, some social psychological research about "superstars and me" suggests that older and more advanced role models in your career field can be inspiring if you feel their success is attainable, whereas superstars in your own peer group might lead to self-deflation if you begin to feel less competent by comparison.[17]

- **Don't play mind games with your mentor.** If you show an unwillingness to learn, act too competitive with or jealous of your mentor, or are deceitful with them, this could easily turn the experience into a negative one for your mentor and he or she might terminate the relationship prematurely.[18]

Section Three

How to Make It Work While Communicating on the Job: Speaking Up and Standing Out

It sounds like a catchy title for a best-selling business book: *All I Needed to Know About Management I Learned from Kindergarteners*. But it turns out there may be some truth behind this idea. Nell Minow—cofounder of the Corporate Library, former principal of a Lens, and former president of Institutional Shareholder Services—had this to say when talking about her leadership philosophy and communication style:

> I also learned a lot about being a manager from being a mom. When I first became a professional manager, I was pregnant for the first time, and so I grew up with both responsibilities at the same time. You have people saying the same two things to you all day long, which is, "Look what I did." And you say: "It's really good. Do some more." Or they say, "He took my stuff." And you have to say, "Tell him to give it back."
>
> You're constantly trying, whether you're raising children or dealing with employees, to get them to take responsibility for their own issues. I'm not saying that in a maternalistic way, just in a way of trying to get people to take responsibility for themselves, to do the best that they can and to learn as much as they can. In both cases, you're trying to make people more independent and bring them along . . .
>
> The book that influenced me the most about management was a book about parenting, called *How to Talk So Children Will Listen and Listen So Children Will Talk*. It was a tremendously educational book for me. In terms of interpersonal skills in dealing with people of all ages and situations, there just isn't a better book.[1]

As Ms. Minow found, to make it at work, women must communicate effectively with supervisors, coworkers, subordinates, and customers. As you may have discovered already for yourself, this is trickier than it looks if you are always wondering "What does he think I think of him?" "Should I send an e-mail, pick up the phone, or walk over to her to deliver this bad news?" "What does my clothing and my cubicle communicate about my professional and personal identity?" "Why do my clients keep using so many sports metaphors?" or "Why does he keep interrupting me during meetings?"

Although some hands-on organizations take positive action to effectively manage communication, at the other extreme are organizations that try so hard to use the most current business jargon that they fall into using clichéd buzzwords that ultimately become overused to the point of being meaningless. Think terms and phrases like "value-added," "customer-focused," "at the end of the day," "forward-leaning," and "bring to the table." No surprise, Scott Adams of *Dilbert* fame was one of the first to spot this concerning trend and captured it in an iconic cartoon that encouraged cubicle dwellers to play "Buzzword Bingo" at the office.[2]

Interested in playing yourself? A variety of Web sites such as Business-BuzzwordBingo.com are all too happy to provide you with bingo cards for your own amusement during your next interminable business meeting.

The occurrence of business buzzwords has become so terrible and pervasive that it received special condemnation in an *Onion* article entitled "Manager Achieves Full Mastery of Pointless Managerial Jargon":

> During what was described to them as "a look-forward meeting to discuss and evaluate the company's event-chain methodology," MediaLine employees stood with mouths agape Wednesday as they witnessed the very moment at which project manager James Atkins attained complete mastery over the fine art of meaningless corporate doublespeak ... When asked to comment on his recent success, Atkins responded in a one-line e-mail, stating, "FYI ETA TBD EOM."[3]

In this section, we will describe research on positive and negative styles of communication and specify techniques for capitalizing on verbal and nonverbal communication that occurs in person and via technology and, importantly, how these styles tend to differ by gender. We'll also discuss issues that have arisen in the digital era, such as communicating at work via instant messenger, e-mail, and text messages. For example, we will point out:

- Women's common language choices ("I'm not sure, but ..." or "don't you think?" or "I'm so sorry" or "I don't know") make us seem less competent and more weak than we are.
- Emoticon usage can be useful if you are trying to come across as warm, but is more often inappropriate in business communications and can even negatively influence whether a company wants to hire you or not. :-)
- E-mail can be a very effective communication tool for women, as it allows them to get right to the point (rather than feeling like they have to "catch up" first) and because they can't be interrupted, which men are more likely to do in face-to-face situations.
- Spending a little bit of time on ESPN.com and watching Sports Center can pay huge dividends when talking with male colleagues and clients.
- Being plugged into your organization's water-cooler rumor network (which are surprisingly quite accurate) can be beneficial for you professionally by giving you insider scoop about the organization, but always steer clear of gossiping about coworkers.
- Dress for success isn't just a cheesy motto—women in high-status jobs who wear sexy attire were seen as less competent and people have a more negative emotional reaction to them than working women who dress more professionally.
- Metaperceptions (or wondering what you think your male colleagues think about you and other women) can eat up the time, energy, and focus needed to effectively do your job.
- Coworkers and bosses can make assumptions (often correct ones at that) about your personality based simply on a quick glance at how you maintain your workspace.

16

"Men Are from Earth, Women Are from Earth. Deal with It": Gendered Verbal and Nonverbal Communication at Work

Veronica: I need this machine so I can watch a tape for a story.

Ron: I'm using the tape. I'm showing Jeffrey my Emmy tape. We are watching history.

Veronica: Mr. Burgundy, I'm a professional, and I would like to be able to do my job.

Ron: Big deal. I am very professional.

Veronica: Mr. Burgundy, you are acting like a baby.

Ron: I'm not a baby, I am a man. I am an anchorman.

Veronica: You are not a man. You are a big fat joke.

Ron: I'm a man who discovered the wheel and built the Eiffel Tower out of metal and brawn. That's what kind of man I am. You're just a woman with a small brain. With a brain a third the size of us. It's science.

—Anchorman: The Legend of Ron Burgundy

The movie *Anchorman* takes place in a sexually charged 70s era newsroom as gender quotas required the inclusion of more diverse newscasters—a move met with initial confusion. When asked what diversity was, Ron replies "Well, I could be wrong, but I believe diversity is an old, old wooden ship that was used during the Civil War era." Next was resistance, as seen in the scene above. Then, finally, acceptance from the originally all-male

Channel 4 anchor team. Part of Ron and Veronica's problem—in addition to blatant sexual harassment, of course—probably stems from gendered differences in communication styles. As sociolinguist Deborah Tannen explains in a series of thoughtful books and tapes, women often use conversations as the "glue" to form and cement relationships, whereas men use it to establish hierarchy and status, much as Ron does to exaggerated and comedic effect.[1, 2, 3]

In this chapter, we'll explore how differences between the genders in verbal and nonverbal communication styles can influence work dynamics, taking care not to veer too much into *Men Are from Mars, Women Are from Venus* stereotypes—as comedian George Carlin allegedly stated: "Men are from Earth, Women are from Earth. Deal with it." Although the research that follows might seem to be just fun bits of trivia, they carry important implications for women because:

> People in powerful positions tend to reward people whose linguistic styles match their own. As a result, in most organizations, where men tend to be in charge, the contributions of women are often downplayed because the things they say tend to be misinterpreted. The woman who politely defers to a dominant male speaker at a meeting may come across (to men, at least) as being passive. As a result, her contributions may never come to the table. However, the woman who breaks from this pattern and interjects her ideas may come across (again, to men) as being pushy and aggressive. And here, too, her contributions may be discounted. In both cases, the communication barrier has caused a situation in which organizations are not only breeding conflict, but they also are not taking advantage of the skills and abilities of their female employees.
>
> —*Behavior in Organizations*, pp. 331–332[4]

He Said, She Said: Verbal Differences in Communication at Work

A large body of psychological and linguistic research explores some of the general ways that male and female employees' approach to verbal communication differs. Interestingly, however, *how much* they speak does not appear to vary, despite the stereotype of women being more chatty than men—research indicates that both men and women generally speak about 16,000 words per day[5]:

- **Ritual Apologies:** How many times have your coworkers shared something negative that happened to them—their alarm clock didn't go off, they spilled coffee on their shirts, they were passed over for a promotion—and your automatic response is to express empathy by saying "I'm so sorry" even when you *clearly* are not at fault for their misfortune. Tannen's research indicates that women use these "ritual apologies" to mean "I'm sorry that happened to you" rather than literally "I apologize."[6] Although sympathizing with others might help build rapport, saying "I'm sorry" is something women commonly do that makes us appear weaker than we are by placing unnecessary blame upon ourselves, and it can lead others to doubt your competence.

- **Hedging Language and Tags:** Have you ever spoken up in a meeting or presentation by saying something like "I'm not sure, but ..." "I guess my question is ..." "I'm not an expert but ..." or "I think that's probably a good idea"? If so, some experts suggest that these "hedges" make you look like you doubt yourself and your ideas.[7] Similarly, adding tags to questions ("This is excellent, isn't it?" "The presentation is well done, don't you think?" or "You would like me to follow up on this, right?") can undermine women's authority and expertise by turning facts into questions.[8]

- **Directness:** Tannen finds that female managers are more likely to downplay their status and couch requests as favors to subordinates ("Are you busy? If not, would you please do me a favor and make 10 copies of this?") whereas male managers are more likely to play up their status be straightforward and direct with requests ("Please make 10 copies.").[9] In a performance evaluation context, females may want to "soften" less than stellar feedback by coupling it with more positive comments—as Dana Levy, founder of DailyCandy.com, says, "[T]here are some basic principle human skills that I learned about this, like the criticism sandwich—praise, constructive criticism, praise."[10] Although we personally see this as an effective approach to giving feedback, a male subordinate may see this as confusing or even "sneaky" because the sequencing is not what he expects (which is that his female manager should be upfront and direct about what work behaviors he needs to change and not bury the bottom line.[11])

- **Interruptions:** Interestingly, research shows that people who interrupt others are perceived to gain status at the expense of those they interrupt—however, these same interrupters, particularly when they are female, are less liked.[12] Interruptions are most likely to occur by men in male dominated groups and least likely to occur by women—the rate of interruptions in a group discussion also appears to decrease as women move from being in the minority to the majority.[13] The phenomenon of alpha-male interruption in asserting dominance is exemplified perfectly by Miranda's d-bag boss in the latest *Sex and the City 2* movie literally putting his hand up to interrupt and silence her. Lest you think this doesn't happen in the real-world, however, check out the recent Stephen Colbert interview with Gloria Steinem—during the four minute interview, he manages to interrupt her five separate times. This is particularly striking in contrast to a later interview she gave to Katie Couric where it was a more egalitarian back-and-forth conversation, and if anything, she was more prone to interrupt Ms. Couric.[14, 15]

- **Filler Language:** We recognize that attacking a reality TV star's workplace demeanor is like shooting proverbial fish in a barrel, but this recent quote from the lead of MTV's show *The City* talking about presenting her fashion designs to her boss is too cringe-worthy to resist: "Joe has so much power, you know what I mean? Like, if he doesn't like my collection and thinks that it doesn't have potential then it's almost like, what am I doing in this industry?"[16] In addition to the unfortunate use of a tag (as discussed previously), it contains a good amount of the filler term "like." Not surprisingly, applicants who overuse "like" in interviews are seen as less professional and less desirable to hire than those who don't use the term.[17]

- **Word Use:** Social psychologist James Pennebaker has used a remarkable program he developed called the Linguistic Inquiry Word Count (LIWC) program to analyze written and spoken language differences between men and women—his research shows that women tend to use more words related to social and psychological processes and positive emotions (words like sister, friends, happy, remember) as well as verbs, pronouns, references to the home, and negations (words like can't or not). In contrast, men are more likely to use words that refer to an object's properties, impersonal topics, current concerns, numbers, swear words, and they were more likely to use longer words[18, 19]

- **Cursing:** No sh*t, men in general are more likely than women to swear in public, to use more offensive expletives than women, and to curse in all-male vs. mixed-gender groups.[20] Although some swearing on the job can help boost morale and increase social cohesion among employees,[21] it can backfire when the expletives are sexual, racial, or homophobic and make employees feel stigmatized or singled out. When cursing in work settings, men may take a paternalistic approach toward swearing by trying to "protect" female colleagues from coarse language—an anecdote from one book about gendered communication in the workplace shows how this can single women out and make them feel uncomfortable by calling unwanted attention to their gender:

  A female senior marketing director for a major toy manufacturer had an experience that was still infuriating her when she told me about it. "The other day the CEO was describing some new plans at a directors meeting. He got annoyed with some idea and started swearing. Two seconds into his tirade, he turned to me and said, 'I'm sorry Sue.' I looked around. Everyone was looking at me. He hadn't apologized to any of them. Why to me? All that does is separate me out. I didn't care for it one bit," she said. (p. 67)[22]

- **Joking:** Like cursing, joking in the workplace can be useful in fostering collegiality, but only to the extent that the humor is supportive and not marginalizing. Luckily, research has found that women are more likely than men to use this type of collaborative humor in the workplace.[23, 24]

- **Deflection of Credit:** Have you ever heard a too modest woman say in response to a work compliment, "Thanks, but it was nothing" or "you are too kind" or "I just got lucky"? Although wanting to appear somewhat self-deprecating seems like it could be a way to guard against being seen as too conceited or arrogant, not accepting credit for legitimate hard work can make it seem like you don't deserve or haven't earned your successes.[25] Instead, next time someone pays you a compliment, instead of downplaying it, you can say something to the effect of "I (or we if it was truly a team effort) have worked really hard on this and I'm really proud of this accomplishment" or simply "thank you."

- **Asking Questions:** Turns out the old stereotype is true—men are less likely to ask for directions when lost and to ask questions than women.[26] As such, you are probably more likely to hear a female employee say, "Should we have a meeting to discuss this issue further?" (perhaps as a way of gathering consensus), whereas a male employee might prefer to directly say "We are going to have a meeting to discuss this issue further" (perhaps to establish his role as "the decider"). Tannen's research finds that men are typically socialized from a young age to believe that asking questions is a sign of weakness and is associated with a loss of status, so asking too many questions in a work setting can unfortunately undermine perceptions of your competence by making it appear that you don't know as much as your colleagues.[27]

- **Reinforcing Hierarchy:** Tannen has found that in business communications, hierarchy is often brought to the foreground.[28] In the first season of *30 Rock*, head comedy writer Liz Lemon thinks that she's developed a budding friendship with her boss at GE, Jack Donaghy. Unfortunately, she doesn't realize that addressing him in familiar terms in front of *his* bosses (two GE executives named Ron and Bob) would compel him to denigrate her to reassert his hierarchical status:

Liz Lemon: Hey, Jack! Sorry to interrupt. Hey, can we eat our pizza outside? Cause those wangs from the *Today Show* eat on the roof garden all the time, you know? And I thought since me and you are best buds maybe you could do me a solid and slip me the key to that thing. This guy's the best. He got me kick ass Chamillionare tickets. You guys like Chamillionare? Anyway, Jack rocks. This guy—A-plus.

Jack: Excuse me for a moment. (whispers to Liz) I'm sorry for what's about to happen right now. Just know that I don't mean it.

Liz: Don't mean what?

Jack: What group home did you escape from that you would dare talk to me like some plumber's wife in front of Ron Gordon and Bob Overmyer?

Liz: I don't even know who those guys are.

Jack: Oh really? Your ignorance was obvious when you waddled up to me with your thin lipped mouth full of greasy peasant food, and addressed me by my Christian name in front of the gentleman from Fairfield. That's Fairfield, Connecticut, Lemon, GE headquarters. But how would you know that with your nigh 40 years of public education and daytime television viewing? If you ever pull a Bush League stunt like that again, I'll have you writing promos for arena football so fast, it'll make your inexplicably small head spin.

Body Language: Nonverbal Differences in Communication

OK, we admit it—we love reading as much as anyone what the "body language experts" in *US Weekly* have to say about the meaning behind Brangelina leaning in together sharing hushed whispers over dinner or Speidi sharing a SMA (Spontaneous Moment of Affection . . . obvi) at a Vegas pool party. But what does the social science literature have to say about men and women's nonverbal behaviors at work? Here are some of the ways the genders typically differ:

- **Touch and Personal Space:** Have you ever noticed two people waging elbow warfare for use of an armrest on an airplane? It's pretty funny until you're the chump stuck in the middle seat without any place to put your arms on a cross-country flight. People of higher traditional status are generally more likely to take up more space, regardless of actual physical body size, and invade the personal space of those who are traditionally considered lower status.[29] One particularly egregious example of this phenomenon comes from the military in a *U.S. News and World Report* article about women's progress up the defense ranks:

  One of their favorite stories, (the Principal Deputy Assistant Secretary of Defense for Homeland Defense and America's Security Affairs Christine) Wormuth says, involved the 1997 Quadrennial Defense Review when (the Under Secretary of Defense for Policy Michele) Flournoy was "very pregnant" with her first child. "QDRs are often very contentious processes here in the department. Michele was calm but was having a very intense discussion with a one-star general." The general "very much wanted to get in her face and use his physical size to intimidate her," Wormuth recalls. But he couldn't: "Her stomach was blocking him."[30]

- **Smiling:** One of our favorite moments in *The Office* came from the always quotable paper salesperson Dwight Schrute who theorized, "I never smile if I can help it. ... Showing one's teeth is a submission signal in primates. When someone smiles at me, all I see is a chimpanzee begging for its life." Oh, Dwight. But his hyper-masculine interpretation of smiling may have some bearing in reality, as a large body of research indicates that women generally smile more than men.[31] This is good news for us since smiling during job interviews is positively related to an interviewer's impressions of interviewees.[32]

- **Body Orientation and Eye Gaze:** Research indicates that female pairs often directly face one another and maintain stronger eye gaze while having a conversation (perhaps to enhance intimacy and emotional connection), whereas male pairs instead sit at angles or even parallel to one another when talking, perhaps to *prevent* emotional intimacy and avoid questions about sexual orientation— Tannen argues that we develop these patterns in same-sex peer groups as children where little girls' best friends are the ones they tell things to and little boys' best friends are the ones they do things with.[33, 34]

In a grown-up employment setting, interviewees who maintain eye contact with the interviewer and lean toward rather than away from the interviewer are positively evaluated.[35] In another stellar Schrute moment at the office, coworker Jim Halpert continues his longstanding series of pranks against Dwight after Jim returns to the Scranton branch of the company and shows just how disconcerting the lack of eye gaze can be during a conversation:

Dwight Schrute: Fact, I am older, I am wiser. Do not mess with me.

Jim Halpert: [staring at Dwight's forehead] Okay. Sounds good.

Dwight: What are you doing?

Jim: I don't know what you're talking about.

Diwght: Do I have sweat on my forehead?

Jim: No. Nothing.

Dwight: Why are you looking at my forehead?

Jim: I'm not.

Dwight: Meet my eyeline, Jim.

Jim: I am.

Dwight: Stop acting like an idiot.

In sum, it's easy to get into "he said, she said" blame games when discussing linguistic differences on the job between the genders, so Tannen argues that we'd be best served that recognizing differences in communication styles can help remove some of that blame to instead focus on understanding and respect and on giving us more awareness and control over our own responses.[36]

Why Is the Sky Blue? Male Answer Syndrome at Work

In this (final, we promise) scene from *Anchorman*, Ron and Veronica are on a date and find themselves discussing the etymology of their city, San Diego.

Ron: Discovered by the Germans in 1904, they named it San Diego, which of course in German means a whale's vagina.

Veronica: No, there's no way that's correct.

Ron: I'm sorry, I was trying to impress you. I don't know what it means. I'll be honest, I don't think anyone knows what it means anymore. Scholars maintain that the translation was lost hundreds of years ago.

Veronica: Doesn't it mean Saint Diego?

Ron: No. No.

Veronica: No, that's—that's what it means. Really.

Ron: Agree to disagree.

Noting this type of pattern in real life, Jennifer's undergraduate mentor, Traci Giuliano, decided to research the phenomenon of men seeming to make up answers to questions (aka, BS-ing) rather than publicly admit they

(Continued)

don't actually know the answer—a phenomenon called "Male Answer Syndrome."[37] As anticipated, they found that men were indeed more likely than women to try to generate a response (and their responses were longer) when there was an actual true answer to a question (like "Do you have any idea why the sky is blue?") Interestingly, they also found that more masculine individuals, regardless of their gender, were the most likely to try to give an answer to these questions, leading them to conclude that it might be more appropriate to call the phenomenon "Masculine Answer Syndrome."

Rachel Ashwell, founder of Shabby Chic, says that this syndrome is a big turn off:

"I think the words 'I don't know'—in a positive way—is a little phrase much avoided, and I don't really know why. I just turned 50 and there's still plenty I don't know and that's something that I often tell my staff. If you don't know something, it's just so much better to say so. Guessing can cause all kinds of problems. But the point is not to be passive either, and to take responsibility and go find out what it is."[38]

17

R U gr8 @ e-comm? ;-) The Growing Role of E-Communication in the Workplace

> I turn on my computer. I wait impatiently as it connects. I go online, and my breath catches in my chest until I hear three little words: You've got mail.
>
> —Kathleen Kelly, *You've Got Mail*

1998—the year that this film starring the perennially perky Meg Ryan and Tom Hanks was released—represented a much simpler time in communication technologies. AOL was actually popular back then and smartphones, online dating, Y2K paranoia, NSFW warnings, tweets, friending someone on Facebook, and sexting were just ideas in the distant future.

As e-communications become cheaper and more pervasive and as the number of telecommuters increases (a phenomenon we discuss in a separate chapter), it is likely that communication technologies such as e-mail, texting, instant messaging, cell phones, video chats, Web conferencing (like on Skype and GoToMeeting.com) and teleconferencing will almost certainly rise as organizations seek ways to keep their employees who are geographically dispersed connected to one another. Indeed, as virtual teams become more in vogue, it is important to know how to positively harness the use of technology to support group effectiveness, as some studies show that they tend to be less cohesive and successful than groups that meet face-to-face.[1] For example, research indicates that it is useful—particularly for male employees—for team members to meet in person and have a social chat or activity before working on a task together to build trust with one another, since trust is especially important to develop in virtual teams.[2]

Interestingly, one study found that asynchronous e-communication such as e-mail where each person takes whatever time they need to formulate a response may give females an advantage because the traditional face-to-face communication pattern of men interrupting doesn't hold in this condition and women are therefore more able to express their points of view. In fact, in this scenario men were more likely to make directive statements ("I'll work up my numbers on a spreadsheet and you guys do the same") and to stop corresponding and putting forth effort into the task after making a final frustrated message ("This is stupid"). Conversely, women were more likely to try to gather consensus and be polite ("I think we should each work up a set of numbers on a spreadsheet and then we can compare results" or "I hope that works for everyone"). This study also found that all-female virtual teams were the most effective and efficient and had the fewest "deadbeats" as compared to all-male or mixed-gender teams.[3]

Given the many technological and gender complexities inherent in computer-mediated communications, in this chapter we'll discuss some of the most common forms of e-communication, gender differences in their use, and ways to make communication technologies positively work for you.

The Interwebs at Work: E-mail and Instant Messaging and Texting, Oh My!

The most popular form of electronic communication in work places today is—no shock here—e-mail, with over 97 percent of workers saying they use it on a daily basis.[4] For workers who want to communicate in real time, however, instant messaging (IM) has become the go-to e-communication device. As of 2002, 29 percent of US-based companies indicated that they officially used IM—a number we suspect has only grown over time.[5]

A major downside of these written e-communication technologies, of course, is that your written words can be forwarded, copied, or monitored without your approval . . . and occasionally might become legal evidence. Just ask the former employees of failed financial services company Lehman Brothers, whose e-mails are currently being combed through by lawyers using search terms like "huge mistake," "serious trouble," "unsalvageable," "don't share this," and "just between us."[6] Doh! This is also why we advised you in the chapter on dating at work to always keep e-mails to your romantic partner PG-rated.

Although efficient and good at quickly communicating unambiguous information, Bobbi Brown, creator of the cosmetics line of the same name, believes that overuse of e-mail can impede the development of meaningful organizational relationships, and instead makes it a point to call or visit with her employees in person: "I just think people need to hear people's voices, and it takes a second. I don't want to have an e-mail relationship. I just think that something is lost."[7] Similarly, the founder of Shabby Chic, Rachel Ashwell, believes that e-mail cal lead to misunderstandings saying, "I said, when our company was bigger, that e-mail cannot be the only way that we're going to communicate. I mean, I think that can be a big downfall, truthfully, because e-mails can really come across not the way that they're supposed to. We've all done it. We've received them wrong and we've sent them wrong."[8]

As a counterpoint to Ms. Brown's and Ms. Ashwell's preferred method of verbal communication, gazillionaire entrepreneur—and owner of Eden's husband's beloved Dallas Mavericks—Mark Cuban almost exclusively uses e-mail to conduct his daily business communications. He argues:

> It keeps me in touch and is much more effective than talking on the phone. I can do e-mail on my schedule. Plus, it gives me documentation. I can do a Google e-mail search going back to 1995 . . . No meetings. No phone calls. Everything is documented so the number of "let's talk again" or "get together to clarify" or "get on the same page" are gone. People learn very quickly to document and get to the point without the "intonation" of trying to sell me that occurs in meetings. I'm a Dragnet type of e-mail guy. Nothing but the facts. Leave the BS for other people.[9]

Research indicates that there are marked differences in the style and content of men and women's e-mail use that are similar to the patterns we discussed in the previous chapter on verbal communication. Specifically, women are more likely to have an expressive tone (like the use of multiple exclamation marks!!), make initial personal inquiries, apologize, make compliments, use intensifying adverbs (like "hugely"), and include relational words, whereas men are more likely to give opinions, use humor and insults, and include offensive words.[10, 11]

Is the E-communication Glass Half Empty?

Our adopted hometown of D.C. is a BlackBerry-centric city with many Capitol Hill, White House, and lobbying staffers (tens of thousands of federal government workers—including 9,140 BlackBerry users in the House alone) who are connected to their crackberries at all hours.[12]

Although e-communications have doubtlessly made their jobs easier, the 24/7 connectivity can come at a price. For example, social psychologists and neuroscientists are increasingly concerned about how juggling multiple types of incoming data can negatively influence our ability to focus, be creative, filter out irrelevant information, and meaningfully connect to our family and friends as our brains literally become addicted to the rush of being so plugged in,[13] not to mention the physical damage, including "frequent headaches, eye twitching, carpal tunnel syndrome, anxiety, and insomnia."[14]

Research shows that employees who use communication technologies after hours report more work-to-life conflict, as do these employees' significant others.[15] Moreover, the employees most likely to use these technologies were those who perceived strong organizational norms and expectations that they should always be available.[16] Gary Mcullough, president and C.E.O. of Career Education Corporation, recognizes this slippery slope and works to create a more positive climate regarding work communication technologies at his organization:

> I live by my BlackBerry, as most of us do. I do make it a point on Friday night to turn it off and I don't turn it on again until Sunday morning. I do that for a couple of reasons. One is, you have to try to separate at some point during the week. Anybody who needs me, whether it's a board member or one of my leaders, they know how to reach me if something comes up that's a crisis. The other reason I turn it off is because when things come in, if I respond, then I've got people in the organization who would see that I've responded on Saturday morning at 8 a.m. And the next thing I know, I have a response to my response at 8:15 and so it goes. And I want people to have a life.[17]

. . . or Half Full?

In the previous chapter we discussed how many women often use communication for building connections—an approach that can be emotionally beneficial and professionally useful for networking, but can impede efficiency when under tight deadlines or when otherwise pressed for time during a busy workday. Recognizing this gendered expectation for rapport building, the C.E.O. of Guilt Groupe Susan Lyne cleverly uses technology to bypass these social rituals and build efficiencies into her schedule:

> My BlackBerry is my best friend. I honestly don't know how I lived without a BlackBerry because I am not a phone person. I mean, I hate getting calls at home. I've never been someone who liked to chat on the phone. I'd rather not take calls at the office if I don't have to, and a BlackBerry is such an efficient way to communicate. You don't have to do the five minutes of chatter at the beginning. You don't have to make the lunch date. It's just a wonderful thing.[18]

Other corporate leaders—perhaps remembering the days of being chained to their desks during 16-hour work days and eating bad Chinese takeout every night—praise communication technologies for the opportunity it provides for teleworking. For example, the chair of CCMP Capital, Greg Brenneman, relishes the fact that e-communication untethers him from his office and gives him the freedom to work from wherever he chooses:

> We're definitely a BlackBerry company and, yes, the answer is I'm totally addicted and rude and typing under the table during dinner with the family—all the horrible behaviors that I thought I'd never do. But it is great. I used to work a lot more weekends in the office. I'm kind of glass-half-full here, and believe that BlackBerrys and all the remote capabilities that we've got now probably give me more flexibility than I ever have had before. I'm not tied to a desk or tied to an office, and that's much more conducive for the way I prefer to work.[19]

Finally, some organizational leaders who must travel frequently for work report using e-communication to actually enhance their work-life balance to stay connected to their families while on the road. Take Brian Dunn, the C.E.O. of Best Buy:

> I'm a gadget freak. I love my gadgets and I've got to tell you why. Many pundits will write that we need to go back into a quieter and simpler

time and the technology is separating us. I think that actually the technology brings us together, if we use it right. We can become prisoners to it if we don't.

I want to give you a real-life example. My sons are big basketball freaks. My wife, too. So I'm in London and I can't sleep. It's 4 in the morning, so I go on NBA.com and I'm watching the Lakers and Utah game. And all of a sudden my little Skype video chirps, and it's my three sons on their computer talking to me and they're whispering. I said, "Why are you guys whispering?" And it's about 11 at night back home. They said, " 'cause Mom will kick our ass if she knows that we're up." And so I said: "Well if she walks in the room, click me off, man. Don't let her know I'm part of it." But I'm sitting there watching the game with the boys and the only thing I can't do is put my arm around them. I'm on the road 100 days a year, so those moments are really important.[20]

Super Cute or Overly Cloying? :-(The Use and Abuse of Emoticons at Work

Because electronic communications often lack the nonverbal richness and nuance of person-to-person or even telephone conversations, many workers have taken to using some variation of the colon-dash-end parentheses to express emotions and strengthen the impact of their message when communicating online.[21] The use of emoticons has become so pervasive—and mocked—that RadioShack recently featured it in a print ad, with spokesperson Lance Armstrong saying: "Men over 30 shouldn't use emoticons. Period. That means no smiley faces, semicolon hotwinks or carrot noses. The Shack and I are just looking out for your best mobile interests here."

So does the use of emoticons differ between men and women? Some research suggests that it in fact does. Interestingly, women seem to use emoticons to express humor, whereas men tend to use emoticons to be teasing and sarcastic.[22] As expected, women use emoticons much more than men, and when men do use them, it is almost always in communicating with another woman as opposed to another man.[23] When applying for jobs, the misguided use of emoticons unfortunately can even influence whether a potential employer wants to hire you or not. One interesting study had participants read the following e-mail message (half of which included the smileys like below and half did not) from a fictitious applicant to a potential employer for a finance internship[24]:

> It was nice to meet you at PSU's career fair last week. I was very excited to find out about the finance internship you have available and read through the position description immediately after we met. :) I feel this internship is a great match for my interests and experience level and would like to be considered for the position. I've attached my resume to this e-mail. I would very much appreciate the opportunity to interview for this internship. Thanks so much! Hope to hear from you soon. :)

Female applicants who used "smileys" in their correspondence to the company were rated as warmer, but they were also unfortunately thought to be less competent and deserved a lower starting salary than those who didn't use the emoticons. What are the practical implications for young women? As the study's author says:

> I certainly think there's a time and place for the smiley. The best rule of thumb is to think about whether you want to portray an impression of warmth and friendliness. If so, then use the smiley. However, if you want to create the impression of someone who is powerful, competent, independent, and a potential leader, don't use smiley faces in your correspondence. Under certain circumstances, like applying for a job that is usually associated with males, using smileys could, quite literally, come at a reduced cost in rates of pay.[25]

18

"You Know You Love Me, X.O.X.O. Gossip Girl": The Pros and Cons of Sharing Dirt at Work

> Studies show that more information is passed through water cooler gossip than through official memos, which puts me at a disadvantage, because I bring my own water to work.
>
> —Dwight Schrute in *The Office*

Though Dwight misses the specifics, he nails the bottom line—*the office scuttlebutt is often not only useful, but a critical component of organizational communication and socialization.* Social scientists for decades have been examining "the strength of weak ties" in connecting individuals and spreading information—we talked more about this theory in the first section on leveraging your network to find a job.[1]

An employee's own direct network is often limited, homogenous, and contains information redundant with what she already knows. Harnessing the networks of more loosely connected individuals, or those two or more degrees removed from her, is likely to provide new info about her job, organization, and industry that can be beneficial through giving her insider knowledge about upcoming organizational changes and helping to increase team cohesion.[2] In fact, by some estimates we learn about 70 percent of what we know about our organizations from this informal water cooler talk, and Gallop researchers say that happy, productive workers spend up to six (!) hours a day socializing and sharing information with their close coworkers on e-mail, instant messaging, and after-work activities.[3, 4]

On the other hand, the dark side of organizational rumors is its tempting, seductive cousin, workplace gossip. As you might suspect, spending too much time transmitting idle office gossip can harm your reputation—one woman in Jennifer's workplace became known as "Us Weekly" because she was always peddling in office gossip about which coworkers she saw having a private coffee together or who thought who was dreamy. Ironically, this nickname she developed seemed to be the one piece of gossip she wasn't privy to.

To help you navigate this maddening minefield, in this chapter we'll present research on rumor transmission and the effect of workplace gossiping in helping women sort out when it is and is not appropriate. Rule of thumb: talking about rumors involving *objects or events* such as whether your team is going to be downsized or will be getting a bonus is always better than spreading organizational gossip about *people*.

Heard it through the Grapevine: How Rumors Get Transmitted . . .

Economics Teacher: Bueller? Bueller? Bueller?

Simone: Um, he's sick. My best friend's sister's boyfriend's brother's girlfriend heard from this guy who knows this kid who's going with the girl who saw Ferris pass out at 31 Flavors last night. I guess it's pretty serious.

Economics Teacher: Thank you, Simone.

Simone: No problem whatsoever.

—Ferris Bueller's Day Off

Perhaps surprisingly and contrary to the Ferris Bueller example, research indicates that rumors that are passed within established informal communication chains in organizations are quite accurate—generally between 80 to almost 100 percent accurate, though the rumors often contain incomplete information.[5] What contributes most to rumors on the job generally being true? When employees are generally trying to make sense of a situation ("I heard that our team is going to layoff 10% of the workforce—what have you heard?"), they will work harder to collect accurate data (for instance, by checking the team's profitability over the last quarter) and seek out credible sources (gathering insights from well-placed sources in the organization).[6]

Furthermore, having an organizational culture that predisposes employees toward skepticism can also ensure rumor accuracy, particularly when the rumor is subject to multiple interaction and iterations in close networks. Additionally, employees are more motivated to get an accurate answer when the outcome is highly relevant to them (such as when hearing layoff rumors) than when they are simply passing along information ("I heard the office holiday party is going to be at David's house this year.")

... and Sometimes Distorted

Although workplace rumors tend to be fairly accurate, there are several processes that can distort them upon retelling—perhaps this is why so many axioms (like "believe half of what you see and none of what you hear" and "a lie can be halfway around the world before the truth gets its boots on") have developed telling us to be weary of them. In a classroom demonstration designed to show how gender stereotypes and expectations can influence how stories are passed along, our graduate school advisor Mikki developed an active learning technique called "Once Upon a Time There Was a Math Contest."[7] To try this yourself at home, simply read the following passage to a friend and then play the "telephone" game until the story has been retold to three or four different people:

> John received a letter in the mail notifying him that he had lost the Texas State Achievement in Math Competition. He had wanted to win and was unhappy with the results. He had been the best student in his math class last year. Losing really hurt his self-esteem. He found out that Terry Browning had done better than him. He hated Terry Browning for that. To make himself feel better he cried, baked cookies, beat pillows, kicked something, took a long bath and talked to his best friend. After that, he went to the mall where he shopped and played video games in the arcade until he had beaten all the records. He then went running and came home to watch *The Princess Bride*.

OK, now repeat that process, but replace "John" with "Sylvia" and all the male pronouns with female ones. Notice any differences? When we've run this exercise in our Psychology of Gender courses, the results are predictable but nonetheless shocking. When John is the protagonist, the story turns into John being mad that another boy named Terry beat him at a math competition, so he punched a pillow, kicked things, and played video games until he felt better. When Sylvia is the protagonist, however, she is upset that another girl named Terry did better than her at math, so she cries, takes a bath, talks to a friend about it, and shops until she felt better.

What are the processes at play here that make the same story come out so differently depending on whether the main character is male or female? In a classic book called *The Psychology of Rumor*, social psychologist Gordon Allport described the concepts of *leveling* (dropping details from a retelling of a story, especially ones that don't fit our expectations, like John watching *The Princess Bride* or Sylvia beating the arcade's video game records) and *sharpening* (highlighting details in the story that do fit our pre-conceived notions).[8]

Additionally, some new details of the story can even be made up upon transmission in a process that psychologists Nicholas DiFonzo and Prashant Bordia call *adding or snowballing* (like John going to Terry's house to confront him or Sylvia losing her interest in math after her poor results).[9] Taken together, leveling, sharpening, and adding lead to *assimilation*, where people unconsciously alter a story to make it more coherent or complete or consciously after it either because of personal self-interests, prejudice, or defensive reasons.

Secrets, Secrets Are No Fun; Secrets, Secrets Hurt Someone

Believing that all gossip is harmful, the online printing company PrintingForLess.com (they look like a pretty cool company to work for if for no other reason than they have a bring-your-dog-to-work-with-you culture[10]) has established a strongly enforced no-gossip policy, described here by their technical service assistant Shayla McKnight:

> At the beginning of my employment interview two years ago, Marne Reed, the human resources manager who interviewed me, mentioned the company's no-gossip policy. She said something like this: "There's no back-stabbing here, and no office politics. Gossiping

and talking behind someone's back are not tolerated." I remember thinking: "Really? That's odd. How is that possible?" Everywhere I've worked people have gossiped, like when someone got into trouble or was laid off.

But I signed the company's "agreement to values" form, and I remember feeling optimistic. The policy sounded refreshing. Now that I've been here for a while, I can say that it makes one heck of a difference in the work environment. At my last job, gossip was rampant. So many people had negative attitudes. Workers would become frustrated if one person was slacking off, so they'd vent about it.[11]

While we agree with this policy in theory, in practice we take a slightly more moderate approach toward rumors and gossip than the one advocated here. If you feel like you must gossip, make sure it is always "positive or praise" gossip ("I heard Veronica received a raise—how exciting!") rather than "negative or blame" gossip ("I heard Alexis got a negative performance review."). In fact, spreading positive gossip may increase what psychologists call your "reward power," since the person you spread positive gossip to may in turn hope you will spread positive gossip about him or her later.[12]

In summary, as DiFonzo says in an interview with the *New York Times Magazine* after his research was highlighted in their annual "Year in Ideas" feature:

In a workplace setting—what we call a stable organizational grapevine—people are very good at figuring out the truth ... If you tell me something and I work closely with you, I know whether you're a credible source. But even if I'm not so sure, in workplace settings the network connections are so dense that it's easy to cross-check information ... [Gossip is] more social in nature, usually personal and usually derogatory. The gossip about the boss's behavior at the Christmas party may or may not be true ... Often it is, since rumors and gossip tend to overlap, but with gossip, truth is beside the point. Spreading gossip is about fun.[13]

Although we know this last statement is certainly true (juicy gossip can liven up a dull workday and make you feel part of the cool kids at work), always make sure to think about the long-term consequences to your professional and personal reputation before becoming a gossip girl yourself.

19

How Dressing for Success Can Show Finesse or Create Duress: What Your Clothing Communicates on the Job

I live by a man's code, designed to fit a man's world, yet at the same time I never forget that a woman's first job is to choose the right shade of lipstick.

—Carole Lombard

It is an interesting time to be a woman in politics, not least of which is because it gives pundits a reason to work themselves into a frenzy talking about these women's fashion choices. A sample of some recent "news" quotes:

- Are vice presidential candidate Sarah Palin's rimless eyeglasses the new Hillary Clinton pantsuit? The glasses, created by Japanese designer Kazuo Kawasaki, are becoming a bipartisan must-have fashion accessory.[1]

- By Day 3, [then Supreme Court nominee Sonia Sotomayor] had stepped away from the bright colors and instead wore a black pinstriped skirt suit that could easily have been used to illustrate the old John T. Molloy "Woman's Dress for Success" book—a manual whose heyday was in the 1980s.[2]

- The image of [Speaker of the House Nancy] Pelosi marching through Washington on Sunday, with her giant gavel and a lock-step herd of Democrats at her back, is the one that will illustrate history textbooks and haunt Rush Limbaugh's dreams. It looked as if America's grandmother ducked out of her Easter brunch, between Bellinis, to dramatically recast the government's approach to national health and welfare. Closeups show her manicure was perfect. Her hair, as always, was neatly coiffed, with five carefully applied blond highlights emanating, just so, from the center of her scalp. Her accessories were lovely, her shoes dyed to match.[3]

- But [then Supreme Court nominee Elena] Kagan took the anti-style offensive several steps further. She put on rouge and lipstick for the formal White House announcement of her nomination, but mostly she embraced dowdy as a mark of brainpower. She walked with authority and stood up straight during her visits to the Hill, but once seated and settled during audiences with senators, she didn't bother maintaining an image of poised perfection. She sat hunched over. She sat with her legs ajar.[4]

Upon reading the last article in this list, Jennifer literally yelled aloud, "Are you kidding me?"

Now we love looking at the gowns displayed at the "First Ladies at the Smithsonian" exhibit and walking the aisles of DSW as much as anyone, but seriously? This is what passes for penetrating analysis by news media outlets these days? Media coverage of male politicians' fashion choices—think former Senator John Edward's expensive haircut and President Barack Obama's "dad jeans"[5]—only seems to surface when there isn't an Argentinean mistress or high price call girl scandal to discuss (we're looking at you, Sandford and Spitzer).

Does this seemingly inordinate focus on female politicians' clothing extend to businesswomen? As former VP candidate Sarah Palin might say, "You betcha." We recognize that this may not feel like the most empowering chapter and certainly struggled with how to present the research on this delicate topic, as no woman wants to feel like her clothes matter more than her ideas in a business setting. Take this example from Nancy McKinstry, the C.E.O. of Wolters Kluwer, a global information services and publishing company—when asked what surprised her most about her position, she said:

Everything you do is evaluated. I remember doing some meeting about our strategy, and the press in Holland wrote that I wore a suit that had the same color as the KLM flight attendants, which I didn't realize when I bought the suit. I remember thinking, "Here we were talking about the plans for the business and that's what they focused on."[6]

Here we'll discuss the scientific literature on how your fashion choices at work influence people's perceptions of you and, more importantly, how they can affect what you think of yourself so you can dress to impress *her* (we know, we know—cue a schlocky *American Idol* coronation song here).

"I'm Too Sexy for My Shirt, Too Sexy for My Shirt, so Sexy It Hurts"

Ah, summer in D.C. This hot and humid season here in our nation's capital is inevitably marked by kamikaze mosquitoes, clueless tourists packing the metro, and the annual invasion of student interns, or "skinturns" as some have become infamously known. These twenty somethings walk the hallways with attire that seems more suited for a "Jersey Shore" casting call, not a stuffy federal government building. Invariably by about July the obligatory HR e-mail goes out to all employees discussing "appropriate work attire."

We can kind of understand some women's desire to raise the skirt hems and lower the necklines in the workplace—after all, we spent a whole chapter talking about how dating at work is on the rise—but women should be aware of the trade-offs of doing so. An interesting series of studies showed participants videos or pictures of a woman who was either professionally dressed (wearing a business jacket, slacks, flats, and minimal makeup) or sexily dressed (wearing a low-buttoned blouse, no jacket, tight skirt, high heels, and noticeable makeup).[7, 8] The research shows that women in high-status jobs (like managerial positions) who wore sexy attire were seen as less competent and participants had a more negative emotional reaction to her than women dressed more professionally. Interestingly, this "I'm so sexy it hurts" impressions of me effect didn't extend to women in low-status jobs like receptionists.

Perhaps if Debrahlee Lorenzana had known about these studies, she might have had a better working experience at Citibank as a business banker. In a fascinating article in *Village Voice* called "Is This Woman Too Hot to Be a Banker," we learn about her lawsuit against the company:

[W]hen she got fired last summer from her job as a banker at a Citibank branch in Midtown—her bosses cited her work performance—she got even hotter. She sued Citigroup, claiming that she was fired solely because her bosses thought she was too hot. This is the way Debbie Lorenzana tells it: Her bosses told her they couldn't concentrate on their work because her appearance was too distracting. They ordered her to stop wearing turtlenecks. She was also forbidden to wear pencil skirts, three-inch heels, or fitted business suits. Lorenzana, a 33-year-old single mom, pointed out female colleagues whose clothing was far more revealing than hers: "They said their body shapes were different from mine, and I drew too much attention," she says.[9]

Note that this case is particularly interesting, as the research shows that Hispanic women more often than white women see professional attire as important for advancement and making a powerful impression on the job.[10]

We certainly don't mean to promote a blame-the-victim mentality here, but women who dress in a sexy manner on the job probably have an expectation that people will talk about them, and not always in a positive way. For example, in *The Office* episode "Body Language," the staff spends the entire half-hour trying to decide whether Donna, a sexy bar manager, is genuinely interested in their boss Michael or whether she was just trying to get a discount on some printers from him. Some key quotes:

- Donna: "Oh. Well, I guess I'm just used to the restaurant business, [removes her sweater revealing a low-cut top] where, if you're in charge, then you can always get discounts for the people that you like." [Later, off camera] "Was it professional, no. But I work in the nightlife industry, I get hit on all the time."
- Usually mild-mannered sales woman Pam: "Most printer sales are done over the phone, Miss Boobshirt!"
- Resident creepy coworker Creed: "You ever notice you can only ooze two things: sexuality and pus?"

"I Look in the Mirror and What Do I See?"

As we've seen, our attire and appearance can certainly influence others' perceptions of us, but it can also impact our own self-perceptions. Some research has shown that when we wear formal business attire, we feel particularly authoritative, trustworthy, and competent; conversely wearing business casual clothing makes use feel more friendly.[11] A separate study found that when people were wearing formal attire, they were more likely to use words like "cultivated" and "accurate" to describe themselves, whereas when they were casually dressed, they were more likely to use words like "easygoing" and "tolerant."[12]

In a series of interviews with female administrative workers, researchers found that the women chose their attire in part to influence their internal psychological states—for example, to feel more self-confident ("If I'm wearing something new and people tell me how nice I look, I feel so much better, like I can go out and do it!") or more comfortable ("I have to dress so I am comfortable, so that I can forget about it and not think about it all day." p.20).[13] Unfortunately, however, women often recognize that looking feminine and looking professional can conflict with feeling comfortable.[14]

Given all these messages about workplace attire, we'll leave you with some final thoughts:

- **Don't Be a Mean Girl.** We know we covered this in the "Queen Bee" chapter, but don't demean other women's appearance—even if accurate, it leaves you looking catty and superficial. Prime example from the June 2010 primaries, here covered by an incredulous reporter from the *Washington Post*:

  What is this, middle school? I was all set to sit down and write about women in politics, and applaud Tuesday's [primary election] results, when off pops the new Republican nominee for senator from California, Carly Fiorina, with a comment that takes you back to the cattiness of the school cafeteria. Fiorina . . . described an aide who saw her opponent, Sen. Barbara Boxer, on television and said what everyone says: "God, what is that hair? Sooo yesterday."[15]

- **Be aware of how your attire might influence women below you.** Because younger and newer women will be looking to you for cues about appropriate workplace norms, always be cognizant of how your dress and appearance might influence them, for better or worse. Here Linda Hudson, president of a group in the military contracting organization BAE Systems, discusses this lesson:

I was the first female president of the General Dynamics Corporation, and I went out and bought my new fancy suits to wear to work and so on. And I'm at work on my very first day, and a lady at Nordstrom's had showed me how to tie a scarf in a very unusual kind of way for my new suit. And I go to work and wear my suit, and I have my first day at work. And then I come back to work the next day, and I run into no fewer than a dozen women in the organization who have on scarves tied exactly like mine. And that's when I realized that life was never going to be the way it had been before, that people were watching everything I did.[16]

- **Give Back**. [PSA alert!] Now that you've seen the research on how important professional attire can be to others' impressions of your competence and your perceptions of your own self-confidence, consider donating some of your time or work clothing to a worthy nonprofit like Dress for Success:

The mission of Dress for Success is to promote the economic independence of disadvantaged women by providing professional attire, a network of support and the career development tools to help women thrive in work and in life ... [It] is an international not-for-profit organization offering services designed to help our clients find jobs and remain employed. Each Dress for Success client receives one suit when she has a job interview and can return for a second suit or separates when she finds work.[17]

20

Put Me in Coach, I'm Ready to Play: Sports Metaphors at Work

Jan: Sports metaphors are one of the ways women feel left out of the language of the office. Now, I know this might sound silly but... many women ask to go over it. So... fumble means...

Phyllis: Mistake.

Meredith: Slip.

Jan: Right. Par for the course is a golf term. It means right on track. Below par means worse. Wait... that should mean better, that doesn't make sense...

Though this exchange on the television show *The Office* is played for laughs, it does reveal how Monday-morning quarterbacking around the water cooler can play an important role in creating rapport with colleagues and gaining you entrance into informal office networks. In an article entitled "Sports Clichés Go from Locker Room to Boardroom," psychologist Don Powell claims that these expressions are actually used in about 50 percent of corporate settings and conversations because they are a shorthand way to "communicate ideas clearly and quickly."[1] Moreover, some social science research studies how leaders look to sports metaphors to help create a unifying organizational vision among their employees.[2]

Full disclosure: before reading further, you should know that your authors are two rabid football fans who were shaped by our early experiences playing soccer, softball, and volleyball and who continue to be active women, having run marathons and played intramurals together. Fun fact: Jennifer's favorite sports saying comes from her soccer coach dad, Ron, who sagely said whenever she would be intimidated before playing a highly ranked team: "Remember, the game always starts out 0-0"—a life lesson she continues to reference as an adult. However, despite our admitted bias, we feel the research on the benefits of sport and exercise to personal and professional success is compelling enough to present here and hope to convince many more women to get out from underneath the fluorescent lights and onto the field.

So If Sports Are So Useful to Female Workers, How Can Women Best Make It Work for Them?

A League of Their Own

Many organizations are increasingly recognizing the importance of physical activity to their employees' mental and physical health—not that this is purely altruistic, as they see the subsequent effect of healthy employees in increased productivity, decreased use of sick days, and lower health care costs.[3] In response, some companies have granted their employees dedicated amounts of time each pay period to exercise. With this allotment, consider joining your workplace intramural team—if no such league exists, consider creating your own, thus showing off your leadership and organizational skills in an informal setting.

Participating in and organizing company sporting events can help diversify your professional network—take this example from the C.E.O. of Saks, Stephen Sadove:

> I was also a reasonably good tennis player back in my college and graduate school days. And when I started work at a company called General Foods, people were always looking for tennis partners. If you were a good tennis player, you were heavily in demand. I found that things like that allowed me to meet people that I otherwise may never have met. I've been amazed over the years how relationships that come out of one thing go toward something else.[4]

Exercise also releases the all-important chemical endorphins in our brains, making us look better and feel better—but this benefit not only works at an individual level, it can carry over to group-level payoffs as well.

In fact, research shows that "emotional contagion," or the transmission of moods within groups, can occur with your teammates—that's right, just like you can catch a cold and you can catch a pop-up fly from your coworkers, you can also catch their positive vibes.[5]

Step Up to the Plate

So what if you don't know the difference between a tight end and a bookend . . . or don't care? In a provocative interview in the *New York Times*, Carol Smith, senior vice president and chief brand officer for the media company Elle Group says:

> Men love to hear themselves talk. I'm so generalizing. I know I am. But in a couple of places I've worked, I would often say, "Call me 15 minutes after the meeting starts and then I'll come," because I will have missed all the football. I will have missed all the "what I did on the golf course." I will miss the four jokes, and I can get into the meeting when it's starting.[6]

Although we empathize with Ms. Smith's desire to get down to business, we also recognize sports talk isn't going anywhere in American workplaces anytime soon. Knowing this, however, the ball is in your court. After picking up a lanyard for her beloved Cowboys last time she was in the DFW airport, Jennifer started wearing it at work and has found it to be a fascinating pseudo-sociological experiment, as people of all ages, races, and genders have commented on it—mostly positively, though a few disgruntled Redskins fans have given her a hard time. This conversation starter not only gives her the opportunity to talk about her favorite team, it also has opened up many new social and professional connections on the job.

Even though a little time spent on ESPN can pay dividends down the road, if the game really isn't for you, don't front—if you genuinely continue to dislike sports after giving it a fair shot, don't pretend to be a superfan or you'll just come off as disingenuous. Just remember that it could be a professional slam dunk, even with a female boss. Take this example from Sharon Napier, the chief executive of the ad agency Partners + Napier—when she was asked about important leadership lessons, she said:

Much of what I learned about leadership I learned playing basketball, whether it was as a player or from my coaches. I use basketball analogies a lot . . . I always tell people it's not about the big game. And what I mean by that is it takes hours and hours of practice to be good. I'll tell a younger person in the agency: "You're going to be at an internal agency meeting to present your work, so practice. Act like it's real. Go home, prepare, practice. Because when you get to the big game, you'll be able to really be good." And I always say that the stats don't lie. It's not subjective. It's just, what are your goals and did you meet them.[7]

From the Cube to the Court—Sporty Female CEOs

Still not convinced of the long-term benefits of sports? The Women's Sport Foundation argues that "it is no accident that 80% of the female executives at Fortune 500 companies identified themselves as former 'tomboys'—having played sports."[8] The Foundation further posits that sports participation helps women learn important life lessons that directly translate into success in business, including the following rules:

- "Teams are chosen based on people's strengths and competencies rather than who is liked or disliked.
- Successful players are skilled in practicing the illusion of confidence.
- Errors are expected of people who are trying to do new things. The most important thing is never make the same mistake twice.
- Loyalty to your teammates is very important.
- 'I will' equals 'I can.'
- In a hierarchical organization, your boss (the head coach) gives the orders and the employees (players) follow the head coach's instructions.
- Winning and losing has nothing to do with your worth as a person.
- Pressure, deadlines, and competition are fun.
- When you are too tired to take one more step, you know you can.
- Perfection is sequential attention to detail."

21

What Do Women Want?: A Glimpse into Men's Perspectives of Interactions with Women

"...Your thoughts are on the AM frequency and I'm only getting FM."

"I can't read your mind. You have to tell me what you're thinking."

"What I wouldn't give to be able to see into your mind for just this one moment."

—Edward Cullen to Bella Swan (in Stephanie Meyer's *Twilight* series)

It's not just fictitious vampire romantic partners that want to read our minds—the people we work with are curious about what we are thinking, too. Indeed, in the workplace as much as the bedroom, people are concerned about what others think about them. One of the most fundamental aspects of being a human is that we want to get along with other humans. Our self-esteem and social success depends to a great degree on how much we think other people like us. As a result, we spend a lot of brainpower (i.e., cognitive resources) trying to figure out what other people think about us.

This is particularly true when we are interacting with people who are different from ourselves in obvious or salient ways like gender. As a woman, then, you should be aware that the men you interact with might be worried about what you think about them. In psychology, the question of "what does she think of me?" refers to a concept called *meta-perception*.

"What Does She Think of Me?"

The notion that men wonder what their female coworkers think may seem somewhat contrary to the stereotype of men as generally disinterested in nonsexual interpersonal relationships; the idea popularized by *When Harry Met Sally* that men have no interest in being friends with women. In addition, you might expect that, because men tend to have the power in companies, they wouldn't give a s*it about what women think about them.

However, research suggests that members of socially advantaged groups worry about being stereotyped just like members of disadvantaged groups. For example, white men and women who were in interactions with African American men and women worried that they may appear to be prejudiced.[1] These concerns also happen when men and women interact; men worry that they may be seen as sexist.

Metaperceptions Are Sometimes Right!

Although psychologists have traditionally thought that people are not very good at guessing what other people think about them, new evidence suggests that we are more accurate than previously thought. A series of studies with undergraduate participants suggests that individuals can tell that their parents see them differently than their friends do.[2] Another study showed that people can sometimes judge new acquaintances' impressions of them; people could guess the personality traits that other people actually saw.[3] This means that the fellas might know if you don't like them, if you think they are not as smart as you, or if you think they are overpaid.

Metaperceptions Are Sometimes Wrong!

Research suggests that guesses about what other people think about you may be least accurate when you are worried about social rejection or when you don't have a lot of experience in the situation. In one study, white students who had not previously had a lot of experience with Chinese students felt that their desire for friendship with a particular Chinese student was misunderstood and overestimated.[4] In another series of studies, people who had strong fears of rejection worried that their behaviors communicated more romantic interest than they intended.[5]

We can extend these ideas to interactions between men and women at work. Men's metaperceptions may be inaccurate when they feel insecure about their position in the office or when they haven't had experience working for a female boss before. This means guys might not always guess correctly about what you think.

What Are the Consequences of Accurate and Inaccurate Metaperceptions?

Lost Opportunities

The three most common strategies for dealing with concerns about what other people think about are: (1) avoid, (2) avoid, and (3) avoid. Men who are worried about what you think about them (particularly if they're worried that you think they are sexist) may simply try to stay away. Unfortunately, the hierarchical system rewards this behavior in men—when men develop social networks with other men (more so than with women), they are more likely to be promoted.[6]

Reciprocal Disliking

We don't really like people who don't like us. If men think you don't like them, they probably won't like you back. Yes, this is the adult equivalent of nanny-nanny-boo-boo.

Uncomfortable Interactions

This may look like a coworker peering around your office doorway to see if you are in a friendly mood before asking for a favor, a supervisor who doesn't use eye contact when he approaches you cautiously after a contentious meeting, or someone trying to make a good impression on you by inauthentically complimenting the artwork in your office. People in these kinds of situations are generally in worse moods and feel worse about themselves than people who aren't worried about what other people think. It follows that these interactions are probably shorter, rockier, and less satisfying.[7]

Problems with Productivity

When all those cognitive resources are being used to try to monitor behavior, it can be hard for people to devote enough resources to the task at hand. In one study, white participants who interacted with an African American participant performed worse on a follow-up cognitive test than did white participants who interacted with white participants, suggesting that they had used up all of the brainpower they had to try to manage the impression they were making.[8]

So Do I Really Need to Worry about What He Is Worrying That I Might Be Worried About?

Is it your job to manage other people's metaperceptions? Probably not. These outcomes may or may not matter to you. However, if the guy in question is someone who is important to your work (e.g., a teammate) or career (e.g., a decision maker), it may be really important to try to manage the impression you are making on him.

If you decide it is important to you to build a positive working relationship with a particular guy, then you might try to get to know each other as people so he doesn't have to worry as much about what you are thinking. This getting-to-know-each-other strategy also has the added benefit of reducing the likelihood that you will judge each other based on gender stereotypes.

If you already do feel positively toward him, you simply need to communicate this in an effective manner. Tell him about your weekend or a project you just finished. Appropriate personal disclosures (not ones involving how wasted you were at a club or the anatomically correct description of childbirth) can facilitate trust and interpersonal friendships.[9] Ask him about his last job, his hobbies, or his family/pets to get him talking and increase his comfort.

If you don't actually like him all that much, getting to know him a bit better might improve your impression of him. Alternatively, you could try to make a list of all the positive things about him. Reframing your perspective of the guy might help you appreciate the good things.

Just as you wonder what your coworkers and romantic partner think about you, the men in your workplace are concerned about what is going on in that brain of yours. Addressing their concerns may make your life just a little bit easier.

22

Room with a Cue: How Your Cubicle Reveals More about You Than You Might Think

Has everyone seen by now that trash-tastic MTV reality show *Room Raiders*? It's the one where a lucky contestant goes through the rooms of three members of the opposite sex looking for clues to determine who they are most attracted to and will ultimately ask out on a date. At this point, the inevitable black light comes out to reveal otherwise hidden stains of questionable origin on the sheets, and everyone recoils in horror on cue.

Though the MTV producers almost certainly don't realize it, there is actually a body of solid social science behind the premise they've concocted—social psychologist Sam Gossling studies how people make inferences about our personalities based on the way we decorate and keep our rooms and work spaces summarized in an excellent book called *Snoop: What Your Stuff Says about You*. In this chapter, we'll discuss the ups and downs of cubicle life and show that your coworkers and bosses can make surprisingly informed estimates of your personality simply based on what your cube looks like.

Life in a Cube Farm

A litany of sardonic Dilbert cartoons chronicles the life of a typical office worker dwelling in a cube culture. Given the number of continuous hours that many workers spend at their desks, researchers have placed emphasis on the extent to which *arrangement* and *location* can facilitate or inhibit communication. Specifically, open spaces (e.g., shared offices, bullpen designs, or co-located workspaces) often facilitate frequent, short, and informal conversations, which subsequently lead to greater sharing of tacit information and stronger social bonds among teammates.[1]

Although open spaces can lead to better communication and innovation, many employees (particularly introverted, older, and high-status ones) react negatively to this change and report a decrease in satisfaction and privacy when moved to open spaces.[2, 3, 4] Designers have consequently worked to find ways to incorporate the positive collaborative nature of open environments with the privacy of closed offices, noting that the oft-demonized cubicle offers the worst of both environments.[5]

If These Old Walls Could Speak

So if cubicles are so terrible, can we at least glean some useful information from them? Gossling's research suggests that we can. You can play along at

home by taking a look at this picture and trying to deduce the gender, age, and personality type of the person who works here:

If you gathered from this picture that the cube belonged to a female worker in her 20s, you'd be correct (in fact, it is Jennifer's younger sister, Katie). If you went on to guess that she is highly extraverted (in fact, she is a laugh-until-your-stomach-hurts kind of funny), open to new experiences, conscientious, and emotionally stable, you would be right on. (If you want to keep playing, GlassDoor.com has a Web page devoted to what offices in different companies look like: www.glassdoor.com/blog/snap-upload -share-office-photos-glassdoor-chance-500.)

What do you have lying around *your* desk that gives away clues about your personality? A *diploma?* (If so, what does the educational institution say about you? Liberal arts degree? Technical or engineering school? Big state school?) *Drinking containers?* (A coffee mug? Multiple old Starbucks cups lying around growing mold cultures? A Kleen Kanteen?) *Travel books?* (If so, are they for regional road trips? Far off exotic locales?) *Pictures of yourself with others?* (If so, with large groups of people at a party? One-on-one pictures? Inside with your grandmother? Outside hiking with a buddy?) *Papers and reports?* (If so, are they scattered about in messy piles or stacked neatly in color-coded files?).

Whether we like it or not, whatever we decide to leave in our cubicle is what Gossling would consider "behavioral residue"—clues that gives observers insight when judging who you are. Some key takeaways from his research:

- Perhaps not surprisingly, it is easier for observers to figure out your personality from seeing your bedroom than your office, where there are more restrictions on what you can and can't do to change the environment—if we could, the ecru-colored walls and fluorescent lighting would be gone in a heartbeat.

- It turns out a cluttered desk really does equal a cluttered mind— observers were accurately able to predict a person's openness to experience, conscientiousness, and extraversion through how decorated and colorful the space was.

- It's not just your bedroom and office that contain this behavioral residue—your music collection, online social networking profile, and clothes do as well, which is why we devoted a whole other chapter in this section to discussing what your work attire says about you.[6, 7, 8, 9]

Gossling warns in an interview on National Public Radio that the stereotypes we have about people and their spaces can sometimes help us make more accurate predictions but in other cases make much worse ones, specifically when it comes to women's rooms:

> There's a stereotype in terms of personality that women are higher on a couple of these big five traits I talked about. One of these is known as agreeableness, if you want to think of it as the—sort of the "Mr. Roger's" factor. This is people who are nice, kind, sympathetic, and so on. So the stereotype is that women are higher on that.
>
> And the other stereotype is that women are higher on the trait of what's known as neuroticism, sort of "Woody Allen" factor. That is, they're more easily stressed, they're more emotional, they're more moody, and so on. So there are these stereotypes about women. And it was true that when our judges went into rooms, they judged those rooms they believed they belonged to females—and they almost always got it right—they judged those rooms to be higher on agreeableness and higher on neuroticism.
>
> However, it turns out that in that sample, the stereotype was only valid in the case of neuroticism, so the women in our study were higher on that trait but they weren't higher on agreeableness. And so it helped in the case of neuroticism, in fact, the stereotype helped it, improved accuracy, whereas it actually got in the way of accuracy in the case of agreeableness. It misled the judges.[10]

Section Four

How to Make It Work While Advancing in the Job: Getting Beyond the Glass Ceiling, the Glass Cliff, and the Sticky Floor

If you are the product of the 80s like we are, you certainly spent a fair share of your formative years playing Milton Bradley, Parker Brothers, and Hasbro board games—the rules were simple, the winners clear, and the objective was simply to have fun. Now that we're all (ostensibly) grown up, the game of work and life doesn't always seem so straightforward. Sometimes our jobs can seem like a big, random game of Chutes and Ladders—an unforeseen turn of events can either chute you back to square one or shooting up the (corporate) ladder. Do you ever feel like:

- After revealing your pregnancy, you find that your boss doesn't give you any challenging work assignments so you can "take it easy" for a few months—do not pass go, do not collect $200
- You nab a huge bonus after working overtime for several months to make sure the project you are leading wraps up on time—Yahtzee!
- A coworker knowingly torpedoes your presentation during a client meeting and takes your ideas as his own—you sunk my battleship!

Although the context may be different, the lessons learned playing these games are real—women who want to get ahead at work need to be aware of several potential roadblocks that may get in their way of success. For instance, working women not only have to contend with the ubiquitous *glass ceiling* (the invisible barriers that can keep women from inhabiting the very top echelon of leadership roles in an organization) but also the *sticky floor* (the subtle barriers that keep women in low-wage jobs), the *glass escalator* (the benefits that men in female-typed jobs in education receive), and the *glass cliff* (the appointment of women to precarious leadership positions only in times of crisis).

The glass cliff is particularly relevant now that the poor financial judgments of many older white men (the "pale, male, Yale club," as some have called it) have brought the world economy to a grinding halt. Or as the *Daily Show*'s Samantha Bee called it when discussing the "ladies' night" victory of several female candidates during the June 2010 primaries: "Apparently last night America got scared and with a poopy in its diaper, cried for its mommy . . . Yeah, I'm just saying it would be nice if the country turned to women when the country wasn't waste deep in tar balls and hobos."

Noting this phenomenon, *Time Magazine* ran a profile looking at the new, female "sheriffs of Wall Street" who have recently been brought in to clean up their mess:

> A few weeks back, at an event to celebrate the role of women in finance, Treasury Secretary Timothy Geithner tried to get things started with a joke. He said he had recently come across a headline that asked, "What If Women Ran Wall Street?"
>
> "Now that's an excellent question, but it's kind of a low bar," Geithner continued, deadpan amid rising laughter. "How, you might ask, could women not have done better?"
>
> It is rarely noted that the financial wreckage littering our world is the creation, almost exclusively, of men, not women. And no wonder: to this day, each of the large banks, from Citigroup to Goldman Sachs, employs fewer than a handful of women in senior positions, and only 3% of Fortune 500 companies have a woman as CEO. Embarrassing tales of a testosterone-filled trading culture tumbled out of the what-went-wrong probes as the Great Recession took hold.[1]

The trouble with women advancing isn't solely relegated to the financial sector, of course. Men's advancement and promotion in math and science continues to outpace women's, in part because of the many reasons we outlined in the first section (stereotype threat, affirmative action stigmas, implicit association biases) and subsequent sections (for example, work-family balance issues). *The New York Times* assesses:

> In computer science, for example, the percentage of female graduates from American universities peaked in the mid-1980s at more than 40 percent and has since dropped to half that, said Sue Rosser, a scholar who has written extensively on women in science. In electrical and mechanical engineering, enrollment percentages remain in the single digits. The number of women who are full science professors at elite universities in the United States has been stuck at 10 percent for the past half century. Throughout the world, only a handful of women preside over a national science academy. Women have been awarded only 16 of the 540 Nobels in science . . .
>
> Many obstacles women face in general are starkly crystallized in scientific and technological professions. Balancing a career with family is particularly tricky when the tenure clock competes with the biological clock or an engineering post requires long stints on an offshore oil rig. For couples, coordinating two careers is especially tough when both are in science. And 83 percent of women scientists in the United States have scientist partners, compared to 54 percent of male scientists . . . In this, too, Pierre and Marie Curie were trailblazers. If she is still an inspiration for women scientists, it is not only because she received two Nobel prizes, one in physics and one in chemistry. She also had a long-time marriage and two successful daughters.[2]

In this section, we will discuss several issues related to advancing in the job—compensation, negotiation, performance appraisal, feedback, developmental opportunities, leadership, effectively dealing with stress, and time management strategies—not just in the financial sector and math and science realms discussed above but across all industries. These aspects of advancement are affected not only by how women are perceived by organizational decision makers, but also by how women see themselves. For example:

- Women feel entitled to less money than men—experiments show they work longer for the same amount of money, and request less money for the same amount of work.

- Sitting at the head of the table helps a man establish to a group that he is the leader, but a woman doesn't receive the same subtle benefit.

- Women are often rated higher than man on certain aspects of job performance like being helpful (bringing in baked goods for everyone in the office to celebrate an organizational success) or having strong interpersonal communication skills ("use your words"), but on the dimensions of performance that really predict promotions (decisive decision making and strategic thinking), our performance ratings lag behind men.

- Organizations are more prone to appoint women to serve on their boards when their company is performing poorly—a situation where almost anyone is doomed to fail, including the newly appointed female leaders.

- Although women receive the same number of developmental work experiences as men, they are often less challenging than the ones men receive, and therefore less likely to help women get ahead professionally.

- When faced with a stressful situation, women don't follow the traditional "fight or flight" response typical of men—instead we are more likely to "tend and befriend" by looking to others for social support. Moreover, women in stressful career fields who successfully use time management techniques may avoid the burnout and emotional exhaustion typically associated with their harried jobs.

23

Gotta Get Better to Get Ahead: Making the Most of Feedback

We have no doubt that many of you are job and career rock stars—like Christina Yang (gotta love the confidence in this *Grey's Anatomy* surgeon) or the female equivalent of Doogie Howser, MD (we heart NPH, especially after his *Glee*-pisode!) for your particular position. Nevertheless, even Christina and Doogie realized that to move beyond the medical intern/resident stage of their careers, they needed to develop new skills. We realize that some of you may be happy as clams in your current roles and jobs, and uninterested in moving up in the organizational hierarchy. Nevertheless, salary increases and bonuses are generally related to the same performance ratings that determine promotions, so the need to improve likely still applies to you! One of primary paths through which you can work on enhancing your skill set and promotability is through receiving and responding to feedback. Sounds easy enough, right?

The most common process through which you will receive formal feedback is in a performance appraisal, A.K.A. performance management system, performance review, annual review, or annual feedback. Unfortunately, giving and receiving feedback is a process fraught with some serious complications.

Reflecting some of these issues, *The New York Times* ran two separate pieces on performance reviews in the span of a few years. The titles speak for themselves:

In 2006: "Performance Reviews: Many Need Improvement"[1]

In 2010: "Time to Review Workplace Reviews?"[2]

Clearly, the *Times* editorial team has unfavorable views of performance reviews. Unfortunately, the research doesn't paint a much prettier picture. An analysis of all the research on performance feedback found that more than one-third of all performance feedback interventions resulted in *worse* performance.[3] Yep, you read that correctly: job performance was worse after receiving feedback than it was before the feedback.

But *don't write off the review process too quickly!* The whole phenomenon (read: cash cow) of "executive coaching" is based on the premise that giving people feedback can help them to improve. Indeed, consultant-researchers at the Center for Creative Leadership find evidence that effective feedback is a critical determinant of success in the form of skill acquisition, performance, *and* promotability.[4] So the heart of the matter may not be about whether feedback is generally good or bad, but what *kind* of feedback is good.

What Is Good Feedback?

A few weeks ago, one of Eden's supervisors engaged in an attempt to give her feedback. In response to Eden's concerns (okay, complaints) about a lack of recognition for her productivity, this supervisor said, "You just need to do *more*." Internal outrage ensued. The internal dialogue was something like: "MORE?!! Do you have any idea how hard I'm working? YOU do more you *&*#@*!!!"

This is an example of ineffective feedback.

Eden did not feel motivated to perform her job better and in fact felt motivated to look for another job altogether. But what made it bad, and on the flip-side, what would have made it good?

Feedback can vary with regard to several dimensions:

1. **Valence:** Is the feedback positive, negative, or neutral?
2. **Specificity:** Is the feedback general or specific?
3. **Frequency:** How often are you getting feedback?
4. **Timing:** Is the setting appropriate (one-on-one)? Is there time for you to address the feedback before personnel actions (promotions, transfers) are made?
5. **Affect:** Is the feeling of the conversation generally positive (constructive, supportive) or negative (dismissive, destructive)?
6. **Basis:** Is the feedback based on good knowledge of your performance?

Most scholars agree that *good feedback is* based on firsthand knowledge of your performance in reference to clear standards of evaluation, includes discussion of both strengths and weaknesses, and is frequent, specific, and appropriately timed.

It follows that Eden's experience with negative feedback was ineffective in part because it was too general to be helpful. Her supervisor could have given her more explicit suggestions about what to do "more" of and how to do it. It was also ineffective because it seemed to be unfounded—it didn't seem to be directly related to any indicator of performance. The focus on negative, without consideration of the positive, aspects of performance may also have been part of the problem.

But let us be clear that *positive feedback can be just as ineffective as negative feedback.* One of the most common problems with feedback sessions is that the individuals giving the feedback are unwilling to state or discuss problems or issues—we avoid conflict by talking about negative things and focus on the positives. So all you might hear is fluff about butterflies and roses (the "pretty" parts of your job performance) rather than the dirt that's underneath it (the "real" view of your job performance). This is a real problem because if our supervisors never talk honestly about what needs to change, then we simply will never know what or how to improve.

Eden has been on both sides of this one. From the feedback-receiving perspective, her formal annual reviews generally consist of her boss's boss telling her, "Keep doing what you are doing." From the feedback-giving perspective, Eden has a hard time giving students less than an A on class assignments. (George Mason University students reading this should immediately forget the previous sentence!!) Even tougher are the one-on-one conversations with graduate students where it is actually really important that she help her graduate students to develop and improve. It is easy to tell people what you like about them. It is extraordinarily, gut-wrenchingly difficult to tell someone who you like, respect, and care about that they need to improve because it sounds a lot like saying "There is something wrong with you." And yes, this does give Eden some perspective on why her supervisor may have given her the crappy feedback described previously. But because it is such a crucial part of professional development, at least once each semester, Eden sucks it up and tries her best to have a constructive conversation with her students about their strengths and weaknesses.

In any given job, you are likely getting some kind of feedback. Because the quality of that feedback can determine your development and success, it is important to understand any gender differences in the feedback that men and women receive.

What Kind of Feedback Do Men and Women Get?

Numerical Ratings

One form of feedback is in the numerical ratings that are associated with many performance reviews. You might get a "4" that means "meets expectations" or a "2" that means "needs improvement." Not so different from the grades you got in elementary school. Experimental studies, in which undergraduate participants rate a fake employee who is either male or female but otherwise identical, sometimes find that the performance of women is rated lower than men, and other times find no differences between the ratings of men and women. In addition, a meta-analysis of 22 studies on performance ratings in field studies (surveys of people in the real world in real jobs) suggested that there were only very small differences in ratings of men and women in real jobs.[5] In other words, across a lot of different people and jobs, there does not seem to be a huge difference in men and women's ratings.

But ... there's always a but, isn't there? ... when researchers look beyond "overall ratings," there may be some important differences in the way that men and women are evaluated. On the bad-news side, performance measures on which gender differences were strongest were those that were stereotypic—women were rated positively on feminine performance outcomes like helpfulness and interpersonal skills and men were rated positively on masculine performance outcomes like decision-making and strategic thinking. This can be problematic because the "masculine" domains are the ones that are typically more valuable in organizations; companies are more likely to give a raise to or promote someone who is seen as a good decision-maker than someone who is helpful. These differences are also problematic because expectations that women should be feminine can lead them to get docked if they *don't* behave in feminine ways.[6] These kinds of expectations may explain findings in a study of people who were recently promoted to managerial positions.[7] The ratings of women who were promoted in this company were higher than the ratings of men who were promoted—women had to outperform men on numerical rating scales to earn the same promotion.

On the good-news side, however, when raters received formal training about objective rating scales and when raters were more familiar with the targets of their evaluations, there was less bias against women. So organizations can reduce some of the problems with rating scales by following the principles of "good" feedback outlined above.

Qualitative Comments

Beyond the numbers, many performance management systems involve verbal or written comments. The "So let's talk about how things are going" conversation. There is some evidence that these conversations may go differently for men and women in meaningful ways.

When there are gender differences in qualitative feedback, it goes one of two ways. The first is that women may get more negative feedback than men. This tends to happen as a form of backlash when women are in highly masculine jobs or positions.[8] This can feel a lot more like criticism than development. When you feel some hostility in an overly negative feedback session, it may mean that you are hearing something that has nothing to do with how well you are performing your job.

The second way it can go is that women get less negative feedback than men. Some of Eden's research suggests that some people believe in paternalistic or "benevolent" ideas about women, including the notion that women should be protected from harm. This desire to protect women can translate into giving less negative feedback to women. Indeed, in a survey about their work experience, women managers indicated that they got less negative feedback than did men.[9]

How Do Men and Women Interpret the Feedback They Get?

It isn't enough to get the feedback—we actually have to *do* something with it. Feedback isn't going to do us any good if we dismiss it, or worse, get defensive about it (as Eden did in the example above). There is some evidence that men and women react differently to the feedback they receive. In one questionnaire study, women reacted more favorably than men to negative feedback. In addition, women's ratings of themselves were influenced by both positive and negative feedback whereas men focused only on the positive aspects of their review.[10]

A survey of bank employees who just had an annual review suggests that women's but not men's self-esteem varied as a function of their evaluation; a negative evaluation was associated with reduced self-esteem and a positive evaluation was associated with increased self-esteem.[11] These results indicate that women tend to see feedback as more indicative of their ability than do men. It might seem that this is evidence that women are oversensitive. However, this same study showed that women were more likely than men to report intentions to change their behavior as a result of the feedback they received. Together these findings suggest that women take feedback seriously and are ready to act on it.

In another study, researchers wanted to consider not only the verbal aspects of feedback but also the nonverbal components of the communication. The authors reasoned that there may be "mixed messages" in feedback settings—a person could get very negative feedback in a very positive tone (and vice versa). To test the ways people respond to these mixed messages, the researchers gave undergraduate participants feedback about how they performed on a sorting task that was either positive or negative in content and either positive or negative in tone. They found that women focused more on the *content* of the messages whereas men tended to be caught up in the tone of the feedback.[12]

Should I Expect Different Feedback from Men and Women?

The gender of the person giving you feedback may affect the nature of the feedback you get. Research suggests that women may ease into feedback slowly and may be more reticent than men to give negative feedback. In a laboratory study, men and women watched a "fake" subordinate perform a task in manner that was either above or below average. Women were less likely to give negative feedback than were men.[13] In a survey, managers indicated their beliefs about the most effective ways to provide subordinates with performance feedback.[14] The results suggest that men and women shared some of the same goals when it comes to feedback, but that women tended to use a more indirect sequence with more interaction cycles that allowed shared discussion. For example, women tended to "set the scene" and put the feedback in context by initially acknowledging the positive aspects of their subordinates' work, and invited the subordinate's reaction to the feedback.

So How Should I React to the Feedback I Get?

Now that you know what you can expect in your next feedback session, here are some ideas about how to make sure you are making the most of it:

Make Sure You Get Your Sandwich

You want to make sure you hear both the good and the bad aspects of the feedback about your performance—the positive tells you what to keep doing and the negative tells you what you need to do to improve. So it may be useful to know that your boss may use the tried-and-true strategy of the "feedback sandwich." This is the tendency to start with positive feedback, quickly mention negative feedback, and then say something positive at the end. If you really *listen* for the whole sandwich and take note of both the positives and the negatives, you will be most likely to maximize the outcomes of the feedback session. Alternatively, if you never *hear* the sandwich (your boss really could be clueless about the need to give you both negative and positive feedback), *ask* for it. You could say something like, "I appreciate that I'm doing a good job at X. Are there ways that I could improve my performance in other areas?" Or in a more indirect fashion, "It is important to me that I develop my skills in ways that are valued in the company. Would you give me some insight about what these competencies/outcomes are?" At the end of the day, you really need that whole sandwich.

Get Motivated

Getting negative feedback can feel like a smackdown. It's okay to reflect (okay, mope) for a couple of days. But get up off the mat! Use the sandwich as fuel to push you forward.

Set SMART Goals

Research suggests that one of the most effective and simplest strategies for motivating behavior change is to set SMART goals.[15] (SMART goals are

Specific, Measurable, Attainable, Realistic, and Timely.) By being very specific about what you would like to accomplish in a particular time frame (e.g., My goal is to finish two chapters of this book by the weekend) you direct your attention towards tasks that support your goals (e.g., reading articles that help me write the chapter), and increase persistence and energy. Seal the deal by making sure you get rewarded for accomplishing your goals—if the organization doesn't do it directly, reward yourself with tickets to a show or a weekend adventure. This may be the ultimate way to turn the stressful or frustrating process of performance reviews into a happy ending.

24

Learning to Fly: Making Work Assignments Developmental

Jenna: Wait, listen to me. I'm 13!

Lucy: Jenna, if you're gonna start lying about your age, I'd go with 27.

—From the movie *13 Going on 30*

When some psychologists talk about "development," they are talking about the process through which infants grow into toddler status or about the joyful phase of adolescence (we cringe at that word!). Being a teenager is unfortunately not all that different from being on the lowest rungs of the organizational ladder—the same feelings of frustration, excitement, and trepidation may be apparent. Jennifer Garner's character Jenna experienced these painful truths when she aged 17 years overnight in the movie *13 Going on 30*. But when organizational psychologists talk about "development," we are talking about the process through which people experience *professional* growth. Who moves up in organizations is often determined by who has gained the necessary knowledge, skills, and abilities to complete the tasks required of the higher hierarchical level. This means that developmental work experiences can be key to your advancement.

Developmental work experiences (noun, plural, abbreviated *DWEs*): incidents individuals encounter at work and learn from in such a way that over time, across multiple experiences, they develop job relevant knowledge and skills.[1]

Am I Growing?

When your parents wanted to know whether you were growing at an appropriate rate physically, they made a mark on the wall to indicate the top of your head and pulled out a ruler. Determining whether you are growing successfully as a professional is a bit more complicated than taking out a measuring stick. What should you be doing to ensure that you are developing professionally? A famous scholar-practitioner from the Center for Creative Leadership, Cynthia McCauley, argued that there are five broad categories of DWEs in management: experiencing a job transition, creating change, managing at high levels of responsibility, managing boundaries, and dealing with diversity.[2] These represent tasks that require individuals to "stretch" beyond their current capabilities and gain new competencies related to managerial positions:

1. tasks requiring you to learn significantly new or unfamiliar responsibilities

2. tasks that require you to start something new in the organization or make strategic changes in business

3. tasks that place you in a position of having to fix problems created by a predecessor

4. tasks that require you to deal with subordinates who lack adequate experience, are incompetent, or are resistant to change

5. high stakes positions where pressure from senior managers, high visibility, clear deadlines, and responsibility for key decisions makes success or failure clearly evident

6. large tasks that include responsibility over multiple functions, groups, products, or services

7. tasks where you are placed in a position where there is a lot of external pressure that requires you to interface with important groups outside the organization, such as customers, unions, or government agencies

8. tasks that require you to influence peers, higher management, or other key people over whom you have no direct authority

9. tasks that require you to work with people from different cultures or with institutions in other countries

10. tasks where you have responsibility for the work of people of both genders and different racial and ethnic backgrounds

You may read this list and think "been there, done that" for each item. If so—awesome! But being there and doing that doesn't necessarily mean you are highly developed. Although a greater number of developmental experiences may be more helpful than a smaller number, the degree to which these experiences are genuinely useful depends on their quality. In an interview about her work in leadership development, Cynthia McCauley stated that:

> The developmental potential of any experience is enhanced when three elements are present: assessment, challenge, and support. Assessment includes the formal and informal processes for getting data about how you are doing in the assignment. Feedback from others is a common source of assessment, although self-reflection and getting reactions from a coach also provide assessment data. Challenge comes from being stretched by the assignment due to encountering new tasks, new responsibilities, increased demands, or more complex situations. Support helps people deal with the struggles of a challenging assignment. Support usually comes from coworkers, but can also come from family and friends.[3]

This means that more important the number of DWEs you amass is the extent to which these DWEs are characterized by challenge, feedback, and support.[4]

What Kind of Developmental Opportunities Can Women Expect?

Social science research has gone back and forth about whether or not there are gender differences in DWEs. On the one hand, some findings suggest that women do not have as much access as men to DWEs like high-risk projects or turning a business around.[5] On the other hand, however, other studies show that men and women who are in executive positions report similar rates of developmental opportunities.[6]

Eden and her colleagues worked to resolve these mixed findings.[7] They believed that part of the reason for the inconsistent results from previous studies is because researchers did not separate the *quantity* of DWEs from the *quality* of the DWEs. Indeed, they argued that, while men and women might encounter a similar *number* of DWEs, the nature of development experienced by men and women might be different. To test these expectations, the research team conducted five separate studies. In the first study, managers in the energy industry reported the number of DWEs they had participated in, as well as the amount of challenge, feedback, and support they received in those DWEs. The results suggested that men and women had a similar number of DWEs, but that women's experiences were less challenging and included less negative feedback than men's experiences.

The second study found a similar pattern in a sample of managers in the health-care industry. But because these studies relied on men and women to report their own perceptions about the nature of DWEs, there were questions about whether men and women perceive the same assignment differently. In addition, these studies couldn't determine whether men and women were *choosing* or being *assigned* different kinds of experiences. So the follow-up studies involved experiments in which participants indicated whether a fake employee ("Kenneth" or "Katherine") should be assigned tasks that were either challenging or easy. The results suggested that "Katherine" was assigned less challenging DWEs than was "Kenneth." The pattern of findings confirms that women get different kinds of developmental opportunities than men that tend to be less challenging.

So How Can I Improve My Development?

Challenge Is a Good Thing. Challenging experiences are "demanding, stimulating, new, and call on [your] ability and determination."[8] These are qualities that enhance learning and skill acquisition. It is therefore quite important that you get challenged! It's kinda like exercise and how you have to get your heart rate pumping to make changes in your body and physical capabilities—in business, you have to expand your mind to make changes in your professional capabilities. This means that if you are interested in developing, you can't get complacent. You need to "work out" as often as possible.

But Watch Out for the Cliff. There's a difference between professional work outs and setting yourself up to fall on your face. Recent research suggests that women sometimes get put into positions that may seem developmental, but actually leave little room for success.[9] A study of 100 top companies suggested that companies were more likely to appoint women to their board of directors when they had experienced a sharp decline in stock market performance than when they were stable or improving in performance. In other words, companies put women in positions of power when it was nearly impossible for *anyone* to succeed. This kind of experience may be good from a learning perspective, but not from the perspective of developing a professional reputation. So watch out for and avoid these "glass cliffs"!

Make Your Own Development

You have the power to shape your own development! McCauley gave useful suggestions about how to reshape your job to ensure that you are developing professionally:

> First is to talk with your boss. Is there something currently on his or her plate that could be delegated to you? Look for things that have become routine for your boss, but would be a stretch for you. Another strategy is to trade a responsibility with a colleague. The added bonus here is that you can serve as each other's coach as you master the new work. A third approach is to take on responsibilities that are currently "falling through the cracks," that is, work that would help your group or the organization but no one is paying attention to it. For example, one manager told us about starting a formal intern program for her organization. The organization sometimes made use of interns, but not in any systematic way. The manager learned more about work processes throughout the organization and honed her ability to spot and develop talent. A final strategy is to devote more time to an aspect of your job that could be developmental if you spent more time focused on it, for example, coaching employees or negotiating with vendors. Sometimes people avoid the parts of their job that they aren't good at—a sure strategy for not improving in these areas.[10]

Don't get stuck in the "kids table" of the working world. Being a teenager once was enough! Be thoughtful and purposeful about your professional growth and you'll develop their socks off.

25

Moving on Up: How Women Become Leaders

Once upon a time (in 1975), a baby named Marissa was born in small town in Wisconsin. She was on the pom-pom squad and the debate team. She went to college, got a masters degree, and took a somewhat risky job in a small startup company. Marissa's story sounds like that of a lot of women we know and count as friends. And like many women, there is more to Marissa's story than is immediately apparent.

The debate team and pom-pom squads won statewide awards. The degrees were in Symbolic Systems and Computer Science from Stanford, specializing in artificial intelligence. And the job was for a company you might have heard about—Google.[1]

Thirty-five-year-old Marissa Mayer was the first female engineer in the company and is now the vice president for search products & user experience. Her work has included defining Gmail and developing Google's search interface. She was the youngest woman ever to be included on *Fortune Magazine*'s list of Most Powerful Women.

We can't all be one of the top 10 women for whatever business we are in. But we *can* all find a path to our own success.

What Is Career Success and How Can I Get Some?

The question of what gets people promoted has been the organizational psychologists' equivalent of a Rubik's cube—we've been working to get all the different colors aligned. And while it may not be very helpful to know that taller people are more likely to get promoted than shorter people[2] (which is very frustrating for the vertically challenged half of the authorship team!), research does point to some important predictors of career success.

However, predictors of "success" may be a little different depending on how it is defined. Marissa undoubtedly has achieved a high salary, prestige, and power. We hope—but cannot know—whether she is also satisfied with her career. An analysis of more than 50 studies on predictors of career success points to somewhat different antecedents of the success-related outcomes of *pay*, *promotions*, and *career satisfaction*.[3] Work experience, education, intelligence, and ability to play organizational politics were among the strongest predictors of success as defined by salary. When success was defined as the number of promotions a person received, training and skill developmental opportunities, networking, and personality were predictors.

Perhaps most importantly, how much people reported being satisfied with their careers was related to quite different factors: career planning which refers to strategic ideas about career path and supervisor support/ mentoring seemed to be most important in determining career satisfaction. This highlights the importance of deciding what success means to *you*. Finding supportive supervisors who will help you plan a career that fits your personal and professional goals may be a good way to ensure that you achieve *your* success.

Based on her current role, we're guessing that Marissa's definition of success may include professional power in the form of leadership positions. According to *San Francisco Magazine*, Marissa is a quintessential example of what organizational psychologists refer to as an "emergent leader", a person who grows into a leadership position through leaderlike behavior[4]:

> "Marissa was hired for a programming job," says Craig Silverstein, Google's technology director and the company's first employee. "Now you look at her, and she's the one deciding what we do." He says Mayer is the most talented person he's ever known.

If you want to be the one deciding what to do in your workplace, you are likely looking for ways that you can move on up to that deluxe corner office in the sky.

Do Women Generally Emerge as Leaders?

Think about the last time you were in a group where there wasn't a clear leader. It might have been a study group in college or a brainstorming team at your job. Somewhere in the course of your discussions with your team-mates, it is very likely that a leader emerged. This person may not have been formally labeled the "leader," but they likely guided the process of the team's work, made decisions on behalf of the team, and/or resolved con-flicts among team members. Who was this leader—got someone in mind? Okay, now answer two questions: Was the leader a woman? Was it you?

When groups are comprised of equal numbers of men and women, men are somewhat more likely than women to emerge as leaders. Indeed, researchers have long theorized that one of the reasons that women are not represented at the highest levels of organizations is because men might engage in and be rewarded for different, more leaderlike, behaviors in group settings. Moreover, a review of the literature before 1990 point sug-gested that women were less likely than men to emerge as leaders, particu-larly in short-term groups that did not involve a lot of social interaction.[5] This tendency is likely a consequence of beliefs that the characteristics of being a woman (e.g., nurturing, kind) are not aligned with the charac-teristics of being a good leader (e.g., assertive, strong).[6] This kind of belief system would make it difficult for women to achieve leadership positions because women are seen as less leaderlike in general and are evaluated differently if they begin to act in more leaderlike ways because these are more masculine and therefore not feminine "enough."

So How Can Women Become Leaders?

How did Marissa make it to the top of the Google world? Research sug-gests that she likely was confident in her professional value, developed appropriate knowledge, skills, and abilities, and balanced feminine and masculine behaviors.

Positive Views of the Self

One factor that probably helped was having a positive view of herself. The U.S. Bureau of Labor Statistics conducted a longitudinal study to track the life and work experiences of young people as they developed. This National

Longitudinal Survey of Youth involved interviews with 12,000 young people at multiple points in time between 1979 and 2004. One report of these data shows that individuals who viewed themselves in a positive manner (who had high "core self-evaluations") tended to have steeper career trajectories (with regard to pay and occupational status) than individuals with lower views of themselves.[7] In other words, people who felt good about themselves actually got paid more and more quickly than people who didn't feel so great about themselves. This suggests that developing a positive view of yourself may be an important first step toward career success.

Get Noticed

The assumption is that you are going to do your job, and you are going to do it well. The chance to get noticed in ways that might help you gain leadership positions is beyond this high level of job performance. In other words, if you want to get promoted, you gotta do more than your job. In some ways this seems ridiculous ("how am I supposed to find time to do more than the job I am already doing?"), but in other ways it makes sense—from your company's perspective, you need to prove that you have the knowledge, skills, and abilities (KSAs) that will ensure you are effective at a higher level of the organization. And the KSAs at that higher level include KSAs that are not part of your current job. Just because you are a stellar salesperson, for example, doesn't mean you'd be great at managing other salespeople.

To get noticed, the first step is to do a personal "gap analysis." Identify the KSAs needed in the job you want and the ways in which your current level of KSAs measure up. Second, engage in high quality developmental experiences (see previous chapter on this topic) that give you the KSAs you need for the promotion you are seeking. Third, find strategies to let organizational decision-makers know that you have gained these KSAs. This can sometimes be a formal part of the annual review process. But if there isn't a formal structure in place through which to communicate your newly-acquired KSAs, you need to find other ways to demonstrate your qualifications.

One route would be to volunteer to take on an assignment that uses these KSAs or to subtly mention that you are excited about what you recently learned through your developmental activity. (Yes, this is kinda like name-dropping except you are dropping your own name/capabilities!) A more direct path would be to set up a meeting with your supervisor to discuss your career trajectory. The bottom line is to get prepared and to communicate your preparedness.

Balance between Masculine and Feminine Behaviors

Stereotypes about women lead to expectations that they are nice and warm, whereas men are expected to be decisive and aggressive. Deviations from these expectations (for example, decisive or aggressive women) are met with disdain (see also our chapter on negotiations). This means that women who order subordinates to do a particular task may be described as bitchy, whereas a man in the same position would be seen as aggressive. So women who aspire to leadership positions walk a thin line between being feminine enough to avoid social backlash, and masculine enough to be taken seriously in a position of power.

Marissa Mayer may have figured out a way to strike this balance. In a profile entirely centered around her success, *Businessweek* claimed that:

> A large part of Mayer's success at Google is due to her ability to travel easily between different worlds. When she first joined, the company had something of a high-school cliquishness, albeit in reverse. At lunch, the coolest kids—in this forum, the smartest geeks—sat together. On the periphery, sales and marketing folks gathered. Mayer could hold her own in either realm. "She's a geek, but her clothes match," says one former employee. Mayer continues to bridge the gap between MBAs and PhDs. She helps decide when employees' pet projects are refined enough to be presented to the company's founders. Such decisions are often made through an established process, with Mayer giving ideas a hearing during her open office hours or during brainstorming sessions. Yet she is also good at drawing out programmers informally, during a chance meeting in the cafeteria or hallway.[8]

According to a quote in the *New York Times*, Marissa herself recognized the need to balance masculine and feminine characteristics:

> "I refuse to be stereotyped," she says. "I think it's very comforting for people to put me in a box. 'Oh, she's a fluffy girlie girl who likes

clothes and cupcakes. Oh, but wait, she is spending her weekends doing hardware electronics.' "[9]

Should Marissa have to worry about how others perceive her interest in hardware electronics, new clothes, or cupcakes? Absolutely not. But the truth is that her comfort in both masculine and feminine domains has probably helped her up the multicolored Google corporate ladder. You may not care about this ladder, or you may feel that the most important thing is to be authentically *you*, whether you are masculine, feminine, or somewhere in between. We celebrate that authenticity—Eden picked a job where she can wear jeans to work almost everyday, bring cookies to class, and voice her opinions in department meetings and loves it. But if impression management or gaining positions of power is important to you, it may be worthwhile to figure out how you can strike a happy balance between the masculine and feminine aspects of your personality.

26

View from the Top: Living the Leader Life

Somewhere out in this audience may even be someone who will one day follow in my footsteps, and preside over the White House as the President's spouse. I wish him well!

—Barbara Bush, First Lady [at Wellesley College Commencement]

On June 8, 2010, political pundits across the country were glued to their computer and TV screens as votes in a primary election were cast in 11 states. One of the most compelling aspects of this particular primary is the fact that four of the major state races involved female front-runners. Why was this newsworthy? Why is the opening quote by Barbara Bush remarkable?

Probably because the representation of women in the highest levels of our government (like the representation of women in organizations) is incredibly small. In the 111th Congress, only 17 of the 100 senators, and 75 of 435 members of the House of Representatives, are women. That means that a group comprising 50 percent of the population only makes up 17 percent of the elected leaders. These women are truly remarkable.

You've Made It! Rock On!

We hereby salute these legislators, the 15 women who are C.E.O.s of the Fortune 500, the three female supreme court justices, and all the other trailblazers (including YOU) who have earned leadership positions! You make us proud.

You've Made It! Now Make it Work!

We realize that our pride in you won't buy you a pack of chewing gum. But we can warn you about the kinds of challenges that you will likely encounter in your leadership positions, as well as strategies for overcoming them.

Likely Challenges in Your New Role

Being (Un)seen as a Leader

You've probably heard stories about or personally experienced cases of mistaken identity. One of our friends, Nicole, told us she overheard people discussing the person who was promoted into a leadership role in the company. They said, "I wonder who *he* is!" Nicole interrupted, "*She* is me!" Another friend, Sharyn, was put in charge of a new team to develop strategy for how the company could survive the recession. At the first meeting, one of the team members (assuming Sharyn was an administrative assistant rather than the team leader) asked her to get them a cup of coffee. These examples typify the invisible, but pervasive, belief that leaders are men. Just think about the last time you read an article about the appointment of a new C.E.O. Was the gender of the C.E.O. mentioned? Chances are that gender was not mentioned in the articles regarding male C.E.O.s, but that gender was an important component of articles regarding female C.E.O.s. Female leaders are still consciously or unconsciously seen as deviations from the norm.

An interesting older experiment demonstrated the challenge of being recognized as a leader.[1] Participants looked at a picture of a group of professionally dressed people sitting around a long table and were asked to identify the leader of the group. The group was comprised of all women, all men, or half and half. In the male group, the man seated at the head of the table was always identified as the leader of the group. In the all female group, the effect was the same—the woman who was at the head of the table was identified as its leader. Importantly, however, in the mixed-gender group, participants tended to pick one of the men seated on the side of the table as the leader of the group. The same cue (sitting at the head of the table) did not convey the position of leadership for women as clearly as it did for men. More recent research suggests that this invisibility may be more pronounced among men; the tendency to guess that a man was the leader of a mixed-gender group emerged in young men but not young women.[2] This means that women likely have to do more than men to be recognized as leaders by men.

Reactions to Your Leadership

Once you have established your leadership of a group, you may face a different kind of challenge. Now you have to deal with how people react to you as a leader. And it ain't always pretty.

In one convincing study about the ways people react to male and female leaders, participants took part in a discussion with three other people.[3] One of the four team members was actually an undercover experimenter—male and female actors who knew about the real purpose of the study and followed scripted dialogue. One undercover actor was assigned to be the "leader" in each group. While the groups completed the task, other experimenters who were not aware of the study's hypotheses evaluated the behaviors of the team members from behind one-way mirrors. These evaluations showed that male and female leaders (who acted in precisely the same ways) got different reactions from their teammates. The teammates of female actor-leaders responded more negatively than did the teammates of male actor-leaders. More specifically, women got more negative, and fewer positive, reactions. This meant things that female leaders were treated with less friendliness, eye contact, gaze, and forward body posture than were male leaders. So if you feel like people are looking at you funny when you begin a meeting or issue an order, you probably aren't imagining it.

These differential reactions extend to leaders' expressions of emotion. A researcher named Victoria Brescoll at Yale University asked the question, "Can an angry woman get ahead?" in three separate experiments. Participants watched videos of fictitious job interviews with men and women who either expressed sadness, anger, or no emotions. Men who expressed anger were rated as more competent, and deserving of higher status positions with larger salaries, than were women who expressed anger. In other words, expressing anger helped men and hurt women. These effects suggest that men and women are perceived differently when engaging in exactly the same behavior.[4]

Penalties for Success

One of the most prominent researchers in the study of women and leadership is Madeline Heilman from NYU. She's written thousands of pages about the factors that constrain women's success in masculine roles, like leadership. In a few of these pages, Madeline and her colleagues were interested in understanding how people evaluate women who have succeeded. They reasoned that stereotypes about women include ideas that women should *not* be self-assertive, achievement-oriented, or tough. One of the reasons these stereotypes are problematic is because a woman's success, particularly in male-typed domains, indicates that she has successfully engaged in male-typed behaviors (like assertiveness, achievement orientation, and toughness). Rather than getting pats on the back for successful performance, women in masculine roles might get backlash.

The researchers tested this basic expectation in a set of three studies.[5] In the first study, participants read about Andrea and James, assistant vice presidents in a masculine job (aircraft company dealing with engine assemblies, fuel tanks, etc.). Andrea and James were described as stellar performers. For half of the participants, the performance evaluations of Andrea and James were based on clear performance outcomes—a recent annual review which designated them as a top performer. For the other half of the participants, Andrea and James were about to undergo the annual performance review process; in other words, the performance evaluations were more ambiguous. The results showed that Andrea was seen as less competent than James when performance evaluations were ambiguous. This suggests that the benefit of the doubt goes to men, rather than women. Perhaps even more importantly, when success was explicit and obvious, Andrea was rated as less likeable and more interpersonally hostile than James. Women seem to face interpersonal penalties when they succeed.

In a second study using a similar experimental design, the researchers were interested in whether this effect only emerged in masculine domains. They compared ratings of Andrea and James as assistant vice presidents of a Financial Planning Division (male-typed), Employee Assistance Division (female-typed), and Training Division (gender-neutral). Andrea was again rated lower than James, but only when they were described as leaders in the Financial Planning Division. This suggests that women may face particularly negative penalties when they succeed in male-typed tasks.

You might be thinking who cares if they *liked* the women? Just like good parents, good leaders can be effective without being liked, right? Unfortunately, the researchers' third study suggested that when participants learned that Andrea and James were not well-liked by their colleagues, they were less likely to support them for promotions or salary increases. Together these studies suggest that, "success can create an additional impediment to women's upward mobility when they have done all the right things to move ahead in their careers" (p. 426). So what can you do when doing all the right things doesn't seem like enough?

How to Overcome These Challenges

Call us optimists, but we believe frowns can be turned upside-down! Even if you want to call the glass half empty, you might be interested in understanding the ways in which being a woman can be to your advantage as a leader.

Overcoming (Baseless) Disliking

Madeline Heilman didn't stop at identifying the interpersonal problems that successful women face when they are in male-typed positions. She went further to determine how women can counteract the backlash she demonstrated. In another set of three studies, Madeline and her student Tyler Okimoto tested the idea that the backlash successful women received can be avoided if these women convinced evaluators that they were not "counternormative"; in other words, successful women might avoid backlash if evaluators believe they are still "feminine" enough. Across the three studies, the researchers informed some participants that Andrea, a successful leader, was "understanding and concerned about others" (Study 1), "placed great importance on understanding the concerns of employees" (Study 2), or that Andrea had children (Study 3). In all cases, when Andrea was described as being not only successful but also feminine, she was seen as more likeable as a leader than when no feminine information was included.[6] This means that, if you want to get past some negative reactions, you can emphasize aspects of your personality that are more feminine in nature. If you go this route, keep in mind that emphasizing feminine traits or behaviors really only helps when you've already established your competence—the first step is to get other people to recognize your success.

A Female Advantage?

We have demonstrated in the previous sections that female leaders are *perceived* differently than male leaders. There's some evidence that they may *behave* slightly differently when it comes to their style of leadership, too. Leadership styles refer to relatively stable patterns of behavior enacted by leaders.

Some have argued that, with increased attention to ideas like "work-life balance" and "corporate social responsibility", women's leadership styles are actually *superior* to those of men. Yup, some people think that the way women lead is actually *better* than the way men lead. This is a pretty sexy idea, and the media has noticed! A quick Google search yields interesting titles: "Women Leaders Smarter, More Honest," "Women Are Better Leaders," and "Women Are Better Leaders than Men. Period." But what does the data about leadership styles actually suggest?

The most recent review of 45 studies on gender and leadership styles suggests that women behave in ways more consistent with a *transformational leadership style* than do men.[7] Leaders who are transformational gain trust, respect, and confidence from their subordinates and act as role models through mentoring and empowerment. Think of Bailey on *Grey's Anatomy* or President Bartlett on *The West Wing*. Men, on the other hand, were more likely to engage in some forms of *transactional leadership*, which involves more standard forms of interactions with subordinates in which roles and goals are clarified and duties distributed, like paying close attention to subordinates' mistakes and failures.

Men were also somewhat more likely to engage in laissez-faire leadership behaviors, which include failures to take responsibility for actions and outcomes. Both transformational and transactional styles of leadership are components of effective leadership, but the data suggested that subordinates of female (and transformational) leaders tended to report being more satisfied and inspired than did subordinates of male (and transactional) leaders. Thus, there may actually be a (small) advantage in the leadership styles that women use when they are able to get beyond the glass ceiling and the sticky floor.[8] And that means that you can get some r-e-s-p-e-c-t that would make us (and Aretha) even prouder.

27

It's about Time: Incorporating Time Management and Planning Practices into Your Workday

A stitch in time saves nine.

The early bird gets the worm.

Plan for the worst, hope for the best.

A penny saved is a penny earned.

Chance favors the prepared mind.

Prior planning prevents poor performance.

Growing up, we are taught myriad proverbs about effective time management, productivity, and the importance of planning by well-meaning adults. Those who internalize these lessons early, it is assumed, go on to be valuable members of society and happy worker bees. But does the organizational research support these axioms? In this chapter, we'll discuss the literature on time management and share the techniques that can best help working women reduce their stress from time demands and improve their productivity on the job.

What Are the Dimensions of Time Management (and Why Do They Matter?)

Therese Macan (a fellow Rice organizational psychology department alum) developed the Time Management Behavior Scale, which has several dimensions[1,2]:

- **Setting Goals and Priorities:** engaging in activities like breaking down tasks into more manageable subtasks, setting deadlines, keeping long-term goals, setting short-term goals, evaluating a daily schedule, setting priorities to determine an order to perform tasks, using waiting time effectively, dealing with incoming mail promptly, avoiding interruptions, and scheduling time daily

- **Mechanics of Time Management:** utilizing skills like making to-do lists and checking off tasks as they are accomplished, carrying an appointment book, writing reminder notes, scheduling events weekly, organizing paperwork, leaving a clean workspace, and keeping a daily log

- **Having a Preference for Organization:** being naturally inclined toward organization, wanting to keep a clean workplace, preplanning tasks, and prioritizing tasks

- **Perceived Control of Time:** not feeling overwhelmed by trivial or unimportant tasks, not underestimating the time required to complete a task, keeping to a set schedule, not procrastinating, not losing sight of objectives, not taking on too many tasks, delegating tasks, and thinking before acting (her research shows this is the most important factor and is more of an outcome of the first three dimensions)

Why should you care about these time management behaviors? Because she found that people who scored higher overall on this time management scale tended to have greater job and life satisfaction, higher performance, less ambiguity about their roles, and less physical tension. Additionally, she found that women scored higher on the overall scale than men, particularly on utilizing the mechanics of time management skills, but there were no gender differences in perceived control of time. In a separate study she found that formal time management training may not be that effective at improving performance; instead, we may be more likely to learn useful techniques informally from watching and learning from successful coworkers or mentors.

Additional psychological research has also shown interesting, and sometimes surprising, findings regarding time management, work, and women:

- Despite the stereotype of the disorganized artist, creativity is actually positively related to daily planning behaviors, perceived control of time, and preference for organization.[3]

- Gender differences in time management probably start early, as some research found that middle school females scored higher than their male counterparts in meeting deadlines and planning.[4]

- One recent review of 32 psychological studies on time management found that engaging in these time management techniques is related to decreased stress, increased health, and higher job satisfaction.[5] The review also found that successful time management was associated with high Conscientiousness scores (yep, the same personality dimension we talked about way back in the first section).

- In particularly stressful jobs where work demands are high and autonomy low (like elementary school teachers), those workers with strong time management skills are less likely to experience job burnout and emotional exhaustion than those without these skills.[6]

- Interestingly, if you are not meeting all of your work demands, creating to-do lists may be counterproductive, because it objectively shows you just exactly how much you still have to do and may lead you to feel that you have little control over your time.[7]

How Do These Techniques Work in the Real World?

The experiences of real-life business leaders seem to validate these psychological findings—listed below are quotes from several successful female managers about successful time management and productivity techniques they have adopted:

Teresa Taylor, C.O.O. of Quest

Well, I would say in the beginning I thought I had to keep work and home very separate. I thought that's what you're supposed to do, especially as a woman. You know, you don't bring up your children and you don't bring up the fact that you're having these issues at home. I think young women think you have to be like a man to succeed. I was like that. I just didn't talk about those things. After a while, when I brought my personal life into the office, it was okay. Turns out, other people have kids, too. And, turns out, other people have these issues. I felt more comfortable when I could intertwine them. Now my calendar is one calendar, everything personal and everything professional is on one calendar. I used to keep literally two separate calendars, and then wonder why I missed a few things.[8]

Maigread Eichten, President and C.E.O. of FRS

I work out really early in the morning, and I use that time to kind of set my key priorities for the day—the two or three work things, the two or three personal things, and what are the key personal relationships that I want to make sure are set. That's usually one of my top priorities— making sure that the team works well together. If I sense something's off a little bit with the team, that's usually one of the first things I zero in on. When I come in, my first priority is to go through the to-do list before anybody's here, and make sure that I've got a list on my desk of no more than 10 key things that I want to get done. I find if you have a to-do list of more than 10, it's just not going to happen, and I pretty much stick to that list.[9]

Sharon Napier, C.E.O. of Partners + Napier

I am really, really good at having 100 things going. None of the tricks seem to work. But I do two things. At the beginning of the year, I say, how has my role evolved, and what are the two or three things that I have to accomplish by the end of the year? So I really do that for myself, and I stay very directed by that.[10]

Anne Mulcahy, C.E.O. of Xerox

I'm at the gym at 6, so I'm usually in my office by 7:15. And I try to not schedule a lot of meetings before 8. So I've got that first hour to get myself organized for the day, and to make sure that I've structured what I want to do. The other thing is, most people in my position would say that as much as we'll whine about traveling, time on planes probably is critically important to us doing our jobs. It's time to be reflective. It's time to catch up. It's time to really be thoughtful and communicate. So I get off a plane with just a ton done, and that's really important in terms of time management.[11]

Carol Smith, Senior VP and Chief Brand Officer for Elle Group

I don't waste time. If you want to chat, if you want to gossip, I'll gossip with anyone, I'll hang out. But when I'm working, I'm working. When you sit here in my office, we work. Men don't do that as well as women do, either. All of sudden they're on football. All of a sudden they're showing videos of their son's soccer game. Then they're telling a couple of jokes. I'm not good at jokes during meetings. I'm very focused. I'm very singularly directed.[12]

Barbara Corcoran, New York Real Estate Agent and Shark Tank Panelist

Make the next day's "to do" list before you leave the office. Rate each item A, B, or C based on its importance, and work on A items first. The productiveness of any meeting depends on the advance thought given the agenda, and you should never leave a meeting without writing a follow-up list with each item assigned to one person. And go outside. All the big ideas are on the outside. You'll never have a creative idea at your desk.[13]

Krissi Barr, Founder of Barr Corporate Success

If I think something is going to take me an hour, I give myself 40 minutes. By shrinking your mental deadlines, you work faster and with greater focus. I also schedule time every week on my calendar for quiet, concentrated PowerTime where I only work on my most important activities. A "Stop Doing" list is as important as a "To Do" list. A "To Do" list is easy, you just keep adding to it and the more you have on it, the more important you may feel. But "Stop Doing" is more difficult because you have to give up some things.[14]

Caterina Fake, Cofounder of Flickr and Hunch

When I used to have meetings, this is how I would do it: There would be an agenda distributed before the meeting. Everybody would stand. At the beginning of the meeting, everyone would drink 16 ounces of water. We would discuss everything on the agenda, make all the decisions that needed to be made, and the meeting would be over when the first person had to go to the bathroom.[15]

(Ok, we'll throw in one male C.E.O., just because we think his advice is so stellar and succinct.)

Richard Anderson, C.E.O. of Delta Air Lines

Only touch paper once. No. 2, always have your homework done. No. 3, return your calls very promptly. No. 4, stick to your schedule. I keep my watch about 10 minutes ahead. It's important to run on time, particularly at an airline. And use your time wisely. And then, once a month, take the rest of the calendar year, or the next six months and re-review how you are using your time and reprioritize what you're doing.[16]

We'll close this chapter with an e-mail forward everyone has probably seen at least once—Jennifer received it from her parents during a particularly stressful time her senior year of college when she was juggling an honors thesis, graduate school applications, part-time work as a psychology teaching assistant, and serving as president of her sorority. It is titled "Big Rocks" (the passage is often attributed to management guru Steven Covey, who said one of his associates heard it at a seminar and passed it along) and is a metaphor that still guides her time management philosophy even a decade later:

An expert in time management was speaking to a group of business students and, to drive home a point, used an illustration those students will never forget. As he stood in front of the group of high-powered overachievers he said, "Okay, time for a quiz" and he pulled out a one-gallon mason jar and set it on the table in front of him. He also produced about a dozen fist-sized rocks and carefully placed them, one at a time, into the jar.

When the jar was filled to the top and no more rocks would fit inside, he asked, "Is this jar full?" Everyone in the class yelled, "Yes." The time management expert replied, "Really?"

He reached under the table and pulled out a bucket of gravel. He dumped some gravel in and shook the jar causing pieces of gravel to work themselves down into the spaces between the big rocks. He then asked the group once more, "Is the jar full?" By this time the class was on to him. "Probably not," one of them answered.

"Good!" he replied. He reached under the table and brought out a bucket of sand. He started dumping the sand in the jar and it went into all of the spaces left between the rocks and the gravel. Once more he asked the question, "Is this jar full?" "No!" the class shouted. Once again he said, "Good." Then he grabbed a pitcher of water and began to pour it in until the jar was filled to the brim.

Then he looked at the class and asked, "What is the point of this illustration?" One eager beaver raised his hand and said, "The point is, no matter how full your schedule is, if you try really hard you can always fit some more things in it!" "No," the speaker replied, "That's not the point. The truth this illustration teaches us is: If you don't put the big rocks in first, you'll never get them in at all."

What are the "big rocks" in your life—time with your loved ones, your faith, your education, your dreams, a worthy cause, teaching or mentoring others? Remember to put these BIG ROCKS in first or you'll never get them in at all. So, tonight, or in the morning, when you are reflecting on this short story, ask yourself this question: What are the "big rocks" in my life? Then, put those in your jar first.[17]

28

"I Got 99 Problems": Dealing with Stress on the Job

Jay-Z may not have the most female-empowering lyrics, but we'll put aside that misogynic debate for now. The hook in his iconic song certainly resonates with many of us who also feel we're constantly juggling 99 problems at work and at home. Stress is one of those pervasive topics that psychologists have studied from almost every perspective: clinical, neurological, physiological, developmental, social, and—you guessed it—organizational.

We'll spend much of the next section on work-family issues talking about these types of specific stresses—for example, negative work-to-family spillover (you have an awful day at work and so are more irritable with your children and partner when you get home) and negative family-to-work spillover (you are worried about your son's grades in school and so have a hard time concentrating while giving a presentation for your clients). Here instead we'll provide a broad framework for thinking about what causes stress on the job, what the outcomes are of experiencing it, and evidence-based strategies for how to cope.

What Causes Stress?

Remember the perturbed little protagonist in the children's book *Alexander and the Terrible, Horrible, No Good, Very Bad Day*? We've all had those days, even in the grown-up world—you're running late for an early morning meeting because you spilled coffee on your suit while getting ready, your boss makes an off-handed comment after the meeting that makes you question your abilities, two of your work friends decide to go to lunch together but forget to invite you, you have to spend the afternoon fecklessly trying to answer phone calls because the economy has forced your organization to lay off most of the customer service department, and your commute on the way home takes an extra 45 minutes because of an accident. In other words, to quote another popular children's book, a series of unfortunate events.

What are some of the most common causes of stress in the workplace?

- **Poor Job Design.** There is a good chance that if your job is causing you stress, than one or more important elements are missing from what organizational psychologists call "job design," or the aspects of people's jobs that best predict employee motivation, productivity, performance, satisfaction, and yes, stress.[1] This line of research reveals the following key core job characteristics and psychological states ultimately support positive work outcomes, particularly those with high growth-need strength (psych-speak for people who have a strong desire to grow in their jobs and develop new skills):

  1. **Skill Variety:** Does the job require a diversity of tasks or skills for you to carry out your work? If not, you may not feel that the job fully utilizes your diverse talents.

  2. **Task Identity:** Does the job allow you to work on a "whole" task from start to finish with a visible outcome? If not, you may be left wondering how what you do fits into a larger picture.

  3. **Task Significance:** Does the job have a substantial effect on the lives or work of others, either within the organization or in society at large? If not, you may feel like your work is meaningless and unfulfilling.

  4. **Autonomy:** Does the job give you the freedom and discretion to schedule your work and choose the procedures needed to carry out the task? If not, you may feel micromanaged and frustrated with a lack of independence.

  5. **Feedback:** Do managers, colleagues, or customers (or even the job itself) provide direct and clear information on how you are performing? If not, you may constantly be wondering how you are

doing (see the chapter in this section that covers the importance of feedback more thoroughly).

6. **Dealing with Others:** Does the job require you to work closely with others within the organization and with external clients to carry out your work? If not, you may feel socially and professionally isolated.

- **Demanding Job Conditions.** Having a job where your work decisions can literally make the difference between life and death clearly contributes to stress (think surgeons, police officers, firefighters, and air traffic controllers) more than a job where the outcomes are more benign (piano tuner, librarian, jeweler, barber).[2] These types of jobs can be particularly hard on the mental and physical health of those workers with Type-A personalities—you know the type: aggressive, hostile, a high sense of urgency, demanding, ambitious, and cynical.[3]

Moreover, these aspects of negative work environments also predict stress—we'll talk about specific types of work-related stress like commuting in other chapters:

1. being overloaded with more work than you can handle (creating long hours and weekend duty), having to be constantly vigilant, feeling "role ambiguity" about what is expected of them at work, and not feeling like you have a say in your work routine, schedule, pay, or decision-making,

2. having poor physical working conditions (too hot, cold, or loud; poor lighting or visibility; confined spaces; poor air quality; exposure to toxic chemicals; heavy lifting; repetitive motion),

3. being constantly concerned about your safety (as in coal mining, war zone service, and bomb diffusing [as we saw in *The Hurt Locker*]) or job security (especially in the middle of companywide layoffs a sluggish economy), and

4. negative relationships with coworkers, bosses, or clients due to personality conflicts or differences in work styles (in fact, a Gallup poll found that most workers cite a bad boss as the number one reason for quitting their job[4]).

- **Shift Work:** One of Jennifer's friends, Brook, was on a temporary shift work schedule for six months where she was advised before she started, "Don't think you're too good for pills." The upside of the work? Extra pay for working night hours, making good friends with fellow shift coworkers, and discovering fascinating new Web sites during their downtime (a favorite: www.cakewrecks.com). The downside? Having an inconsistent schedule made sleep difficult and social activities tricky to plan, plus her nightly duties weren't nearly as intellectually challenging for this M.I.T.-trained engineer.

Some recent national employment data suggests that Brook was in the minority, as the majority of workers working very early or very late are men, meaning the Dolly Parton song is true—women really are "working 9 to 5."[5] To some economists this helps explain part of the persistent pay gap between men and women, since shift work often pays higher and many women might choose or feel forced to forgo that pay incentive and keep more traditional hours so that they can care for their families in the mornings and evenings.

What Are the Effects of Workplace Stress?

Everyone remembers from 9th grade biology that the typical reaction to a stressor is "fight or flight"—that is, our focus narrows, our heart rate and blood pressure go up, our pupils dilate, and our muscles tense—so our bodies are physically prepared to either fight an enemy or flee from it. However, research by social psychologist Shelley Taylor shows that this traditional model is only based on men's reactions to stress—women, her research shows, are more likely to follow the model of "tend and befriend."[6] Specifically, when faced with a stressor, women instead of fighting or fleeing are more likely to tend to their offspring and other loved ones to protect them from harm and to befriend others so they collectively can counter a threat.

In a work setting, this model has implications for how women might experience stress on the job—common negative reactions to stress among working women include increased alcohol or drug abuse, difficulty sleeping and concentrating, irritability, fatigue, being easily distracted, and depression.[7] Why should organizations care about individual employees' stress levels? Because when workers experience high amounts of stress, organizations face higher turnover, more sick days, reduced productivity, and lowered job satisfaction and commitment from their employees—it can even lead to physical violence or emotional abuse at work.[8]

Over time, workers who experience chronic stress are likely to have feelings of burnout, particularly in jobs that require responsibility for and constant attention to the physical, social, and cognitive needs of others such as nursing and teaching. Research by Christina Maslach shows that burnout generally has three specific components[9]:

- **Emotional Exhaustion:** Employees report feeling "used up at the end of the workday," feeling like they are "at the end of my rope," and "emotionally drained from work."

- **Depersonalization:** Employees report feeling "callous towards other people," treating people "as if they were impersonal 'objects,' " and worrying that the job is "hardening me emotionally."

- **Lack of Personal Accomplishment:** Employees report feeling like they are not "effectively dealing with work problems," not "accomplishing many worthwhile things in this job," and not "positively influencing peoples lives."

What Can I Do about It?

OK, now that we're all thoroughly depressed thinking about the many ways that our jobs can bring us down, what can we personally do—short of changing bosses, jobs, or careers—to help mitigate the effects?

- **Talk about It.** Just like that craptastic 80s song "Funkytown" said, you gotta "talk about it, talk about it, talk about it, talk about it." For chronic life or work stressors, consider working with your organization's wellness program or EAP (Employee Assistance Program) if they offer one to find a clinical psychologist who can help you cope with severe stress or burnout. EAPs can also provide helpful literature on managing stress—hopefully more useful than the brochures in guidance counselor Emma Pilsbury's office in *Glee*, containing such gems as "Wow! There's a Hair Down There!"

    For milder forms of stress, find a trusted coworker, family member, or friend to discuss your stresses with and brainstorm solutions (or hug it out). Indeed, social support is a huge buffer against stress through giving you new perspectives or coping strategies to think about, offering you a sense of belonging, and providing a diversion from a stressful situation.[10]

- **Write About It.** Not to get all "Are You There God? It's Me Margaret" about it, but a robust body of research by social psychologist Jamie Pennebaker shows that writing about a traumatic or stressful event is a surprisingly effective way to cope. Interestingly, the benefits aren't just psychological and mental, as our physical health can even be improved through this expressive writing.[11, 12, 13]

- **Exercise.** We covered the myriad benefits of exercise in the previous chapter about sports and communication, but we'll also reiterate them here. Many organizations offer onsite fitness classes, so even if the treadmill isn't for you, you might be enticed by kickboxing, pilates, zumba, or spinning classes. In fact, one of Jennifer's favorite parts about her work at OMNI Research and Training—a top-notch evaluation and consulting firm in Denver—was the weekly yoga sessions over the lunch hour in the conference room and the annual company hike up one of Colorado's 14,000 foot mountains. Even if your organization doesn't offer these benefits, take 30 minutes during lunch to walk around outside or in the building when feeling stressed.

- **Don't Cry (at least not while at work).** To tweak a line from *A League of Their Own*: there is no crying in business. As social psychologist Alice Eagly points out in her excellent book *Through the Labyrinth: The Truth about How Women Become Leaders*, emotional displays like crying can connote weakness, especially in male-typed jobs.[14] If you must cry, a separate line of research shows that having your eyes brim with tears is perceived more favorably than a full on office bawl because it shows control over your emotions.[15]

Section Five

How to Make It Work While Balancing Work and Family: The Grand Canyon or a Line in the Sand?

The iPhone4G has been called "moms' new best friend." We love our Apples, but really? And then there is the iPad ...

> Not only does the new Apple iPad tablet hold a lot of opportunity for new and improved business applications, but it also has a lot of potential to unleash apps that allow business people to be people again. Channel Insider's top 10 iPad apps for work-life balance help busy executives keep their busy work, home and travel schedules in order while at the same time aiding them in maintaining their health and sanity, too.[1]

These "top 10 apps for work-life balance" help users access their systems while away from the office, evaluate the diagnosis associated with their kids' cold or flu symptoms, plan trips, engage in yoga, track food and exercise, watch videos, set up databases, and track sleep cycles.[2] We're exhausted just *thinking* about all these suckers, much less needing to use them. Is this what we are supposed to be doing to "be people again"? Is this what it takes to have work-life balance?

These apps are symptoms of an experience that many women encounter—trying to balance the responsibilities of work with a life outside of work. Nearly 90 percent of parents with children under the age of 18 in the United States are employed and the vast majority of these working parents (86%) work full-time.[3] According to Arlie Hochschild, author of *The Second Shift: Working Parents and the Revolution at Home*, despite women's involvement in paid work outside the home, women's primary social and family responsibility continues to be the raising of children and care of the home. As breadwinners, men are "done" with their job at the end of the work day. Women's "true work" starts when they clock out of their jobs. Don't believe us? Have you ever heard a guy say he "babysat" his kids? Or "helped" with the dishes/cleaning/grocery shopping? These activities are central to women's roles, but are considered "extra" for most men.

Moreover, there is clear data to support the idea that women take on more responsibilities at home than do men. In one study, participants kept track every day of the amount of time they spent doing different household chores such as the amount of time they spent cooking meals, cleaning up from meals, housecleaning, doing laundry, completing outdoor chores, making repairs, garden and animal care, and bills and other financial accounting. The results showed that, on average, women spent 17.5 hours per week on these chores whereas men spent only 10.[4] While this gap is smaller than it was 20 years ago, it adds up to more than two weeks of time every year. A similar study examining the time parents spend with their kids found that men spend about two and half hours each day with their kids, whereas women spend closer to five hours.[5]

Taken together, this evidence supports what you probably already know: the intersection of work and family is particularly important and challenging for women. The goal of this section of the book is to discuss major questions that arise when women balance work and nonwork responsibilities and activities. This section addresses questions like the following:

- **Think that deciding whether to keep your name or taking your husband is purely a family matter?** Think again! We'll discuss research that shows *either* choice can have consequences for how you are perceived at work.

- **Thinking about having kids?** You're not alone. As much as 80–90 percent of women will become pregnant while they are employed.[6] This section includes advice about how to handle telling your boss that you are expecting, and research about when you might want to ask for an extended maternity leave.

- **Wondering what work-life balance is and how to get some?** In this chapter, you'll learn about research that shows your spouse/partner's conflict about work and family can be a stressor for you. We'll also tell you about the specific kinds of behaviors you should ask your supervisor to do to support your work-life balance.

- **Worried that people at work might see you differently because you are a mom?** This section will describe evidence that moms are seen as nice, but incompetent. We'll also describe family responsibilities discrimination and what you can do about it.

- **Realizing your parents are getting older every year?** Many women become caretakers for not only their children, but also their parents. We'll give you tips for making decisions about how to care for elderly family members and remind you to care for the caretaker.

- **Have a long commute?** We'll discuss alternatives you should consider to lower your blood pressure (literally!).

- **Considering an international work assignment?** Many people who work abroad crash and burn (figuratively speaking!). We'll help you figure out whether your personality is well-suited for working in another country and give you the scoop on what to expect from different kinds of cultures.

The overarching goal of this section of the book is to let you know about some of the issues that may emerge when work intersects with life outside of work, and to give you some ideas about how to make this work for you!

29

What's in a Name? The Decision among Married Working Women to Change or Keep Their Names

Susan B. Anthony. Amelia Earhart. Pocahontas. Sally Ride. Harriet Tubman. Sandra Day O'Connor. Marie Curie. Sojourner Truth. Jane Addams. Rosa Parks. Mother Theresa. Elizabeth Caddy Stanton. Maya Angelou. Charlotte Bronte.

These are all famous women you doubtlessly learned about in grade school for their pioneering work advocating for the rights of women or for their inspiring accomplishments. But one less famous though no less impressive woman's name isn't included in most history books: Lucy Stone. Though her work as a suffragist and abolitionist in the 1800s is remarkable enough, she is most remembered today for her advocacy in promoting so-called name choice, or a woman's right to retain her last name after getting married. Her classic quote, "A wife should no more take her husband's name than he should hers. My name is my identity and must not be lost" is featured prominently on the Web site of the League named for her, along with merchandise adorned with slogans like "Surnames, not *Sir*names" and "~~Mrs.~~"[1]

What does Ms. Stone have to do with contemporary women in the workplace? Just as a first name like Mary Kathleen, Ayesha, or Celina can say much about your gender, race, class, and age (and can impact how potential employers perceive you, as we discussed in the first section), so too can the choices you make about your last name after getting married influence perceptions about you, your personality, and your values. Here we'll talk about the social science research on the issues surrounding name choice and what they mean for you as a young professional woman.

What Factors Help Predict Who Will Change Her Name vs. Keep Her Name?

One psychological study reviewed the *New York Times* wedding announcements—surely you remember Carrie in *Sex and the City* describing this section as "the single woman's sports page"—over the last several decades to test several hypotheses about what types of women were most likely to (1) keep their name exactly as is (e.g., "Jane Smith"), (2) keep their name in modified form (e.g., "Jane Smith-Doe" or "Jane Smith Doe"), or (3) take their husband's name in full (e.g., "Jane Doe").[2] What did they find?

- The percentage of brides keeping their name exactly as-is was 1 percent in the 1970s, 9 percent in the 1980s, 23 percent in the 1990s, and 18 percent in the 2000s (though the study only looked through 2005).
- Women in occupations where professional "branding" is important (e.g., arts and entertainment) or that are considered professional or high-powered (e.g., C.E.O.s and doctors) were much more likely to keep their surnames than women in other occupations.
- The higher the level of the bride's educational attainment, the more likely she was to keep her name.
- Older brides were more likely than younger brides to retain their surnames.
- Women married in religious ceremonies were more likely to change their name than those married in a civil or nonreligious ceremony.

How Does My Name Choice Influence Impressions about Me?

Do these seemingly personal choices that all these brides make have professional consequences? Some new research suggests that they might. Female job applicants who kept their surname were seen as more independent, ambitious, intelligent, and competent (yea!) but as less caring (boo). Conversely, female job applicants who took their husband's name were viewed as more caring, dependent, and emotional and less intelligent, competent and ambitious.[3] Moreover, a woman who took her husband's name was seen as less desirable to hire and was believed to have a lower salary than a woman who kept her surname. Note: A couple of important caveats before you run to court to change your name back if you are in this latter group—the study was conducted in the Netherlands with student participants making the judgments. In the United States, of course, it would be illegal for any employer to make decisions about you based on your marital status, but they may unconsciously look for clues on your ring finger during an interview.

What about hyphenators (e.g., the Courtney Cox-Arquettes and Jackie Joyner-Kersees of the world)? The research is somewhat mixed on this group of women—one study found that they were perceived as less stereotypically feminine and more stereotypically masculine than women who took their husband's name, similar to how women who kept their name were perceived.[4] A separate study described how women who hyphenated their surnames were seen as more friendly, good-natured, industrious, and intellectually curious than "the average married woman."[5]

Are these impressions that others have about them the same perceptions that women have of themselves? Well . . . kind of. It turns out that women who keep vs. women who change their names after marriage describe themselves as equally "feminine" in self-reports. However, women who keep their surnames are more likely to describe themselves as "masculine" than are women who take their husband's name.[6]

Why Keep or Change Your Surname? Women Respond . . .

When asked why they took their husband's name, women who change their name often cite tradition and concerns about not having the same last name as their children, and they report wanting to forge a new family "unit" unified by the same last name.[7, 8, 9] Some of these concerns are valid—when Jennifer's aunt Shelley (an impressive judge who proudly kept her surname) tried to board an international flight with her son Evan (who had his father/ her husband Paul's last name), there was all kinds of madness at the gate, as the airline wouldn't let them board, because they thought she was trying to flee the country with a young boy who did not appear to be related to her since they had different last names.

Women who keep their surnames, on the other hand, often say they feel that their last name is a part of their self-identity that they don't want to lose. A less vocal minority also mentions "hedging their bets" to avoid the hassle and embarrassment of changing their name back if things in the marriage don't work out as well as they'd hoped. A good number of Eden and Jennifer's graduate school colleagues from Rice, in fact, have kept their names after marriage, not the least of which is because that is the name on their hard-earned diploma and on their résumé. Happily bucking this trend is a good friend from Rice named Stefanie—she decided to change her name after getting married and was able to cleverly show the change on her CV by putting an asterisk next to her earlier articles that were published her surname with an explanatory note at the bottom of the CV.

What about women who want to try to have it all by using their surname at work but their husband's name in all other contexts, like family situations? These women are what the married research team Laurie Scheuble and David Johnson call "situational last name users"—they've found that about 12 percent of women fall in this category.[10] Women who were most likely to engage in situational last name use were full-time workers, those with higher levels of education, and those who were older when they married. The researchers argue that this dual persona can be perceived as ambiguity over family vs. nonfamily roles in women's lives.

30

Waddle It Up, Women! Balancing Pregnancy and Work

We remember very clearly a hot, humid summer day in graduate school when we learned how to waddle. Why on earth would we learn how to waddle in graduate school? Because we needed to be believable pregnant women, and it seemed important to recognize that carrying around an extra-large bowling ball in your belly requires some serious waddling.

We wore pregnancy prostheses (fake bellies) and pretended to be pregnant (or not) while applying for jobs and shopping. Yup, we waddled our "pregnant" selves around to dozens of retail stores to find out how we would be treated when we applied for jobs or shopped for a gift. We and other nonpregnant observers filled out questionnaires about each interaction, and we carried hidden tape recorders to capture the conversations to be coded later by people who didn't know whether or not we were "pregnant."

The results of our study illustrate just one of the many issues that pregnant women encounter. When we "shopped," we were treated with extra-friendly service (people called us "honey" and "sweetie," offered us a place to sit, started long conversations, and smiled). When we applied for jobs, people tended to look at us like we were crazy, to be somewhat hostile, and to spend as little time talking to us as possible. Pregnant women, it seems, evoke very positive reactions when they are doing something feminine (shopping) but negative reactions when they do something more masculine (apply for a job). This study points to pregnancy as a time when women might face tough questions like those detailed below.

To Whom, How, and When Should I Announce I'm Pregnant?

One of the first sets of questions you will probably consider deals with how to let the people you are working with know that you are pregnant. Yup, at some point you have to "come out" of the pregnancy closet.

On the one hand, many pregnant workers are likely excited about the baby growing inside them and want to share this news with the world. In addition, research suggests that people generally prefer to be authentic (fully honest) in their interactions with others. In addition, women have to disclose their pregnancy if they want to take advantage of relevant accommodations.[1] On the other hand, however, pregnant women may fear that their supervisor, coworkers, and subordinates will view and treat them differently the moment the cat is out of the bag. This sets up a "disclosure dilemma" that brings with the questions of how, when, and to whom pregnancy should be disclosed. Here's one possibility:

> **Boss:** I don't want to shock you but we know what's under that jacket. You're pregnant and have been for awhile. From my count you're right around eight months, and I don't know why you felt you couldn't tell us.
>
> **Allison:** I'm really sorry.
>
> **Coworker:** This is Hollywood. We don't like liars.
>
> **Allison:** I wasn't expecting this and I didn't know how to handle it and I didn't want to lose my job. I'm really sorry.
>
> **Boss:** It's unfortunate you didn't tell us because you would've found out that we think its great! . . . It turns out that people like pregnant! The bigger you are, the bigger your numbers.
>
> **Coworker:** I was surprised. Because I feel the opposite.
>
> —From the movie *Knocked Up*

The movie business seems to have some opinions about pregnancy. Unfortunately, the research on balancing pregnancy and work is scarce— we don't yet have a lot of evidenced-based information about the best strategies. (Eden is working to fill this gap in the literature with a grant from the Sloan Foundation to study women over the course of their pregnancies!

Stay tuned for those results.[2]) But here is the best information we can give you now:

1. The Federal Medical Leave Act (see more below) requires that employees give 30 days notice for intent to leave, but the average pregnancy is more than 250 days. There is a lot of wiggle room for deciding when to disclose.

2. Given the unfortunate incidence of miscarriage and potential for physical challenges in the early stages of pregnancy, women are generally advised to wait until after their first trimester to share the news of their pregnancy widely.[3]

3. After your first trimester, it may be better to tell your supervisors and coworkers sooner rather than later. Giving your colleagues time to think about, get accustomed to, and develop strategies for dealing with the change (that will likely affect them to some extent, particularly if/when you take maternity leave) may help them to feel that the process is more fair.[4] Ultimately, the choice is absolutely yours—you get to decide what feels right to you!

4. Some supervisors may prefer that you tell them before you tell other people at work. They may like to have a plan in place so that if your subordinates or teammates have concerns, they can address them.

5. It is probably best to tell your supervisor, subordinates, and coworkers who rely on you but not casual work acquaintances in formal, one-on-one settings. If you treat the disclosure process as "no big deal" and tell people casually about your due date, you could run the risk of people feeling like you haven't been thoughtful about how your major life event can affect them. We suggest you set up a meeting.

6. In this meeting, you should get to the point quickly, take a deep breath, and take the plunge, so you can go on to describe how you plan to balance pregnancy and motherhood and work. Be as specific as you can about your expectations for work hours, length of maternity leave, and workload issues—ambiguity leads to confusion and stress. Note that this means you need to have an idea of what it is you want to do before you have these meetings! See section on maternity leave below.

7. Follow up with these folks as your due date approaches to determine how the process is going from their perspective and to deal with any changes in your plans and expectations.

We've discussed pregnancy in a "traditional" manner, but recognize that women can be "expecting" a child in many ways.[5] For example, women can become mothers through surrogacy, adoption, and partners' pregnancies. In addition, some women may have children in "nontraditional" ways that are not consistent with societal expectations that only young, married women have children. Clearly, women can be older or single and have kids. We think the same basic strategies described above apply, but we also would expect that, unfortunately, reactions might be somewhat less positive. If this is the case for you, it may be helpful to find allies who will advocate on your behalf through formal channels (e.g., requests for HR policy changes) or informal ways (e.g., squelching gossip), and who will be excited for you becoming a mom regardless of how it might be happening.

How Should I Handle Maternity Leave?

According to the Federal Medical Leave Act (FMLA), companies with 50 or more employees have to provide new parents 12 weeks of unpaid leave if they have worked for at least 1250 hours (about a year). Unfortunately, some women can't afford to take FMLA leave because they need to maintain their income or because they are afraid of losing future promotion/pay opportunities. Many women work in small companies for which FMLA does not apply.[6] In other words, for many women, the FMLA-mandated leave is not working. Some companies go a lot further! For example, in their description of American Express (a "Best Companies to Work For" Hall of Fame-r), *Working Mother Magazine* stated that,

> Juggling a busy schedule and the birth of a first child can be tricky, but new moms who work for this financial firm quickly learn how to handle it all, thanks to their employer's interactive Parenting 101 seminars. Professional parenting coaches demonstrate various child-care approaches and explain how to handle challenging situations, providing advice from pregnancy through age 3. But that's just the start of how this New York City–based firm steps up to assist its working-mother

employees: It also provides them with up to six paid weeks of time off after a birth or adoption and 20 free visits to a childcare center (or in-home visits) for backup care each year. Last January, servicecenter employees in Fort Lauderdale, FL, rejoiced when the firm opened a backup-care facility on-site; it now serves more than 1,300 children under 13.[7]

Even if you are fortunate enough to work for a company with these awesome benefits for expecting parents, you'll still have to make decisions about how you want to handle your time away from work.

Real Women Say . . .

Eden's college next-door-neighbor (Tamara) has an interesting perspective on maternity leave. She has been working as a regional supervisor for a small media consulting firm for more than five years. In that time, two of her subordinates got pregnant and delivered babies. One of these women approached the process of negotiating leave from the perspective of "how much time can I get off?" The other saw the question somewhat differently: "How can I spend time with my baby *and* make sure I am fulfilling my job responsibilities?" Ultimately, both women got the same amount of time off. As their boss, however, Tamara felt it was much easier to deal with the second new mom. From Tamara's perspective, she appreciated that the second mom recognized that her absence would create more work for everyone else and expressed gratitude for their support. Tamara also liked knowing that it was okay to call the second new mom if absolutely necessary even while she was on leave. This made Tamara less resentful of doing the extra work, and more willing to help out—she actually never called either mom.

Now Tamara is expecting her own kid and she says she is trying to emulate those behaviors she appreciated. For example, because Tamara wants to continue to move up in the company, she is thinking about advice recently published in *The New York Times*; "Keep your foot in the door while you are on maternity leave by calling in to see how projects are progressing and stopping by with the baby for a visit."[8] This will help to overcome the possibility that absence will lead to being overlooked; she'll make sure her bosses remember she is a valuable employee who is invested in the company in addition to her family.

And the Research Says . . .

Interviews with women who had recently taken maternity leave provide additional insight about the experience.[9] All of the women reported feeling stressed about taking leave, but half of the women felt "encouraged" by their experience and the other half felt "discouraged." The women who had more positive experiences seemed to achieve that through a few common "conflict management" strategies. Yep, this is another time to put on your master-negotiator hat.

> **First,** they worked with their supervisors to overcome seemingly incompatible goals before the leave began. For example, some women wanted to take an extended maternity leave so that they could spend more time with their new infant, but found their supervisors reticent to "lose them" for longer than 12 weeks. To overcome these conflicting perspectives, women compromised with their supervisors by taking additional time off without pay, working from home for the extended part of their leave, or by bringing their baby with them to the office. The compromise involves meeting organizational goals in exchange for fulfilling personal needs.

> **Second,** women who described more positive experiences tended to focus on a narrow set of underlying needs rather than trying to engage in tit-for-tat negotiations. One of our friends, Rachel, was happy to go back to work at the end of the standard 12 week leave, but it was very important to her that she was able to continue breast feeding for at least 6 months. This was a little tricky because Rachel is a family doctor and has back-to-back patient appointments scheduled all day long, and pumping takes quite a bit of time every few hours. Focusing on this one central need and request helped her to negotiate for breaks in her schedule and a space to pump in privacy rather than try to extend the length of her leave.

> *(FYI: The Patient Protection and Affordable Care Act (AKA health care reform) of 2010 actually now includes a provision that states that companies with more than 50 employees have to provide "(a) a reasonable*

break time for an employee to express breast milk for her nursing child for 1 year after the child's birth each time such employee has need to express the milk; and (b) a place, other than a bathroom, that is shielded from view and free from intrusion from co-workers and the public, which may be used by an employee to express breast milk.")

Third, women with more positive maternity leave experiences reported being assertive about their needs without being aggressive. In this way, they were able to get what they really needed without damaging their relationship with their supervisors. In fact, these women reported a sustained positive relationship with their boss.

How Do I Deal with Changed Expectations about My Work?

Unfortunately, people have some negative perceptions about pregnant workers. Some people think that pregnant employees reduce team productivity, and thus should not be hired, promoted, or given help by organizations.[10, 11] This may be because being pregnant is, in some sense, the epitome of femininity or the ultimate womanly action. This means that pregnant women are seen as uber-feminine. And "feminine" isn't always seen as consistent with "productive."

In addition, people have concerns about what will happen to the work and workload when a woman takes maternity leave; your colleagues may really rely on *you* to be able to do their own jobs. In many cases, the work you do will still have to be done—probably by your teammates—while you are on leave.

Given these perceptions and concerns, women who are pregnant may want to try to manage the impressions of their coworkers, supervisors, and subordinates in two ways:

First, it may be helpful to develop and implement a plan that allows you to continue your current level of performance as long as possible while simultaneously transitioning off of projects and tasks that have deadlines during your leave. This approach will have the effect of demonstrating your competence while also making things easier on your colleagues.

Second, it can't hurt to express your gratitude for your any support you receive. Emily Post was right—thank yous go a long way! Your colleagues will probably feel less resentful about picking up a little slack for 12 weeks if you let them know that you are grateful and that you will be back at work to make it up to them.

How Should I Manage Returning to Work after Maternity Leave?

The overwhelming majority of women (more than 90%) who worked before maternity leave do return to their jobs at the conclusion of the leave period.[12] The transition back to work requires both personal and professional considerations.

On the Personal Side ...

Data from the Wisconsin Maternity Leave and Health (WMLH) Project involved 530 pregnant women who were interviewed during their pregnancies and one year after giving birth to their children. At four months post-childbirth, there were some differences in the depression, anxiety, anger, and self-esteem reported by women who decided to stay at home compared to those who worked part-time and full-time. For example, women who took short leaves of four–six weeks and had concerns about their marriages were more stressed out than other women.

However, at one year after giving birth, moms' ratings on measures of depression, anxiety, anger, and self-esteem did not differ as a function of job status. The extent to which moms felt stressed out was most highly related to the temperament of their kids; stressed kids made moms more stressed. In addition, among women who valued work as central to their identity but took a long leave of absence were more likely to be depressed than other women. This evidence jives with other studies that show women with less "feminine" attitudes are those more likely to return to work quickly.[13] Perhaps most importantly, the results of this study show that moms' anxiety and anger were most likely to be elevated when their employment status was not what they would have personally chosen. In other words, women were less anxious and happier when they were doing what they wanted to be doing (working when they liked to work, not working when they didn't want to work). *These data highlight something we've heard before—when it comes to maternity leave, we really should do whatever we think is best for us.*[14]

This is also consistent with stories our girlfriends have shared. One of Eden's friends, Tracy, had a beautiful baby boy about six months ago. She loves working at her job (she is a counselor for people who are severely mentally ill), but finds the long hours when she is on call at night and on weekends are too much to manage. She's realizing that what would be best for *her* is to work in a job that has more flexible hours, or perhaps to even work part-time. She doesn't want to give up that part of her life— she finds it both enriching and financially necessary—but she needs to find a situation that will work better for her new goals. Another friend with an 18-month-old, Amelia, confessed that she likes going to work because it feels like a break from baby-talk and allows her to appreciate the time she has with her son. She decided to take a short maternity leave so that she could stay involved in work and go up for promotion. Amelia loves her son as much as Tracy does, but they have made different decisions about what will work for them.

On the Professional Side ...

Unfortunately, research suggests that taking a leave of absence—whether for illness or maternity—can have a negative impact on your advancement prospects. A survey of over 11,000 financial services managers suggested that taking a leave was negatively related to promotions and salary increases. This negative effect of leave-taking held even after accounting for performance ratings; in other words, equating for how well they performed when they were at their job, people who took a leave of absence were less likely to be promoted or get a bonus.[15] It may be that people who take leave, including new moms like Tracy, experience a shift in priorities—some women really do make conscious decisions to spend more time/energy/effort with their families once they have kids. They may maintain performance but refrain from doing extra activities like networking and helping out that would otherwise help them to advance. However, it is also possible that instead of "opting out" of the work role, some women may be "*pushed* out" through unfair policies and experiences.

Eden's very first doctoral student, Whitney Botsford Morgan, studied the experiences that women have when they return to work after maternity leave for her award-winning dissertation. After a series of interviews and focus groups, Whitney surveyed several hundred first-time-moms who had given birth in the previous year. Across the interviews, focus groups, and surveys, Whitney noticed a common theme: many new moms felt that they had been informally promised one thing before maternity leave (e.g., ability to work from home, flexible hours) and found something totally different once they got back to work (e.g., no telecommuting, no flex-work). These women had experienced what researchers call "psychological contract breach." The feeling of unmet expectations or being misled made some of these women consider leaving work altogether. These findings suggest a crucial aspect of returning to work after maternity leave is to *formalize your intended arrangements with your supervisor*—make sure you are both on exactly the same page and get it in writing. The whole "my word is stronger than oak" thing doesn't really work here any more than it did in Jerry Maguire.

In Conclusion . . .

One woman who participated in interviews about pregnancy summed up her experience by stating, "Pregnancy, bringing a life into the world, is a normal occurrence . . . You shouldn't feel ashamed of it, you shouldn't feel like you're different or you're going to lose your job over it or anything else. You shouldn't feel awkward about going to your supervisor about it. If that had been spelled out a little bit more, it would have made things just slightly easier. You know?"[16] We hope this information makes managing work and pregnancy just a little bit easier.

31

Can Work and Family Be Like Peas and Carrots?

Policies that support families aren't political issues. They're personal. They're the causes I carry with me every single day.

—Michelle Obama

For many, many, many years (we're talking Neanderthal era here) the overwhelming trend was for women to be responsible for household and childcare labor and men to be responsible for hunter-gathering (i.e., bringing home the bacon). The separation of labor made the notion of "work-family balance" less relevant. Today, however, women actually outnumber men in the workforce; now the homemaker-breadwinner distinction is largely irrelevant in many families.[1]

Indeed, public opinion surveys show meaningful change in how people see these roles. In 1977, 66 percent of people thought that women should be homemakers and men should be breadwinners. In 2006, only 35 percent of people held that belief. Similarly, 67 percent of people now believe that children are not harmed when their mothers decide to work outside the home. However, 41 percent of people still believe that preschool-aged children are better off if their mother doesn't work.[2]

So where does this leave women? The opening quote from the self-proclaimed "mom-in-chief" is suggestive of the importance of this issue. Most women work outside the home. Most women have a life outside of work, whether that life involves kids or parents or siblings or a partner or hobbies. And even when women and their partners both work full time, women tend to be responsible for the majority of the household tasks and taking care of kids. So *work-life balance* is a concept with special meaning and unique challenges for women.

What Is Work-Life Balance?

The notion of work-life balance grew out of ideas about role theory, which addresses the different roles that people have in their lives. *Role conflict* exists when the pressures that a person feels in one role make it difficult to fulfill the responsibilities of another role. (For example, you stay up late talking to a friend [a friend role] who is having marital problems, and you are too sleepy to lead a meeting the next day at work [a work role].) *Role enhancement* exists when the emotions or experiences gained in one role positively affect experiences in another role. (For example, your spouse/ partner helps you talk through how to handle a conflict [in your wife role] with your supervisor [in your work role].[3])

Thus, *work-life conflict* can be considered a type of interrole conflict that occurs when pressures at work interfere with family, or when pressures within the family interfere with work. *Work-life enhancement* is a form of interrole enhancement where experiences at home positively affect experiences at work or vice versa. *Work- life balance* can be considered the absence of conflict and/or the presence of enhancement.

An implicit aspect of this definition is that *work-family balance is subjective*—it means different things to different people. Some people may feel a good level of balance by working full time five days a week and hanging out with friends on the weekend. Other people feel more balance on weeks where they work 20 hours and get to pick up their kids from school every day. There's no "right" way to have balance. Only you can decide for yourself what "balance" means to you. And bonus points: this should lead to a peaceful solution in the "mommy wars" between stay-at-home moms and moms who work outside the home!

We have to point out that the idea of work-life balance may be a luxury. A report from the Center for WorkLife Law and the Center for American Progress reminds us that families with few economic resources—low- and middle-income families—face additional burdens of finding full-time work, consistent and predictable schedules, access to reliable and high-quality childcare, and health benefits.[4] Women in these families feel like they are running as fast as they can just to stay in the same place. The report suggests that all families could benefit from enhanced flexibility; short-term, episodic, and extended time off; childcare, afterschool care, and elder care, and eliminating discrimination based on family responsibilities. Even though we all define balance in different ways, it can still be helpful to consider some of the factors that generally lead to more positive experiences balancing work and nonwork roles for most people.

How Can I Get Balanced?

A review of over 60 studies points to factors that can make things harder.[5] For example, participants in these studies reported more work-family conflict when they spent more hours at work and were highly involved in their jobs, and when they had more and younger children. Participants reported less conflict, however, when they had a flexible schedule and a high income. A few themes can be extracted from the research literature on the work-life balance:

Find a Good Partner

If you decide to pursue a long-term relationship, your choice has major implications for your work-life interface. Your spouse or partner can be a source of enhancement or a source of conflict. Of course, there is bound to be conflict in any relationship, but finding someone who makes you happy on most days is a good starting point! Eden looks forward to seeing her hubby at the end of the day (they really do the cheesy "what was your high/low today?"), and appreciates that they split household responsibilities (she cooks, he cleans). Jennifer and her man just trained together for their first triathlon. Three times the awesomeness.

The positive spillover from our relationships (on most days) is valuable for our psychological well-being and even our productivity at work. If/ when we have kids, or have to take care of our too-quickly aging parents, we are confident that these fellas will be there to have our backs and share the load. We're not saying every moment will be blissful or even easy, but when we add it all up, these guys make our lives better and make it easier for us to feel balanced.

This is particularly important because work-family conflict can be contagious—your partner's experience of work-family conflict can affect whether or not you are late to work, absent from work, and interrupted while at work and vice versa.[6] This points to the shared experience of conflict and the importance of finding a partner who you work well with. Go team!

Another aspect of your choice in partners is the extent to which they will support your career and any career opportunities that come your way. Women are more likely than men to be "trailing spouses," moving to new cities for their partners' jobs rather than their own. This has obvious implications for your career trajectory. Depending on your personal views about your family and career priorities, this may not be problematic. However, if you have lofty goals about getting to the top of your company, this is something you should talk about with potential romantic partners. Yep, in addition to conversations about kids and money, you should talk about jobs, too!

Find a Good Supervisor

Supervisors have the opportunity to enhance your work-life interface by providing emotional support, instrumental support, role modeling behaviors, and creative work-family management.[7] Indeed, the degree to which supervisors engage in these behaviors improves work-family enrichment and job satisfaction, and reduces work-family conflict and turnover intentions. Items that assess these kinds of behaviors include: (1) my supervisor is willing to listen to my problems in juggling work and nonwork life, (2) I can depend on my supervisor to help me with scheduling conflicts if I need it, (3) my supervisor demonstrates effective behaviors in how to juggle work and nonwork balance, and (4) my supervisor is creative in reallocating job duties to help my department work better as a team. If your supervisor doesn't do these things, keep your eyes open for other leader/mentors who might be able to help you with these aspects of work.

Get Flexible

Organizations have begun to offer "flexible work arrangements" as a simple and low-cost strategy for helping to improve employees' work-life balance. According to a recent survey of 230 women in a range of jobs and occupations, having flexibility in the scheduling of work and in the location of work was particularly useful in reducing the degree to which work interferes with family.[8] This flexibility seems especially important for people with more family responsibilities; women who have kids may benefit most from flexible work. If your organization does not formally offer flextime or flexwork, try talking to your supervisor about an informal trial period to see how you, and they, like the arrangement.

Make Use of Resources

One of the biggest determinants of how satisfied parents feel with their work-life interface is the quality of childcare they have access to. Parents who are worried about their kids during the workday are distracted and anxious, whereas parents who feel comfortable with their kids' childcare arrangements can typically focus better at work and are less worried. So whether you use the referral service at work, your friends' recommendations, or ask your own parents to help you take care of the kids, find what works for you.

And every good girl scout has a back-up plan! When your primary childcare provider gets sick or has a holiday, when your meeting runs late or you have to travel, you'll need to have some last-minute strategy options. Other kinds of resources to support your work-life balance can come from your friends and communities (e.g., church, volunteering) that you find nourishing—get connected to people who help you reenergize you after a long day at work.

Figure Out Your Coping Strategies

People deal with the work-life interface in different ways. For example, some people prefer to keep their work and families very separate while others like the boundaries between their roles to be blurred.[9] Our grad school mentor Mikki is definitely the latter—she brings her kids to work with her occasionally and often invites her students to visit her home. Another grad school mentor, Margaret, likes to keep the worlds separate—when she's home, she doesn't work and when she's at work, she's not with her kids. Both Margaret and Mikki have figured out how to match their personality to their approach to the work-life interface.

Think about where you might be on the integration-segmentation continuum. If you are on the "*integration*" side like Mikki, you'll need to look for policies and procedures that support that style (e.g., on-site childcare facilities). If you are on the *"segmentation"* side like Margaret, you'll need to use policies that help you make the separation easy to manage (e.g., flextime). In either case, it might be helpful to let the people you work with know your viewpoint—as grad students, we needed to know that there may occasionally be a couple of (amazing) kids in our weekly mentoring sessions with Mikki, and that Margaret would not respond to e-mail after 5 p.m.

Beyond these individual preferences, researchers have identified three general strategies that people use to deal with stress: *problem-focused coping, emotion-focused coping, and avoidance.*[10] A survey of over 300 working adults suggests that problem-focused coping, which includes taking direct action and seeking help (e.g., "I try to work harder and more efficiently" and "I decide what should be done and explain this to the people who are affected"), can be an effective way to deal with work-life stress.

An alternative would be to engage in emotion-focused coping, which involves managing the feelings and emotions associated with the stressor (e.g., "I tell myself things will probably work out to my advantage"). If people engage in emotion-focused coping but don't actually deal with the problem by changing their behavior, it may not be as effective. A third coping strategy would be to avoid the stressor and hope the problem will fix itself (e.g., "I accept the situation because there is little I can do to change it"). This was actually associated with *more* work-family conflict. For most people, then, it would be most useful to take direct action and seek help when it is needed. Avoidance strategies should be avoided—pun intended.

Beyond the research evidence, popular wisdom suggests strategies like prioritizing your activities, dropping unnecessary tasks, and planning specific and protected "fun time" and "you time" can help people feel more balance between work and nonwork. Try these out and see what works for you!

Final Thoughts on Work and Life . . .

> Like all working mothers, sometimes I feel like a terrible mother and sometimes I feel like a terrible employee. But for the most part, I try to give myself a break, which is something I urge all mothers to do —to live your life with a cloud of guilt about everything you are doing is just not good for anybody.
>
> —Katie Couric

I was surrounded by plenty of working moms, including my grand-mother, a pediatrician, and my mother, a writer and producer . . . I just thought, Well, that's what moms do. They work and raise their kids. I was brought up to believe I could do anything I wanted professionally and, of course, be a mother at the same time. But I'm finding out that it's complicated. It requires a lot of thought and planning and I haven't figured it out yet.

—Maggie Gyllenhaal

Finding balance may feel like an impossible task. Some people think it's one of those things that sounds great but doesn't actually exist. When it comes down to it, you have choices about how to approach both work and family that can affect your experience. Don't worry, we're not going to quote Miley Cyrus and say "it's all about the climb." Instead, we're going to suggest that you do have (some degree of) control in how you create the work-life interface that works for you.

32

She's Nice, but Incompetent: Misperceptions of Moms and How to Correct Them

Do you want to have babies or do you want a career here?
—An employer who passed over a new mom for a promotion

Look at this as an opportunity to stay home with your new baby.
—A supervisor who fired a new mom because he believed
she would no longer be able to cover her sales territory

A senior Vice President of a law firm complained about the "incompetence and laziness of women who are also working mothers." The general counsel of the same firm believed that women could not be good mothers and good lawyers at the same time, stating, "I don't see how you could do either job well."

— www.worklifelaw.org

The Center for WorkLife Law cited these quotes that appeared in recent cases of *family responsibilities discrimination*—unfair treatment of employees based on their status as caretakers of children or aging parents.[1] While federal law does not explicitly include family responsibilities in its protective statutes, family responsibilities discrimination can be prosecuted under Title VII of the Civil Rights Act, the Pregnancy Discrimination Act, the Family Medical Leave Act, the Americans with Disabilities Act, or the Equal Pay Act. The moms targeted in the opening quotes were successful in their lawsuits, winning millions of dollars in damages.

Indeed, when the First Circuit Court of Appeals remanded a recent case for trial, they stated that "[an] employer is not free to assume that a woman, because she is a woman, will necessarily be a poor worker because of family responsibilities. The essence of Title VII in this context is that women have the right to prove their mettle in the work arena without the burden of stereotypes regarding whether they can fulfill their responsibilities."[2]

What's So Bad About Family Responsibilities?

We still talk about "glass ceilings," but more and more of the evidence is suggesting that we should first talk about "maternal walls." The "maternal wall" is a metaphor for the experience that many women who work outside their home have when they become mothers—running into a brick wall in their career trajectories. We've discussed the challenges women face in returning to work after maternity leave. The extent of these difficulties is also indicated by research suggests that the "pay gap" in the salaries of men and women is actually driven primarily by the low salaries of working moms—the gap between mothers and women without children is actually bigger than the gap between women and men.[3] What is driving this?

A series of studies by psychologists, sociologists, and management scholars suggest that stereotypes about mothers contribute to the maternal wall. In one experiment, undergraduate students were asked to provide their "first impressions" of a consultant at a large company.[4] The consultant was either named Kate or Dan. In half of the conditions, participants learned that "Kate and her husband [or Dan and his wife] recently had their first baby." Dan and Kate were otherwise entirely identical. The results suggested that women without children were rated as high in competence (capable, efficient, organized, skillful) but low in interpersonal warmth (good-natured, sincere, trustworthy, warm).

Mothers, on the other hand, were rated as highly warm but lacking competence. In other words, women faced a trade-off between warmth and competence. Men without children were rated as high in competence and low in warmth, whereas fathers were rated high in both. That is, men got a "warmth bonus" when they became fathers. This is important because the degree to which the consultants were seen as competent was related to whether participants thought they should be promoted and given developmental opportunities. These findings suggest that, unfortunately, *people see moms as nice but incompetent.*

Sociologists conducted an "audit" of hiring practices to determine whether the tendency to favor fathers over mothers happens in the real world.[5] The researchers sent pairs of résumés and cover letters that reflected equally qualified candidates to business and marketing job openings. The applicants had either male or female names (e.g., Kenneth or Katherine). In addition, half of the applicants were described as officers in a parent-teacher association (the other half were officers in a college alumni association). By tracking callbacks that each "applicant" received, the researchers found that being a parent decreased the odds that female (but not male) applicants would get interviewed for a job. *Being a mom makes it harder for women to get jobs.*

This tendency to rate mothers negatively *extends beyond hiring decisions to promotion-oriented evaluations.* In experiments using both undergraduate and working adult samples, participants evaluated employees who were applying for promotions. These employees were described as male or female, and as parents or not parents. Parental status was indicated in a fake personal information perform by circling either "children" or "no children." Parents were rated as less committed to their jobs, less interested in achievement, and less dependable than nonparents. Moreover, mothers were rated particularly negatively on these dimensions—worse than fathers.[6]

You might be thinking, "I'm a mom, but I handle it well! There's no way my supervisor thinks I'm incompetent!" To consider this, researchers asked supervisors to evaluate the performance and "fit" with the organization of their male and female subordinates. Their results suggest that supervisors think women have more work-family conflict than men, and that these perceptions influence performance and promotability ratings.[7] Eden's dissertation actually found that supervisors perceive that mothers have more conflict and less commitment to and availability for work than fathers even after accounting for what mothers and fathers themselves report; in other words, *supervisors perceive mothers and fathers differently even when they are not different.*[8]

How Can I Overcome These Stereotypes?

We realize we've painted a pretty bleak picture about the influence of motherhood on a career trajectory. But never fear—there is still hope!

As we've discussed throughout the book, one strategy for overcoming stereotypes is to provide positive, counter-stereotypic information. For female leaders, this means balancing feminine characteristics (niceness) with masculine, leader-like characteristics (assertiveness). For working moms, the "nice" stereotypes are covered, and you'll need to focus on the "competence" ones. This can *start by doing high quality work and making sure your supervisors and coworkers notice.*

You could also build on this by compensating for associated stereotypes—people don't just believe that moms are lacking competence, they also believe that that moms are less committed to their jobs, less interested in advancement and development, and less available for unscheduled activities than are fathers and people without children. So *speak up about your interest in developmental opportunities* if these things are appealing to you and *demonstrate your commitment to your job* by making choices that reflect its importance to you.

Lynette on *Desperate Housewives* did this by taking work home with her when she was working for an advertising company. Julia on *Parenthood* does this every day by having multiple working lunches to keep her clients happy. But both Lynette and Julia feel the pull of their family responsibilities—Lynette ended up leaving one job to spend more time with her kids and Julia stopped working late so she could coach her daughter's soccer team. This suggests you should try to *keep track of your personal boundaries*—with each decision you make, you may be giving preference to your "work" life or your "home" life. These choices should be made depending on what kind of balance makes you happiest. Eden's boundary happens before 8 a.m. and after 6 p.m. every day; she doesn't meet with students, write papers, or read journal articles except during that time. So to address stereotypes that she likely faces, she has to demonstrate commitment and engage in development between the hours of 8 and 6.

Another useful example of balancing "mom" and "professional" roles can be derived from the mom-in-chief, who also happens to be a successful lawyer:

Before moving to the White House, Mrs. Obama said that as First Lady she planned to make herself an advocate for working parents, particularly military families, and to urge better access to child care for all. Trying to juggle public duties with two young children, she would become a living illustration of the very issue she describes . . . Mrs. Obama has given coveted interviews primarily to women's magazines and news outlets that have allowed her to highlight her domestic side: her focus on motherhood and her efforts to settle her family in the White House; her interest in gardening and healthy living; her affinity for mixing off-the-rack and designer goods; and her efforts to open up the White House to ordinary Americans.[9]

Like FLOTUS—First Lady of the United States for those of you not inundated with acronyms here in the nation's capital—our good friend from graduate school, Steph, works hard to balance these dual personal and professional roles and to effectively manage perceptions at work:

> I have work friends that are usually outside of my direct reporting structure that I share funny kid stories with, but with people in my unit or reporting relationship I keep it professional. If they ask about kids I will be pleasant and say "great" or something short like "James [her son] started preschool," but I won't go into stories of sleepless nights or whatever adorable thing they did last week—typically people are being nice and asking to try to connect, but I don't want them to only think of the latest baby story when they think of me.

What Do I Do If I Think I've Been Discriminated against because of My Family?

Sometimes stereotypes manifest in discrimination. You may find yourself in situations like those described in the opening quotes. The Center for WorkLife Law makes the following recommendations for this kind of experience:

> If you think you have been discriminated against because of your family responsibilities, make sure your understanding of the circumstances is accurate. Keep notes about statements and actions that you believe are discriminatory. How other people like you have been treated is usually very important, so ask around. Talk with your supervisor, if appropriate, and tell him or her that it appears that you have been discriminated against. If your company has a grievance

procedure, use it. The law does not allow your supervisor to retaliate against you for making a complaint. If the situation is not resolved, contact a local attorney or WorkLife Law (hotline@worklifelaw.org, 800-981-9495) to get an objective view on whether you have been discriminated against. If you decide to pursue legal action, you must file a complaint with an EEOC office or a local EEO office, and you may have as few as 180 days within which to file.

Is There Such a Thing as "Supermom"?

Research and anecdotes point to a common experience—few moms feel like they really "have it all." This may be due in part to the high standards we have for ourselves as mothers and as workers, and in part to the fact that, "For men, having a family is an asset when pursuing a demanding career. For women, it is still a complication."[10] We think we should create a new standard and expectation: every mom who loves her kids and shows them this the best way she can is already a Supermom.

33

Nowhere Near PB and J, but Still the Sandwich Generation: Balancing Child and Elder Care

More women than ever before are caught between taking care of their kids and taking care of their parents while maintaining a full-time job. The term "sandwich generation" refers to people, currently mostly in Generation X (mid-30s to 40s), who are simultaneously raising children under the age of 18 and supporting elderly parents. This phenomenon has increased partly because of the "graying" of the American population; the Baby Boomers represent a large and aging segment of our country. Also contributing to the sandwich effect is the tendency of women to delay having kids until somewhat later in life than was historically traditional. As many as one in four Americans[1] and 1.7 million women in the United States are taking care of their parents and their kids.[2]

Challenges of Sandwichers

Time- and Strain-Based Conflict

At this point, it probably won't surprise you a single bit that research shows women devote more time to caregiving and are more likely to be caregivers for spouses, parents, parents-in-law, relatives and friends than are men.[3] According to one national telephone survey, women in the sandwich generation spend $10,000 and 1,350 hours on average helping their children and parents every year.[4] This means that women have 1,350 fewer hours to do other things (like work!). It is therefore a mathematical certainty that women in the sandwich generation have substantial demands on their time. Ever felt like you have to be in two places at once? Women in the sandwich generation almost *have* to find more hours in the day or be in two places at the same time. It is not surprising, then, that these women also report more stress and strain than men as a result of these responsibilities.[5]

A story reported in *The Huffington Post* illustrates these challenges[6]:

> Carol, 54, is a family caregiver who quit her job as a health club manager to care for her aging parents. While she was comfortable at her job, and had accepted increasing responsibility over the years, she struggled daily and then made the hard decision to leave work after it was clear that both of her parents required daily assistance . . .

> At work, I was spending a couple of hours a day on the phone helping my parents. While my boss certainly didn't stand over me all the time, it just became too much. I could not handle my job responsibilities and meet my parents' needs.

Caretaking Decisions

One of the major aspects of elder care is figuring out how to help aging people in their daily lives. For example, many people run errands, do household chores, or help their parents with personal care. Other people provide direct financial support. A survey of nearly 500 employees at a large university found that decisions about how to care for an elderly family member affected employees' psychological well-being even more than did decisions about how to care for children.[7]

Family Responsibilities Discrimination

People who take time off to care for elderly family members are penalized in much the same way as are moms and women who take maternity leave (see previous chapters). Caretakers are seen as less committed to work and less available for work, and so are less likely to be given promotions and developmental opportunities.[8]

How to Take Care of Business AND Your Parents

Since you can't *actually* be in two places at once or add more hours to the day, you need to find other strategies for coping.

Considerations for Caretaking

When it comes to elder care, there are a lot of housing and care arrangement options (e.g., independent living, assisted living, continuous care, companion, chore work, nursing). It can be difficult to make these decisions because of the emotional and psychological weight of the choice. However, the choice can be made in a somewhat objective manner. What kind of care your loved one needs depends on things like their mobility (Can they walk? Drive?), nutrition (Can they prepare and eat meals on their own?), hygiene (Can they take baths on their own?), dressing (Can they dress themselves?), toileting (Can they use the bathroom on their own?), medications (Do they need help keeping track of medication?), mental status (How is their memory for daily tasks?), and behavioral status (How well do they interact with others in social situations?). Answers to these questions should determine what kind of care you seek.[9] Financial considerations are also important factors—check your and your loved ones' insurance policies to see if any coverage is available. (If you have the luxury of thinking ahead, buy long-term health insurance in your 40s or 50s.) Look to your community for low-cost alternatives.[10]

Additional ideas[11] about caring for aging people include:

- Purchase a Medic Alert bracelet so that healthcare professionals will know of any special medical needs.

- Educate yourself about the types of medications necessary and keep a list to avoid possible interactions with over-the-counter drugs.

- Identify potential hazards or obstacles within the home and correct them.

- Keep a list of daily routines and activities.

- Develop a support system of other family members, friends, and neighbors that can help out with occasional errands or chores.

- Set up automatic bill payment and direct deposit for income like pensions or social security that your parents receive.

- Consider having a power of attorney written up for the right to handle any additional financial or medical matters that may come up.

- Encourage them to do things they enjoy, like cooking or gardening.

- Check out activities/organizations they'd like to get involved in so they can meet people.

Care for the Caretaker

One of the toughest parts about being a caretaker is that no one is taking care of *you*. No matter how much you love and want to be with the person you are caring for, you need a break. Actually, you need a lot of breaks—big ones (vacations) and little ones (throughout the day). Eden's aunt Linda is the primary caretaker for her uncle Tommy (who has ALS). Linda is amazingly devoted to Tommy, and is wise enough to know that she can't do it all herself. One of her friends helped the family by giving the generous gift of in-home daytime care so that Linda can leave for short periods of time (to go for a walk, out with friends, or to the grocery store). This kind of help is even more necessary for women who have to (or want to) keep their jobs. You might also need the kind of help that comes with people who will ask about *you* and listen to your part of the story. This may be friends, people from church, or coworkers in an Employee Resource Group. Finding sources of social support for you will help you care for your loved ones.

Addressing Family Responsibilities Discrimination

Employees have filed lawsuits on the basis of discrimination for elder care in increasing numbers (23 cases before 2000, 181 cases since 2000).[12] Thus, you have the option of seeking legal recourse (or seeking formal help within your company) if you feel you have been unfairly treated because of your caregiving responsibilities.

Bring on the PB and J with a Side of Milk!

Family responsibilities can make it harder to do your work, and work can get in the way of time with your family. If you're lucky, you'll figure out a way to find happiness in both parts of your life. After all, "Being happy doesn't mean everything is perfect. It means that you've decided to look beyond the imperfections."

34

On the Road Again: The Hidden (and Not So Hidden) Costs of Commuting

Viewers of the cult hit movie *Office Space* invariably remember the opening scene where IT worker Peter sits in morning commuter traffic growing increasingly frustrated as he sees an elderly man with a walker moving faster on the sidewalk than he is in his idling car. Similar to Peter, studies of major stressors at work find that commuting is often a primary source of frustration and can negatively affect job performance and physical and mental health.[1, 2]

Moreover, the number of employees making extreme commutes—spending at least three hours everyday day traveling to their workplaces—is on the rise, as is the number of "commuter couples" who live in different cities or even countries to accommodate dual careers.[3] Unfortunately, the stress and anxiety of commuting can affect working women more than men—research has shown that women's blood pressure takes longer to come down after work and they report feeling more exhausted, possibly because of the competing pressures of balancing work and family obligations,[4] or "the second shift."

Not only can commuting have negative effects on individual workers' health, it can also have unfortunate environmental and financial consequences. In Arlington, Virginia, the country has set up an innovative Web site called carfreediet.com, which helps residents estimate how much they spend every week commuting, how much carbon dioxide is released during this drive, and how many calories are (not) burned while in the car. In comparison, they can see how much money they would save, how much less their emissions would be, and how many more calories they would burn a week if they biked, walked, telecommuted, or took mass transit to work. Hint: the differences are pretty stark.

Given the personal and societal downsides of commuting, how can working women best accommodate these challenges?

How to Cope

Investigate Flex Schedules or Telecommuting

Many companies are willing to let workers set their own schedules, so long as they are there for core business hours, usually between 10 a.m and 3 p.m. Such flexibility can put you on the road during off-peak (i.e., less crowded) hours and can be especially useful for working moms if they want to pick their children up right after school.

Telecommuting has also been found to generally have beneficial consequences for workers—namely, telecommuters feel they have higher autonomy and lower work-family conflict, and it can even lead to higher job satisfaction, stronger job performance, and less stress.[5] Moreover, it appears that telecommuting for women, more than for men, is associated with improved job performance and career prospects, most likely because it gives women more control over both their jobs and their family life.

One of Jennifer's friends, Katie, can be labeled a high-intensity telecommuter (someone who works from home more than 2.5 days a week), as she lives and works out of her home in Texas though her company is based in California. Psychological research shows that workers like Katie who engage in high-intensity telecommuting experience even less work-family conflict and stress, but the lack of everyday face-time with coworkers can lead to a deterioration in relationships with them.[6] To combat this potential downside, Katie takes a special effort to connect to her coworkers everyday via some combination of instant messaging, phone calls, video conferencing, or e-mail, and she flies to California on a regular basis to see them in person.

Explore Transportation Alternatives

If sitting in traffic everyday doesn't appeal to you, consider exploring different methods of getting to work. For example, here in the D.C. area many organizations and government departments and agencies utilize the SmartBenefits program to reimburse employees for using public transportation—a solution that can be better on the nerves *and* the wallet than the traditional car ride. Some psychological studies have found that workers who use the bus or train to commute are somewhat more likely to be less stressed about their commute than those who drive in to work, though these effects are moderate.[7] If public transportation isn't an option at your place of work, many larger cities have developed van pools, which gives workers the added benefit of being able to split transportation costs and take advantage of HOV lanes.

For those workers looking for an extreme change in commuting, many workers have turned to biking as a way to lower commuting transportation costs and simultaneously get a fantastic workout. However, women are less likely to do this than men, probably because (1) they are more concerned about their personal safety on busy streets, and (2) in families they are disproportionately responsible for running errands, grocery shopping, and picking up children from day care—tasks that can be more difficult without a car.[8]

If All Else Fails

In the unfortunate event that telecommuting, flex schedules, or transportation alternatives aren't solutions for you, try to make the most of your time in the car—one of our coworkers listens to books on CD that her sons are reading in school so that she's prepared to discuss the themes with them when she gets home every day. Additionally, Jennifer and her husband have used their daily commute together to listen to and discuss the morning news on their way into work and catch up on their respective days on the way home, all while saving on gas money and wear-and-tear on their cars.

Perhaps the extremes of dealing with a commute can be best summarized by two of our favorite country singers—if your commute now is stressful and sounds like this lyric from a Tim McGraw song ("Six lanes, tail lights, red ants marching into the night"), hopefully the research on reducing commuting stress can instead help you feel more like this iconic Willie Nelson tune: "On the road again, just can't wait to get on the road again."

35

Leaving on a Jet Plane: Navigating the Ups and Downs of Working Abroad as Women

2004 was a big year. HUGE. There was the Bush vs. Kerry presidential vote, the Summer Olympics in Athens were a resounding success, and Pakistan confirmed Pervez Musharraf as its new president. But an arguably more memorable pop culture milestone occurred that year as well—both *Friends* and *Sex and the City* aired their series finales. The major plot tensions involved two of America's favorite television heroines dealing with the realities of leaving New York to live and work abroad in Paris, with Rachel planning to leave the gang in New York to pursue a career at Louis Vuitton and Carrie doing the same to be with her new artist boyfriend in the City of Light.

Although neither of these plans worked out so well for the ladies, their fictional experiences shed light on the excitement but concurrent road-blocks that come with a move abroad. These workers, or expatriates (aka expats), generally are folks who move to a related unit in their organization within a different country for a specified amount of time—generally more than six months but less than five years.[1] Unfortunately, however, many employees sent on these jobs terminate the assignment early, leading organizational psychologists to study what type of individuals make the most successful expats and what can be done to make the experience max-imally productive and positive. Here we'll review that literature and talk about how it specifically applies to female workers:

Is Your Personality Right for the Gig?

A growing body of research looks at how the "big five" personality traits (we discussed these in Chapter 1 on self-assessment) can predict expatriate performance. Specifically, a study that summarized over 30 previous studies found that high levels of extraversion, agreeableness, and conscientiousness and low levels of neuroticism predict how well an individual will perform abroad.[2]

- Moreover, the researchers also found in exploratory analyses that cultural sensitivity and flexibility, local language ability, tolerance for ambiguity, leadership skills related to both tasks and people, and social adaptability also seemed to be important to expatriates' success. On the flip side, employees who are low in extroversion and agreeableness and high in neuroticism seem more likely to terminate their assignments prematurely.[3]
- A separate study found that those expats who adjusted the best to their assignments additionally had high levels of openness to new experiences, were not ethnocentric, were oriented to achieve their assigned goals, and were motivated to interact well with their coworkers.[4]

What Are the Cultural Factors at Play in the Country?

Your organization will hopefully give you lots of helpful and specific information about the culture where you are moving—perhaps language training, guidelines about appropriate etiquette and nonverbal behavior, taboos to avoid, norms and traditions to recognize, and other types of cross-cultural training. Above and beyond what they provide you, however, try to do some research to determine more specific information about your new society's culture—as the old saying goes, "the fish does not recognize the water in which it swims" and many of us are probably not aware of how our own national culture influences our thoughts and behaviors until we are "fish out of water" when immersed in another.

To help guide your research, several organizational psychologists embarked on a multiyear, 62 nation study called the GLOBE research project to determine how societal culture is related to organizational effectiveness and found that the following dimensions are important to consider when assessing a nation's culture (learn more about the project at their Web site: www.thunderbird.edu/sites/globe/)[5]:

- **Performance Orientation:** Does the society encourage innovation, high standards, results, competitiveness, feedback, training, control, direct communications, and a sense of urgency or does it value relationships, belongingness, quality of life, harmony, loyalty, cooperation, tradition, subtle communications, and a slower pace of life and work?

- **Future Orientation:** Does the society promote saving for the future, being intrinsically motivated (valuing tasks for their own worth), strategic planning, flexible organizations, deferment of gratification, and visionary leadership or does it value spending now, being extrinsically motivated (valuing external rewards for completing tasks), tactical planning, inflexible organizations, instant gratification, and status quo leadership?

- **Humane Orientation:** Does the society endorse altruism, benevolence, kindness, generosity, support for others, affiliation, sensitivity to discrimination, paternalistic norms, and obedience or does it desire self-interest, self-enjoyment, material positions, self-enhancement, less sensitivity to discrimination, self-reliance, independence, and autonomy?

- **Individualism vs. Collectivism:** Does the society encourage individuals to look after themselves, autonomy, individual goals, more nuclear family interaction, individual activities, and shorter and less intimate communication or does the society desire cohesive groups that look out for members, an interdependent sense of self, fulfillment of social obligations, longer and more intimate communication, and more extended family interaction?

- **Power Distance:** Does the society advocate class stratification, stable bases of power, limited upward mobility, localized and restricted access to information, weak civil liberties, and high growth rates of consumption or does the society desire a large middle class, sharable power, high upward mobility, shared and open access to information, strong social liberties, and mature growth rates of consumption?

- **Uncertainty Avoidance:** Does the society support formal interactions, documents to formalize agreements, meticulous records, formalized policies and rules, strong resistance to change, risk-adverse decision-making, and low tolerance for breaking rules or does the society appreciate informal interactions, "gentlemen's agreements" to seal deals, less resistance to change, higher tolerance for breaking rules, and less calculation when taking risk?

- **Assertiveness:** Does the society encourage domination, toughness, competition, success, expressive thoughts, positive connotations about aggression, belief in a just world, equity, demanding goals, and opportunistic behaviors or does it value modesty, tenderness, warm relationships, face-saving communication, and negative connotations about aggression, equality, and seniority?

- **Gender Egalitarianism:** Does the society have many women in positions of authority, accord them a high status, give them a prominent role in decision-making, have them working in high numbers in the labor force, afford them equal opportunity to pursue education, and have less occupational gender segregation or does the society have fewer women in authoritative positions, accord them lower status, given them less of a role in decision-making, have a lower percentage of women in the labor force, give them less opportunity to pursue education, and have more occupational gender segregation?

FYI, here are several interesting findings on the last dimension:

- Americans generally say they *value* gender egalitarianism, but in practice the United States was right in the middle in terms of our actual practice of gender egalitarianism.

- The societies in the 62-country study that practiced the most gender egalitarianism were Hungary, Russia, Poland, Slovenia, and Denmark, and the countries that practiced the least gender egalitarianism were South Korea, Kuwait, Egypt, Morocco, and Zambia.

- Interestingly, a society's climate and ambient temperature is a strong predictor of gender egalitarianism. Why? The study's authors posit that "because both men and women must master complex survival skills in cold climates, inequality between them is less likely in countries that lie closer to the poles" (p. 371) and "the colder and less hospitable the climate, the greater the need for both women and men to invest in their offspring . . . this greater need for cooperation between men and women is thought to result in a more egalitarian division of roles between the sexes" (p. 373).[6]

- Why should societies care about gender equality? Because those societies that value and practice gender egalitarianism achieve greater longevity, reach higher standards of living, enjoy greater economic prosperity, and have higher levels of general satisfaction. Note that these results are correlational and not causal, however, so we can't say gender equality *causes* these favorable outcomes, just that they are related.

How Will the Move Affect Your Partner and Children?

If you are going over with a partner or family, how do they feel about the move? What are their career and educational prospects in the new country? Will the quality of schools, childcare, and health care be the same? Does the organization have the same policies and regulations regarding maternity/paternity leave, sexual harassment, evaluation, and promotion in their overseas office? How safe is the new country? Will your family be able to reestablish networks of friends in their new city to minimize feelings of loneliness, alienation, and resentment? These questions are critical to ask, as one of the most common reasons for terminating an overseas assignment early is a spouse's dissatisfaction.[7] Unfortunately, because so many of the female expats who work abroad are single, organizations may not have strong career and personal support systems or groups in place to address the unique needs of so-called "male trailing spouses."[8]

For example, Jennifer's friend Marie, a United States diplomat, discovered once she and her husband Eric arrived in their new country within the Persian Gulf region that he was having a hard time getting a work visa, despite his being insanely qualified in financial consulting and even having an offer in hand from a large multinational corporation in the country. Why? Because the host government's laws stipulated that male "guests of the country" such as diplomats could sponsor their wives for a work visa, but female expats were not legally allowed to do the same for their husbands. Don't worry—there is still a happy ending despite months of being in diplomatic limbo. Although he didn't get the job with the corporation, he was able to find an interesting job at the U.S. Embassy and now is enjoying a much-welcomed work-life balance that he didn't have in his previous high-stress position.

What factors seem to influence a trailing partner's adjustment? One study found that it was the size and diversity of their new social networks, particularly with host country nationals, their reaction to the new culture's novelty, their new living conditions, and their fluency in the new language.[9] Interestingly, those spouses who had preschool-aged children reported feeling more adjusted than those with school-aged children or no children in country—perhaps because children at this age require so much more time and resources, this might help the nuclear family maintain some of its core identity in a foreign setting. As one research participant said:

> It's difficult to make close friends. So many expats have their guard up, not wanting to become too close. Too many have been hurt, too many times to become emotionally dependent on a friend only to have the inevitable happen—one or the other of you gets transferred. It's also difficult to watch your children get hurt when their best friend gets transferred. Although I have many acquaintances, I have nowhere near the close friends I had in the States. My spouse, therefore, has become my rock. (pp. 250–51)

How Will the Assignment Affect Your Future Career Prospects? .

Before accepting an international assignment, it is important not to look at just the immediate payoff (compensation, benefits, title) but the long-term implications as well. For example, several new State Department foreign service officers Jennifer knows feel that if they do a first tour in a hardship post like Iraq or Afghanistan, they will be rewarded down the road for their service in a war zone with a more lucrative posting. In a corporate context, one of the leaders of General Motors, Susan Docherty, also believes in the broadening experience of overseas work:

> I like building teams with people who come from very different backgrounds and have very different experiences. I don't just mean diverse teams, in terms of men and women or people of different color or origin. I like people who have worked in different places in the world

than I have because they bring a lot more context to the discussion. That's something that I value a tremendous amount.[10]

But do the long-term benefits of expatriate assignments accrue equally for men and women in organizations? Virginia Valian, a psychology professor and author of the impactful book *Why So Slow? The Advancement of Women* discusses economic research, looking at the 17 possible factors that influence male and female employees salaries in internationally-related occupations and finds that 14 seem to help men more than women. Specifically related to working abroad, she reports:

> For example, having lived outside the U.S. added $9,200 for men but subtracted $7,700 for women. Having deliberately chosen international work added $5,300 for men but subtracted $4,200 for women. Speaking another language added $2,600 for men but subtracted $5,100 for women ... We can now understand that speaking another language and living outside the U.S. are interpreted differently for males and females. As expected with gender schemas, employers only interpret such qualifications as career preparation when men have them. The gender schema for men would see a man as choosing to be abroad or learn a language not for the intrinsic pleasures of those activities but for their instrumental benefits. But the gender schema for women would see them as choosing such activities for their own sake. When men go abroad, their choice signals career commitment. When women go abroad, their choice signals indifference to a career.[11]

Though the data from the original study are somewhat dated by now (1991), the research and implications still raise important questions about how women's work abroad is perceived. For example, when Elizabeth Gilbert of *Eat, Pray, Love* Fame decided to travel to Italy, India, and Indonesia as part of an advance for a book deal, she describes her motivations going into it:

> I wanted to explore one aspect of myself set against the backdrop of each country, in a place that has traditionally done that one thing very well. I wanted to explore the art of pleasure in Italy, the art of devotion in India and, in Indonesia, the art of balancing the two.

Don't get us wrong—the book was as fun a read as anything, but these descriptions unfortunately came across to many critics more as looking for an interesting way to spend a year and learn a beautiful language (Italian) than as a serious career investment. Similarly, a few years working abroad leading a startup Costa Rican ecotourism company might be perceived like a fun way to get a nice tan and hang out with monkeys if you are a woman but as an entrepreneurial endeavor where you learn about international economies if you are a man.

Why So Low?

Despite now constituting about 50 percent of the U.S. workforce, female workers only comprise 17 percent of the expat workforce—the lowest point since 2001, according to the *2010 Global Relocation Trends Survey Report* published by Brookfield Global Relocation Services.[12] Some researchers have dubbed this barrier the "expatriate glass ceiling: the second layer of glass."[13] Why the lag? There are any number of (erroneous) stereotypes that might prevent managers from assigning an international account to a woman: the country is too dangerous, since women aren't generally the main breadwinners their husbands won't want to move, women might be less likely to want to disrupt their families by moving, they won't be able to work the long hours required for many expat jobs, or the host country's culture is not accepting of businesswomen—all opinions that lead supervisors to think she wouldn't be interested or suitable.[14, 15, 16, 17]

Despite these stereotypes about female expats, how do they actually perform once they get there? Some research has found that female employees assigned to a country generally perceived as unfriendly to women performed just as well in their new environment, even when rated by their host country national coworkers.[18, 19] As such, we encourage organizations—and the women and men who work in them—to develop better and more equitable selection procedures, more robust predeparture training, and more effective organizational support structures to further develop this valuable pool of potential expatriates.

Section Six

How Women of All Stripes Can Make It Work: Special Issues for Subgroups

A Hispanic female dispatcher filed suit against her employer. According to the EEOC, her complaint alleged that Hispanic employees were told by not to speak Spanish at work. Specifically, they were told, "This is America and they should learn to speak English." In addition, supervisors yelled and whistled at Hispanic employees over a loudspeaker, asked the plaintiff whether she missed getting up late and having siestas, and asked the plaintiff if she would be making burritos for Thanksgiving. The employer agreed to pay $125,000 in compensatory damages.[1]

That same year, the EEOC also filed suit against another company on behalf of an African American woman who was harassed by her bosses, taunted by coworkers, and denied a bonus after she complained about manager comments that "black people are lazy and move too slowly." The total amount of damages in this case was $3.3 million.[2]

It is clear from these cases that the experience of women at work is affected not only by their gender but also by other aspects of their identities. Being both a woman and a member of another stigmatized group can be doubly difficult. We will devote this section of the book to issues that may be central to women with potentially stigmatized identities.

Indeed, researchers have studied the "double jeopardy hypothesis," which is based on the idea that minority women will face a "double whammy." One survey of 800 employees in five companies found that minority women reported more racial and gender harassment than did men who are minorities, white women, and white men.[3] Unfortunately, research has also shown that harassment on the basis of race and gender can independently affect psychological and physical health.[4] In other words, experiencing both types of harassment can truly be a double whammy.

With hope of identifying the challenges and coping strategies that are unique to subgroups of women, we will consider the unique experiences of lesbian and bisexual women, disabled women, women from ethnic minority backgrounds, and single moms. For example, we'll discuss research on each of these different subpopulations that shows that:

- Women with physical disabilities may best succeed on a job interview if they acknowledge their disability at the beginning rather than the end of an interview.

- When people think about a "leader" they don't only think "male", they also think "white."

- Lesbian and bisexual women can benefit most by seeking both traditional mentors (older men who can help develop their networks and provide professional support) and demographically similar mentors (older lesbian women who can help navigate the complexities of "coming out" on the job and provide personal support).

- Single moms take networking to a whole new level. Their family and community networks can help them to juggle their work and home responsibilities.

- White, heterosexual, childless women can help! Confronting people about their biases can actually reduce the likelihood that they will use stereotypes.

Read on for more info!

36

Perfectly Capable: Workplace Considerations of Women with Disabilities

Brooke Shields. Princesss Diana. Frida Kahlo. Joni Mitchell. Harriet Tubman.

You may have heard of these women. Indeed, their achievements are irrefutable. But you may be surprised to learn that each of these famous women had some sort of disability:

Depression. Eating disorder. Spina bifida. Polio. Sight impaired.

These names are indicative of the prevalence of disability, which affects one in five Americans, more than half of whom are women.[1] In addition, these names exemplify the potential that every woman has for achievement regardless of whether she is disabled. This achievement potential can be stifled by challenges facing women with disabilities, but it can also be supported by individual, organizational, and societal efforts. With the hope of identifying strategies that women with disabilities might engage, we first describe research on what they might expect and then discuss evidence about how to make it work.

What Do We Mean by "Disability"?

According to the Department of Labor, a disability is a physical or mental impairment that substantially limits one or more of a person's major life activities. This can include a range of attributes such as learning disabilities, mental illness, or physical impairments.

There are three important dimensions of disability that affect workplace experiences. The first is *severity*: To what extent does the disability limit your ability to perform the duties of your job? The second is *visibility*: can other people tell that you have a disability when they first meet you, or do you have to decide whether and when to tell people about your disability? The third is *controllability*, or whether or not other people generally blame you for your disability—do people think it is your fault that you are disabled?

For example, asthma is usually seen as an uncontrollable, invisible disability that may not be particularly severe and so may have little impact on your daily work experiences. As another example, however, being confined to a wheelchair can reflect a severe, visible disability that may or may not have been controllable. These kinds of distinctions are important because they imply a different set of psychological processes. For individuals with visible disabilities, for example, they have to deal with the fact that other people will immediately notice their disability and possibly judge them on this basis. People with concealable disabilities, however, have to make decisions about whether (and when and how) to tell their supervisors, coworkers, and clients. People with disabilities that are perceived to be controllable (even though they might not have actually been controllable, like HIV or lung cancer) have to deal with the fact that others might be hostile and unsympathetic, whereas people with uncontrollable disabilities may feel helpless and have to deal with other people's pity.[2] The workplace experiences of people with asthma are likely very different than those who are paraplegic. Unfortunately, the research suggests that women who have a range of disabilities are likely to face some challenges at work.

What Can Women with Disabilities Expect at Work?

Women who have disabilities may face difficulties getting a job, getting paid, and getting promoted. As much as 80 percent of people with disabilities report trouble finding a job.[3] Some disabilities increase the likelihood of missing work, which is often interpreted as a sign of a lack of commitment to the job or company. In addition, there is some evidence to suggest that salaries decrease at the onset of a disabling condition, and although there is some recovery in the paycheck, there is often a decline in wages over time.[4]

Women who have disabilities may have challenges in their interpersonal relationships at work. Many people who do not have disabilities will hold stereotypes about people with disabilities that can interfere with their interpersonal relationships. Laurie Block, from National Public Radio, described contradictory yet overlapping stereotypes in six forms[5]:

1. People with disabilities are different from fully human people; they are partial or limited people.
2. The successful "handicapped" person is superhuman, triumphing over adversity in a way which serves as an example.
3. The burden of disability is unending; life with a disabled person is a life of constant sorrow.
4. A disability is a sickness, something to be fixed, an abnormality to be corrected or cured.
5. People with disabilities are a menace to others, to themselves, to society.
6. People with disabilities . . . are holy innocents endowed with special grace.

Indeed, research shows that people feel pressured by competing motivations when they interact with people with disabilities. On the one hand, people are motivated by general social norms about being kind and politically correct. On the other hand, however, people are also motivated to believe they live in a world that is just and fair. The former motivation leads to overly solicitous (fake nice!) behavior, and the latter can lead to harsh treatment and evaluations of individuals with disabilities.[6]

Beliefs about disability as illness or burden may limit the extent to which coworkers build friendships with workers with disabilities. Stereotypes that people with disabilities are "other" or "holy innocents" may limit access to challenging work assignments, constructive feedback, and useful kinds of conflict. Each of these stereotypic beliefs can lead to strained relationships.

How Can Women with Disabilities Make It Work?

Take Advantage of Programs Designed to Help

The feds tell us that:

Currently, over 209,284 people with disabilities, seven percent of the total federal civilian workforce, work for the federal government.

Opportunities exist at all levels of government and in hundreds of occupations. Total disabled federal employment has remained constant at seven percent since 1980. Executive Order 13078 and the Americans With Disabilities Act (ADA) has increased awareness of hiring options by federal managers. These initiatives should expand total disabled employment opportunities throughout government. All agencies are required by law to develop outreach efforts to identify qualified candidates to meet agency workforce diversity goals.[7]

This is just one example of an effort by the nation's largest employer to hire people with disabilities. Don't let long application processes or fears about how you might be seen by employers stop you from trying to find a job that is a good fit for you.

Take Matters into Your Own Hands

Sometimes being direct about your disability can help other people get over themselves. In one study, a sample of 137 students and working adults watched a video of an interview with a job applicant in a wheelchair. This applicant discussed their disability at the beginning, middle, or end of the interview (or not at all). Participants gave the lowest ratings to job applicants who did not discuss their disability at all, and those who waited until the end of the interview. In other words, participants favored the job applicants who brought up their disability earlier in the interview.[8] This acknowledgement of the disability seemed to convey that the interviewee was well-adjusted and socially competent, and therefore ready for work.

In an impressive personal example of taking matters into your own hands, Jennifer's sister Vickie (who uses walking braces and has a little bit of difficulty articulating words after undergoing radiation treatments to her jaw area during a courageous battle with cancer when she was 16) found that after she got a job as a child life specialist at a children's hospital, some young patients and their parents were having a hard time understanding her name, thinking she was saying "Mikki." Rather than simply be frustrated or upset about it, she asked the person who makes her name badge to print her name as "Victoria" instead, and she happily uses that name on the job now and is able to serve as a great role model to the children she helps by showing that whatever medical problem they might face, *nothing* is insurmountable with a little creativity and determination.

Use Your Rights

The law is on your side. The Americans with Disabilities Act of 1990 prohibits discrimination "against a qualified individual with a disability because of the disability of such individual in regard to job application procedures, the hiring, advancement, or discharge of employees, employee compensation, job training, and other terms, conditions, and privileges of employment." Indeed, the Equal Employment Opportunity office reported that discrimination claims on the basis of disability went up 10 percent between 2008 and 2009—over 21,000 claims were filed. This means that there are no excuses—if you are equally qualified as another applicant or employee, you cannot be hired, fired, promoted, or compensated differently. This also means that employers are required to make reasonable accommodations to make sure you can do your job.

Accommodate Accommodation

We're guessing that some of you are like us—we don't like to ask for help with anything (except maybe doing the dishes and laundry). Research suggests that people with disabilities are sometimes reluctant to ask for accommodations because they are worried that other people might perceive it to be unfair, that people will view them more negatively, or that the accommodations might not actually be all that useful.[9]

In one recent experiment, participants competed or cooperated for rewards (cash money!) with an undercover experimenter who was described as being dyslexic. In half of the conditions, the undercover experimenter got extra time on the task (an "accommodation"), and in the other half they did not get this accommodation. Participants' responses on a survey after the task showed that (regardless of whether they were competing or cooperating) felt cheated when the undercover experimenter performed the best. This supports other evidence that shows giving and taking accommodations can be a tricky business.[10]

Nevertheless, other research suggests that these fears can be overcome by involving employee input in the accommodation process.[11] When people have a say over what happens, they tend to find that it isn't a big deal. If possible, you might consider requesting accommodations through a group decision-making process so that everyone feels they get a say in the outcome.

On the positive side of things—since we like to go out on a high note—many women with and without disabilities find that the workplace is a setting in which they can engage in meaningful activities and forge positive relationships, and these are actually life-extending activities![12] We hope you get to the good stuff.

37

Minority Report: Workplace Considerations of African American, Hispanic, and Asian Women

The woman in question became a lawyer after some years as a community organizer, married a corporate lawyer and is the mother of two little girls, ages 9 and 6. Herself the daughter of a white American mother and a black African father—in this race-conscious country, she is considered black—she served as a state legislator for eight years, and became an inspirational voice for national unity. Be honest: Do you think this is the biography of someone who could be elected to the United States Senate? After less than one term there, do you believe she could be a viable candidate to head the most powerful nation on earth?

—Gloria Steinem[1]

People often wonder: which is worse, racism or sexism? This was certainly discussed in the 2008 presidential primary season when Hillary Clinton and Barack Obama battled for the democratic nomination. Gloria Steinem's Op Ed in *The New York Times* provided one perspective of the issue in which she concluded that, "Gender is probably the most restricting force in American life, whether the question is who must be in the kitchen or who could be in the White House."

But a question that is too often forgotten in these debates is obvious: what about people who are socially disadvantaged with regard to both gender and race? In other words, what about women of color? Data from the U.S. Census clearly demonstrate that the representation of African American, Latina, and Asian women in the workplace is growing rapidly. Research is just beginning to scratch the surface in understanding how these women experience work.

What Are Women of Color Likely to Encounter at Work?

Hurdles for Getting Hired

According to the Department of Labor, the overall unemployment rate was 10.3 percent for men and 8.1 percent for women in 2009.[2] However, these figures varied substantially across women of color. Specifically, unemployment was greatest among African American women (12.4%), followed by Hispanic women (11.5%), white women (7.3%) and Asian women (6.6%). Women of color are also likely to get pigeonholed in particular types of jobs. Whereas large proportions of Asian (47%), Caucasian (41%), and African American women (34%) worked in management, professional, and related occupations, Hispanic women were more likely to work in sales and office occupations (32%).

Research shows that having a name that *sounds* black, Hispanic, or Asian can influence whether or not people are interviewed for jobs. Audit studies, in which résumé with matched credentials are sent to job offers, show that people with Black and Latino-sounding names are less likely to get jobs in 20 percent of cases.[3]

Problems Getting Paid and Promoted

You'll remember the emphatic message in our chapter on negotiations—women get paid less than men. But we got another one to lay on you: the wage gap is bigger for ethnic minorities. Asian American women earn 78 percent of white men's salaries, followed by Caucasian women (73%), African American women (63%), Native American women (60%) and Hispanic women (52%). Yep, you read that correctly. The average Hispanic woman earns HALF the salary of the average Caucasian man.

Given these sad statistics, it probably won't surprise you to learn that surveys of over 2000 managers in a Fortune 500 company suggest that being female and being African American or Asian negatively influenced ratings of promotion potential. In other words, African American and Asian women were penalized for being female, in addition to being penalized for their race. The bias toward women of colors reflects the combination of bias toward women AND bias toward racial minorities.[4]

Unfortunately, the promotion problems are part of a self-fulfilling cycle. The results of an analysis of 74 studies showed that supervisors give higher ratings to members of their own ethnic groups than they do to people from other ethnic backgrounds.[5] Since ethnic minorities have a harder time getting promoted, they are likely not to be in positions to give positive evaluations of members of their own ethnic groups. This means it may be harder for them to get promoted, which feeds back into the cycle.

Challenge to Be Seen as in Charge

You wouldn't know it from *Grey's Anatomy*'s cast (which includes an African American in the role of chief of surgery, and has featured both a Latina and an African American woman as the chief resident), but it is difficult for racial minorities to be seen as leaders. In general, people assume that leaders are white men. In one series of studies, participants read a description of a leader whose race was not mentioned and were then asked to indicate the ethnicity of that leader. People guessed that the leader was white. Follow-up studies suggested that, regardless of industry, white leaders were rated more favorably than African American leaders. In addition, the career prospects of successful fake leaders who indicated their race was "white" were higher than successful fake leaders who were described as being African American, Hispanic, or Asian.[6]

Rocky Relationships

One of the hardest parts about being in the numerical minority is that it can be difficult to fit in with everyone else. To explore these experiences, the Center for Women's Policy Studies conducted a survey of over 1,500 women of color from 16 Fortune 1000 companies. Their results suggested that many ethnic minority women felt that the managers at the top of their company's hierarchy were not committed to diversity. Similarly, a survey of African American and Caucasian managers in three different organizations suggested that African Americans felt less accepted by their organizations than did Caucasians.[7]

In addition, many women reported that they felt like they had to downplay their gender and ethnicity in order to advance in their companies.[8] This need to ignore ethnicity may be due to specific stereotypes about ethnic minorities. For example, African American women are perceived to be more likely to engage in conflict than Caucasian women.[9] This could lead people to avoid interactions with African American coworkers that could become contentious.

Sexual harassment may be experienced differently by women of color compared to white women. A survey of 184 Latina women enrolled in adult schools or job-training centers suggested that Latina women were particularly susceptible to harassment when the perpetrator power was substantial. The researchers interpreted this finding through the Latino tradition of "respeto" which reflect deference to people with power.[10]

The work-life interface may also be experienced differently for women of color. For example, Asian women are stereotyped as being part of the "model minority" for whom work ethic is central.[11] As a result, when Asian women make decisions that reflect commitment to their families above their work they may be doubly penalized. Being treated negatively or even just differently than everyone else can have a negative effect on work-life balance.

How Can These Experiences Be Improved?

Capitalize on Connections

One thing that women of color often have that white women don't is connections with their ethnic group. Being part of a larger community can be an important source of pride in one's self and of emotional support. In addition, women of color can serve as sources for networking.[12] You can complain to your friends about your dumbass boss, or you can find a friend who has a boss she likes and ask her to recommend you for the next opening.

Shake Things Up

Pull together a group of women of color (and allies!) to form an employee resource group that can decide what can be done to improve the experiences of ethnic minorities in your workplace.[13] Nominate (or become!) a champion who will pursue the goals of the group with organizational managers. There can be power in these kinds of numbers—if you convince management that it is in the best interest of the company to transform the organization's policies, procedures, or practices, it's all downhill from there.

Make Your Own Workplace

More women of color than ever before are turning to entrepreneurship to find their happy place. These women start their own companies, often out of their own homes, to ensure that they get to create the kind of culture that will support them.[14] This can be a risky endeavor, but when it is successful it can have the biggest possible payoff—financial security AND job satisfaction. Take the example of Gail Warrior, the C.E.O. and president of the construction business Warrior Group and founder of the Warrior Small Business Academy, a group she began to help other female and minority business owners—when talking about mentoring and networking with other women, she says, "It's so energizing ... we really learn from each other."[15]

In Conclusion . . .

Research by the Center for Survey Research and Analysis which included over 1,000 participants across the United Sates suggested that racism was more strongly related to votes in the 2008 election than was sexism.[16] This and the other research described in this chapter suggests that, although the basic premise described in Gloria Steinem's opening quote stands, we must push beyond the conclusion that sexism is a dominant phenomenon in our society. Instead, we must recognize that women of color are particularly vulnerable to the dual effects of sexism and racism are particularly in need of efforts to improve these experiences.

This is reflected in the statement of one woman of color:

> We occupy many of the seats on the 5:30 P.M. Metrolink train from downtown Los Angeles to San Bernardino. We are behind the counters at the Department of Motor Vehicles and on both sides of the desks at the Department of Social Services. We push wheelchairs in parks and hospitals and hug children at day-care centers. Black women, who in

2006 constituted 7 percent of the working-age population, represented 14 percent of women workers and 53 percent of black workers, yet we are largely invisible in the policy discourse about both race and gender. Like black men, black women live in neighborhoods far from employment opportunities and with low-performing schools. Like white women, black women experience occupational segregation, a gender wage gap and the challenge of balancing family and work.

We are discriminated against because we are black. We are discriminated against because we are women. We are discriminated against because we are both.[17]

38

Coming Out and Standing Up: Workplace Considerations of Lesbians and Bisexual Women

As much as 21 percent of women are attracted to other women. Somewhere around 10 percent of women have engaged in sexual behavior with other women. Around 5 percent of women consider themselves to be "lesbian" or "bisexual."[1] So it's not just Rosie and Ellen—millions of women across the globe are gay. And when these women go to work, they face a set of unique challenges that deserve unique solutions.

The Three Challenges

Just a few months ago, Eden was lucky enough to collaborate with Belle Rose Ragins, a famous management scholar and inspirational presenter, in presenting a workshop on lesbian, gay, and bisexual (LGB) issues in the workplace. In that session, Belle identified three challenges that LGB workers will encounter.

The First Challenge: The Invisibility of a Gay or Lesbian Identity

No matter how good you think your "gaydar" is, we're here to tell that you simply cannot know a person's sexual orientation by looking at them. This concealability may be comforting in some cases, but it comes with a serious set of baggage.

One problem is the common presumption of heterosexuality—when lesbians interact with people who don't know their sexual orientation, they often get asked things like "are you married?" or "what does your husband do?" Perhaps even worse, lesbians might be exposed to jokes or crude language about gay people because people assume that they are straight. This is an indirect form of discrimination that can be just as harmful as someone making fun of you directly.

Another problem is that lesbians have to decide whether, how, when, and to whom they should disclose their sexual identity. They have to juggle the balance between wanting to be authentic and genuine in their interactions with other people and wanting to avoid potential discrimination. This "disclosure dilemma" can be incredibly stressful.[2]

Once disclosure dilemmas are decided and women tell their coworkers or boss they are gay, they might face backlash. Some disclosure recipients will go into denial mode, avoiding all discussion of sex, families, and marriage forever. Other disclosure recipients will be angry or hurt and feel that they had been "lied to." In some cases, this is a lose-lose situation. An unintended consequence of disclosure decisions is that women can lose control over the disclosure process—it's just like the middle school rumor mill: once one person knows, it is possible that everyone else will find out.

The Second Challenge: Negative Coworker Reactions

So what happens when you tell or everyone finds out? Unfortunately, evidence suggests that many Americans continue to hold negative views toward LGB people. A 2010 Gallup survey found that, when respondents were asked whether sexual relations between two adults of the same sex are "always wrong," "almost always wrong," "wrong only sometimes," or "not wrong at all," more than 40 percent of Americans chose "always wrong."[3]

Studies also show that these attitudes translate into negative behaviors toward LGB workers. In a study by our amazing mentor, students applied for retail jobs wearing a hat that either said "gay and proud" and hats that said "Texan and proud." They were in Texas, so all you anti-Texas people should know that this was seen as a very good thing! They didn't know which hat they were wearing. After they filled out job applications in the retail stores, they filled out questionnaires about how they were treated. The results of these questionnaires and coding of their tape recorded conversations suggest that people were treated more negatively when they wore the "gay and proud" hat than when they wore the "Texan and proud" hat. They were treated with more hostility and rudeness, and less eye contact and friendliness. In addition, the store managers spent less time talking to them in the "gay" condition.[4]

Moreover, surveys of LGB workers show clear patterns of persistent discrimination. One comprehensive study showed that over a third of LGB people experienced verbal or physical harassment or discrimination in their jobs.[5] In addition, some evidence suggests that lesbians may be more susceptible than heterosexual women to sexual assaults at work.[6]

The negativity of reactions to LGB people can be traced to beliefs about the controllability of sexual orientation—the more people think that people can choose whether or not to be gay, the more negative their attitudes toward gay people. In addition, people have fears tied to morality and religion.[7] Together, these forces lead to the likelihood of negative reactions to lesbians at work.

The Third Challenge: Lack of Support

Whereas members of ethnic minority groups can look to their families and communities for support, many gay people are ostracized from these same sources of support. Some lesbians may be "out" at work, but "in the closet" with their families. This means that they may have fewer places to get the emotional and task-related support that they need.

> While many minority groups are the target for prejudice . . . and discrimination . . . in our society, few persons face this hostility without the support and acceptance of their family . . .
>
> —Virginia Uribe and Karen Harbeck

Gay people also lack access to legal support. For example, in contrast to the United Kingdom, Germany, Israel, Belgium, Canada, Spain, and South Africa, there is no federal legislation protecting LGB workers from employment discrimination in the United States. Lesbians can also face challenges outside of work with regard to having or adopting children, filing taxes, and getting married. The lack of legal recourse for negative events serves as an additional challenge for LGB people.

What Individuals and Organizations Can Do to Meet These Challenges

Organizational Steps

Despite the fact that federal legislation has not been enacted to support LGB workers, the Human Rights Campaign reported that protections based on sexual orientation are becoming commonplace among the most competitive businesses: 85 percent of Fortune 500 businesses prohibit discrimination based on sexual orientation. In 2000, only 51 percent of these businesses had such protections.

What do these protections look like? The first step is to include LGB people as protected members of the organization in diversity/equity statements. But beyond this, organizations can go further to create an inclusive workplace by setting up employee resource groups, supporting LGB-outreach efforts (e.g., sponsoring PRIDE events), and setting norms that support inclusive language (e.g., inviting all partners or significant others to company social events). Indeed, research suggests it is these sorts of efforts that can have the biggest impact on how gay people experience work and life.[8]

Individual Efforts

An interview study suggests that there may be several ways that lesbians can improve their work experiences. Women in these interviews reported that they engaged in three primary strategies. First, *they "pre-screened" their coworkers and supervisors* to determine their likely receptivity to the issue of lesbianism. For example, one woman reported that, "I listen to people before I engage with them. So if I sense a lack of tolerance for certain kinds of things, people, music, art, a total focus on themselves, who they peer with, kinda gives me give me a clue that these are people are . . . there's a vibe. There's just a vibe."

Second, they *came out as lesbians in a strategic way.* For example, one woman was strategic in telling her boss so that her boss would not feel embarrassed to be the last one to find out: "I wanted to tell my boss. Now, up to this point I had just told my peers. I didn't tell my boss . . . she's one of these people like if someone were to walk up to her and say 'I just heard, I just read that Susan was gay.' She would say 'Absolutely not! I can't believe you'd say that!' You know, she'd defend me. And I didn't want her to embarrass herself by thinking she was being protective and in reality, it's like 'no, I am'. So I told her about it and she was fine with it."

Third, they *educated others* in their organization about the issues facing lesbians by dealing with human resources, engaging in committees and support groups, and participating in social events within the company. For example, one woman was subjected to a lengthy security clearance. A conversation with her boss demonstrates how she used this as a "teaching moment":

> And it was funny too 'cause when I went back to the office [Butch], my boss says: "You were there five and a half hours?" And I went "yes. Why?" He was trying to figure out what was it about me that was so special that I was there five and a half hours. And I said "[Butch], because I'm gay." And he just stared at me like Oh shit you know? There's another thing going on here. A part of me just loves teaching people that. I just really being able to say OK, open your friggin' eyes to what other people go through—especially white males. Because when you think about it they have privilege because they're male and because they're white and they just don't understand. They don't have a clue what it's like not to have that privilege . . . So you have to constantly sort of—it took me five and a half hours because I'm queer, Butch. You know. Obviously, it took you 30 minutes because you're a white male.[9]

Our friends/colleagues Mikki and Scott (Dr. T!) are working on a paper now looking at the *kinds of mentors that are in the best position to help LGB employees*. The results of their survey of LGB workers suggest that LGB people will be best served by having both heterosexual and LGB mentors. Heterosexual mentors can help get access to good resources and information, and LGB mentors can provide advice about how to handle your sexual orientation in the office by pointing out sensitive topics and close-minded colleagues.

If you want to make *more formal attempts at organizational change*, you might try this kind of argument with the powers-that-be:

> Research from scientists across the country has shown that individuals who encounter discrimination report physical, stress-related symptoms

and are at risk for depression. More directly related to the bottom-line, discrimination is associated with outcomes that affect worker productivity and organizational performance: decreased job satisfaction, decreased job commitment, and increased stress and turnover. Institutions that make employment decisions on the basis of sexual orientation will encounter problems not only with employee health and retention, but also with performance. Given that there is no evidence that LGB workers perform any less well than heterosexual workers, personnel decisions made on the basis of sexual orientation will be faulty, ineffective, and costly for institutions. The presence of LGB-supportive policies (particularly when paired with a supportive culture for LGB workers) is associated with reductions in discrimination, and thus can help to avoid the negative outcomes described above.

And you can quote us on it.

39

All the Single Ladies: Workplace Considerations of Single Moms

Beyonce made single-dom sound fabulous, but the research suggests that being a single, working mom isn't always bootylicious.

Instead, single moms, "characterize their lives as involving a paradoxical bind which emerges from their needs to survive in the male-oriented work world and succeed in their roles as heads of households while searching for the ideal of the ever-happy two-parent family they feel they have been promised."[1] Sheesh, talk about mission impossible.

Who Are These Single Ladies?

According to the Census Bureau, there are 13.7 million single parents in the United States—84 percent of these are mothers. Moreover, the incidence of out-of-wedlock births (representing 4 out of 10 births in the United States as of 2007) is rapidly increasing, with a high of 59 percent in D.C. and a low of 20 percent in Utah.[2] Most of these women (45%) are single through divorce, though 34 percent were never married. The overwhelming majority (80%) of these single moms are working—50 percent of them work full-time.[3]

What Are the Common Challenges?

Single moms who work outside the home talk about three primary challenges: *time, money, and energy.* These concerns are similar to those reported by women from dual-earner households,[4] but the experiences of single mothers seem to reflect heightened anxiety about each of these issues.

Among participants in one interview study, lack of money was the primary concern for 80 percent of women, and all of the moms mentioned that they needed more time to do everything they wanted to do.[5] In a blog about motherhood, Jeannette from Santa Barbara described her experience as follows:

> I am a single mother, a teacher, with 3 sons in grad school. I have to say that though I was not poor, I was always struggling with financial worries. I was fortunate to have three smart boys and I knew if we could get scholarships, they could go onto college. It took our nights and our weekends, my one car shared for their part time jobs and dates, many pick ups, late night homework help, and many, many weekends with homework, scholarship papers, college apps, and endless sports games, reports, papers, and classwork. My memory of it all was just determination and really, really hard work on all our parts . . . It is one very long road of debt and late nights and missed holidays, etc. I think we are all doing it on faith, that somehow it will pay off.

This quote points to the challenges that single moms face, as well as the decisions that many make to try to handle it. These women report making compromises—like keeping not-so-perfect jobs to stay in a good school district, putting off their own education, sacrificing social life—to support their children.[6] Among women with more financial resources, the choices look somewhat different. One manager/single mom explained her decision to take a new job in the following way:

> I'm going to have one-third of the number of people reporting to me than I used to and I'm going to walk out of work at 5:15 p.m. . . . And that was a very conscious choice. I didn't want a job that was going to consume me right now because I know that my priority needs to be taking care of Ben . . . So it's constantly this balance of how much time a to spend at work and with my child. How deep does the foot go in? Is it the toe; up to the ankle; up to the knee? How deep am I in the work world with still my arms and head free to be with Ben and it's a balance that I anticipate continually needing to adjust as the years play out.[7]

How Can Single Moms Make It Work?

Researchers have identified a few factors that seem to be particularly useful for single moms who are juggling work and family responsibilities. One of these strategies involves *cultivating external resources*. Since women can't share the burden of childcare or earning a living with a partner, they share these tasks with a larger social network. Indeed, parents.com recommends that single moms assemble a reliable support team. For example, one mom reported that she reached out to her network when she had to work longer hours:

> It's very hard to find any (daycare facilities) that are open that late . . . So when Ben first started going to daycare, at that time I actually had 5 people. I had somebody every day of the week who picked him up. They would pick him up at 4 or 4:30 and have him for a couple of hours until I got home. There was my roommate, the two people with older kids, then my friends Joan and Mary.[8]

Single mothers also try to *make special accommodations* with bosses and coworkers. Data from a longitudinal study of households receiving public assistance included 851 single mothers. The responses of these women suggest that one of the factors that was most strongly related to their success was support from their coworkers. That is, separate from support from community and familial sources, coworker support positively impacted the lives of single mothers.[9] This means that single moms might benefit from frank conversations with their colleagues about what they need to get their jobs done effectively.

One of the factors that may help single moms juggle their work and family is flexibility. Surveys of single moms also suggest that *having flexible schedules*, or at least schedules that are predictable and controllable, is an important predictor of work satisfaction.[10] This means that flexibility may be an important characteristic to look for in your next job, or a goal for changing your current job. Single moms' schedules often revolve around their children's childcare schedules. Try to work out a schedule that is parallel by offering to come in early (as soon as you drop off your kids) so you can leave early. You might also want to talk with your boss about backup plans in case your childcare provider is sick or your kids' school is closed for teacher in-service (e.g., can you work from home?). Having a plan in place for these disruptions in childcare might help you and your colleagues cope.

And Don't Forget . . .

One more thing to keep in mind—*give yourself a break*. This means that you need to make sure you are taking care of yourself and spending time doing things that genuinely make you happy, whether that means making time for a run before you kid wakes up, reading a book before you go to bed, or sleeping in on Saturdays. It also means that you should let go of guilt, whether it is about buying cupcakes instead of making them, missing your daughter's softball game, or being a few minutes late to work. Your kid and your boss will appreciate having a happier version of you even if the cupcakes aren't homemade.

40

We All Need Somebody to Lean On: How Allies Can Support Each Other

---

> They came first for the Communists, and I didn't speak up because I wasn;t a Communist. Then they came for the trade unionists, and I didn't speak up because I wasn't a trade unionist. Then they came for the Jews, and I didn't speak up because I wasn't a Jew. Then they came for me and by that time no one was left to speak up.
>
> —Martin Niemöller

You may be currently healthy, heterosexual, married, and childless, but that doesn't mean there isn't work for you to do! The most powerful agents of change are sometimes the ones who are not directly affected by the change efforts. In other words, we can and should be advocates for each other. We know it isn't always clear what women should do to help each other, so we're going to make it simple with a three-step strategy for ready and willing allies. Think of this as a workplace-ready version of stop-drop-and roll! LISTEN. CONFRONT. ADVOCATE.

Step 1: Listen

We need to listen for two things. First, we need to *listen for stereotyping* and discrimination—we need to *notice* when it happens. This is the first step for any kind of change (even the stop-drop-and-roll metaphor requires that you pay attention to the beginning signs of fire).[1] It's easy to brush things off or pretend like stuff didn't happen, particularly when it isn't about *us*. But the people it is happening to might not be able to brush it off. Eden remembers a meeting in which a female, Asian coworker mentioned an idea for a new project that was basically ignored. A few minutes later, another coworker who happened to be a Caucasian man made a very similar suggestion and everyone jumped on board. Eden noticed that the initial idea was forgotten and wondered if it might have been overlooked because of gender and ethnic dynamics.

The second thing we need to *listen for is guidance about the ways we can help*. This kind of listening is sometimes more straightforward—our coworkers and subordinates may come to us with their concerns and ask us for their help. If the request for help is this direct, your response is equally obvious: *be there*. Make time to provide the kind of support they are requesting, and help them find the resources that will provide long-term solutions. But when requests for support are not as obvious, it is also okay to check in with your colleagues who may feel powerless. Respectfully ask the women of color and lesbians and women with disabilities with whom you work about what things are like for them in your office. We all know about the trouble with assumptions (the "ass" out of "u" and "me"), so rather than assume things are good or bad for any particular group, just ask! This can feel a little awkward and it might border on being patronizing, so the "respectful" component of the ask is key.

Step 2: Confront

If you are really listening, you may hear a lot. It is hugely important that you call it out—don't let things slide. An important study examined the effects of simple statements condemning or condoning racism. People were approached on three different college campuses and asked to indicate their beliefs about racially charged situations. When these people heard someone else condemn racism, they were more supportive of antiracist statements. This was contrasted with a condition in which participants heard someone else condone racism (say that it's "no big deal"); in these situations, people indicated less agreement with antiracist statements. Thus, acting like racism is no big deal can perpetuate it.[2]

Allies can help not only by generally condemning prejudice and discrimination, but also by confronting the instances that they witness. In the example described above, Eden could have mentioned to her team that her Asian coworker had the same idea that the white coworker did to ensure that she got the credit she deserved. (Eden wishes she had done this, but didn't get as far past the "listening" step as she would've hoped!) Confronting bias when it happens is a powerful way to reduce stereotyping. Indeed, a series of three experiments showed that when undergraduate students were confronted about behavior that could be biased, they later expressed fewer stereotypes and prejudice. It is important to note that, although these confrontations reduced participants' bias, they also negatively affected perceptions of the person who did the confronting.[3] This suggests that there can be interpersonal risks associated with confronting, so you have to make decisions about when the benefits of reducing discrimination outweigh the risks of negative interpersonal evaluations.

Step 3: Advocate

Remember that people who are the recipients of unfair treatment are often those who lack the power to change it. Think about the fact that, in 30 states, your lesbian coworkers could be fired simply because of their sexual orientation. Or think about how a victim of sexual harassment may have to work with the same boss who made sexual advances toward her. You have the opportunity to advocate on behalf of these women within and outside the company.

Within the company (and typically only after securing the permission/encouragement of the targets of bias), you can file complaints, push for company-wide culture change, or propose formal policy changes. Outside the company, you can write letters, call your congressional representatives, make donations, and tell your friends about the changes that need to be made.

Take Three Steps to Make the Change!

We all like to think of ourselves as good people who stand up for what is right. We believe we will confront perpetrators of prejudice and advocate for people whose rights are violated. But research shows again and again that this kind of standing up is an incredibly difficult task that can be cognitively and emotionally draining.[4] Luckily, every journey starts with one step, and we can take that step together. In this way, we hope we can fulfill Ghandi's pronouncement: "We must be the change we wish to see in the world."

Conclusion

What's the Bottom Line about How to Make It Work? What You *Can* Take with You

If you made it this far, you've probably got all kinds of numbers and findings and ideas doing Zumba in your brain. We're all for our brains getting a workout, but we'd like to minimize the forgetting that will inevitably occur and maximize the utility of this book. So, like any organizational psychologist worth their paycheck, we will give you a few bottom-line, not-to-be-forgotten, tattoo-on-the-back-of-your-hand highlights. And you'll get your money's worth from these organizational psychologists, Joss Whedon (*Buffy the Vampire Slayer*) style.

- **Despite progress, women face challenges at work**. The biggest of these challenges are grounded in stereotypes about men and women— these stereotypes affect our own behavior and the behavior of others toward us. We don't ask for raises, we perform worse on tests when we think they measure our math ability, and we sugarcoat negative feedback. Other people try to protect us from challenging assignments, assume that we are more interested in being at home than at work, and think our work is less valuable than that of our male counterparts. The dynamics of these stereotypes have to be recognized and addressed before gender equality can exist. Faith, an undeniably powerful woman (and vampire slayer), responded to the question, "Why are slayers always girls?" by directly addressing the stereotypic basis of the question, "Because we're better at it."

- **It's all about fit.** We're not talking about prince-on-a-horse-glass-slipper fit. We're talking about that feeling you get in your stomach on your way to work or at the end of a long day. Are you filled with dread, uncertainty, and anxiety, or do you get the warm and fuzzy butterflies of excitement and enthusiasm? Figure out what makes the fuzzy butterflies for *you*. Our favorite vampire slayer considered a poor-fitting career change after a bad breakup:

Buffy: So, um, about being a nun. You know, um, with the whole abjuring the company of men, you know? How's that working for you? The abjuring.

Nun: Um, good.

Buffy: Yeah, do you have to be, like, super-religious?

Nun: Well, uh . . .

Buffy: How's the food?

- **The people really do make the place.** The relationships we forge are central to our lives and jobs. Your teammates, supervisors, and mentors will *make* your day-to-day work experience. (Buffy wouldn't have made it out of the ground to the series finale without pals Willow and Xander and watcher-mentor Giles.) So find that work-BFF, identify a mentor who will support you, go the opposite direction when bullies enter the room, and build and use (nonelectronic) networks.

- **You can stand on the shoulders of giants.** There is a huge field of social science that is filled with precious gems of useful information. We're not talking about Dr. Phil or Dr. Laura (sorry, folks!)—we're talking about researchers who are dedicated to understanding the world of work. The social scientists cited in this book are giants who can help you see the world in a new way and develop strategies for tackling the toughest problems you are facing. We hope you finish this book knowing that not all psychology professors are like Buffy's Professor Walsh, who infamously introduced herself by stating, "Okay, this is Psych 105. Introduction to Psychology. I am Professor Walsh. Those of you who fall into my good graces will come to know me as Maggie, those of you who don't will come to know me by the name my T.A.'s use and think I don't know about: The Evil Bitch-Monster of Death."

And in the End . . .

A memorable Buffy moment sums up the importance of our day-to-day lives at work:

> If there's no great glorious end to all this, if nothing we do matters . . . then all that matters is what we do. 'Cause that's all there is. What we do. Now. Today.

We hope you spend every day doing something that matters *to you*.

Notes

Introduction

1. Notes from the Cracked Ceiling. *The Washington Post.* Retrieved from www.washingtonpost.com/wp-srv/special/politics.

2. The White House Project. (2009). The White House Project Report: Benchmarking women's leadership. Retrieved from www.thewhitehouseproject.org/documents.

3. Mulligan, C. B. (February 5, 2010). In a first, women surpass men on U.S. payrolls. *The New York Times.* Retrieved from: http://economix.blogs.nytimes.com.

4. Rosin, H. (July/August, 2010). The end of men. *The Atlantic.* Retrieved from: www.theatlantic.com/magazine/archive/2010/07/the-end-of-men/8135/1/.

5. Accenture (2010). 2010 Women's Research: Millennial Women in the Workplace Success Index: Striving for Balance. Retrieved from: www.accenture.com/Global/About_Accenture/Company_Overview/Our_People/Women_at_Accenture/Research/Striving-for-Balance.htm.

6. Ledbetter, L., and Hallman, L. (January 29, 2010). For Women, What a Difference a Year Almost Made. The Huffington Post. Retrieved from: www.huffingtonpost.com/lilly-ledbetter/for-women-what-a-differen_b_436113.html.

7. Dezso, C. L. and Ross, D. G. (August, 2008) "Girl power": Female Participation in Top Management and Firm Performance. Retrieved from: http://ssrn.com/abstract=1088182.

8. McKinsey & Company (2009). Women Matter Reports. Retrieved from: www.mckinsey.com/locations/paris/home/womenmatter.asp.

9. U.S. Department of Labor Bureau of Labor Statistics (2009). Highlights of women's earnings in 2008. Washington, DC.

10. Brown, H., and DeCarlo, S. (September 23, 2009). America's Top-Paid Female CEOs. Forbes. Retrieved from: www.forbes.com/2009/09/23/corporate -america-ceo-paycheck-forbes-woman-power-salary-bonus.html.

11. Sharma, R., and Givens-Skeaton, S. (2009). Ranking the top 100 firms according to gender diversity. *Advancing Women in Leadership Journal*, 30(3). Retrieved from: www.advancingwomen.com/awl/2010/RajnesshSharma_SusanGivens -Skeaton.pdf.

12. McKinsey & Company, Women Matter Reports.

13. Accenture, 2010 Women's Research.

14. www.forbes.com/2010/07/01/lisbeth-salander-stieg-larsson-action-hero -forbes-woman-time-feminist.html.

Chapter 1

1. Barrick, M. R., and Mount, M. K. (1991). The Big Five personality dimensions and job performance: A meta-analysis. *Personnel Psychology* 44: 1–26.

2. Mount, M. K., and Barrick, M. R. (1998). Five reasons why the "Big Five" article has been frequently cited. *Personnel Psychology* 51: 849–57.

3. Hurtz, G. M., and Donovan, J. J. (2000). Personality and job performance: The Big Five revisited. *Journal of Applied Psychology* 85: 869–79.

4. Feist, G. J. (1998). A meta-analysis of personality in scientific and artistic creativity. *Personality and Social Psychology Review* 2: 290–309.

5. Costa, P. T. Jr., Terracciano, A., and McCrae, R. R. (2001). Gender differences in personality traits across cultures: Robust and surprising findings. *Journal of Personality and Social Psychology* 81: 322–31.

6. Schmitt, D. P., Realo, A., Voracek, M., and Allik, J. (2008). Why can't a man be more like a woman? Sex differences in Big Five personality traits across 55 cultures. *Journal of Personality and Social Psychology* 94: 168–82.

7. Barrick, M. R., Mount, M. K., and Gupta, R. (2003). Meta-analysis of the relationship between the five-factor model of personality and Holland's occupational types. *Personnel Psychology* 56: 45–74.

8. Ibid.

9. Su, R., Rounds, J., and Armstrong, P. I. (2009). Men and things, women and people: A meta-analysis of sex differences in interests. *Psychological Bulletin* 135: 859–84.

10. Rounds, J. B., Dawis, R. V., and Lofquist, L. H. (1979). Life history correlates of vocational needs for a female adult sample. *Journal of Counseling Psychology* 26: 6487–96.

11. Dawis, R. V., and Lofquist, L. H. (1984). *A psychological theory of work adjustment*, Minneapolis: University of Minnesota Press.

12. Amabile, T. M., Hill, K. G., Hennessey, B. A., and Tighe, E. M., (1994), The Work Preference Inventory: Assessing intrinsic and extrinsic motivational orientations. *Journal of Personality and Social Psychology* 66(5): 950–67.

Chapter 2

1. Melcher, M. (November 17, 2008). They never write, they never call. *The New York Times*. Retrieved from: http://shiftingcareers.blogs.nytimes.com.

2. Granovetter, M. S. (1973). The strength of weak ties. *The American Journal of Sociology* 78: 1360–80.

3. Greenhouse, S. (May 24, 2010). "Glimmers of hope" for grads. *The New York Times*. Retrieved from: www.nytimes.com.

4. Christakis, N. A., and Fowler, J. H. (2009). *Connected: The surprising power of our social networks and how they shape our lives*. New York: Little Brown and Company.

5. Alboher, M. (July 30, 2007). A global view of reinventing careers. *The New York Times*. Retrieved from: www.nytimes.com.

6. Rice University Career Services Center: Liberal Arts Job Search Guide. Retrieved from: http://cspd.rice.edu/emplibrary.

7. Bryant, A. (April 18, 2009). Think "we" for best results. *The New York Times*. Retrieved from: www.nytimes.com.

8. Bryant, A. (October 3, 2009). Want to talk to the chief? Book your half-hour. *The New York Times*. Retrieved from: www.nytimes.com.

Chapter 3

1. Kristof, A. L. (1996). Person-organization fit: An integrative review of its conceptualizations, measurement, and implications. *Personnel Psychology* 49: 1–49.

2. Verquer, M. L., Beehr, T. A., and Wagner, S. H. (2003). A meta-analysis of relations between person-organization fit and work attitudes. *Journal of Vocational Behavior* 63: 473–89.

3. Peters, W., and Waterman, R. (1982). *In search of excellence*. New York: Harper and Row.

4. www.workingmother.com/BestCompanies.

5. http://articles.moneycentral.msn.com/CollegeAndFamily/RaiseKids/10-best-places-for-working-moms.aspx.

6. www.usatoday.com/money/workplace/2006-09-25-working-momschart_x.htm.

7. www.nafe.com/?service=vpage/3846.

8. Heilman, M. E., and Blader, S. L. (2001). Assuming preferential selection when admissions policy is unknown: The effects of gender rarity. *Journal of Applied Psychology* 86: 188–93.

9. Kanter, R. M. (1977). *Men and women of the corporation*. New York: Basic Books.

10. Valian, V. (1999). *Why so slow? The advancement of women*. Boston: MIT Press.

11. Catalyst. (2008). *Advancing women leaders: The connection between women board directors and women corporate officers*. www.catalyst.org/publication/273.

12. Kalev, A., Dobbin, F., and Kelley, E. (2006). Best practices or best guesses? Assessing the efficacy of corporate affirmative action and diversity policies. *American Sociological Review* 71: 589–617.

13. Biernat, M., and Wortman, C. B. (1991). Sharing of home responsibilities between professionally-employed women and their husbands. *Journal of Personality and Social Psychology* 60: 844–60.

14. Thompson, C. A., Beauvais, L. L., and Lyness, K. S. (1999). When work-family benefits are not enough: The influence of work-family culture on benefit utilization, organizational attachment, and work-family conflict. *Journal of Vocational Behavior* 24: 392–415.

Chapter 4

1. Amare, N., and Manning, A. (2009). Writing for the robot: How employer search tools have influenced résumé rhetoric and ethics. *Business Communication Quarterly* 72: 35–60.

2. Bryant, A. (April 11, 2009). Knock-knock: It's the C.E.O. *The New York Times*. Retrieved from: www.nytimes.com.

3. Bright, J. (November 25, 2006). The top 10 job myths—busted. *The Sydney Morning Herald*. Retrieved from: www.smh.com.au.

4. Valian, V. (1999). *Why so slow? The advancement of women*. The MIT Press.

5. Bright, J. E. H., and Hutton, S. (2000). The impact of competency statements on résumés for short-listing decisions. *International Journal of Selection and Assessment* 8: 41–53.

6. Cole, M. S., Feild, H. S., and Giles, W. F. (2003). Using recruiter assessments of applicants' resume content to predict applicant mental ability and Big Five personality dimensions. *International Journal of Selection and Assessment* 11: 78–88.

7. Cole, M. S., Feild, H. S., and Giles, W. F. (2003). What can we uncover about applicants based on their resumes? A field study. *Applied H.R.M. Research* 8: 51–62.

8. Cole, M. S., Rubin, R. S., Feild, H. S., and Giles, W. F. (2007). Recruiters' perceptions and use of applicant résumé information: Screening the recent graduate. *Applied Psychology: An International Review* 56: 319–43.

9. Cole, M. S., Feild, H. S., Giles, W. F., and Harris, S. G. (2004). Job type and recruiters' inferences of applicant personality drawn from resume biodata: Their relationships with hiring recommendations. *International Journal of Selection and Assessment* 12: 363–67.

10. Cole, M. S., Feild, H. S., and Giles, W. F. (2004). Interaction of recruiter and applicant gender in resume evaluation: A field study. *Sex Roles* 51: 597–608.

11. Korkki, P. (February 27, 2010). Writing a résumé that shouts "hire me." *The New York Times*. Retrieved from: www.nytimes.com.

12. Fried, J. (June, 2010). Never read another résumé. *Inc*. Retrieved from: www.inc.com.

13. Bright, J. E. H., and Hutton, S. (2000). The impact of competency statements on résumés for short-listing decisions. *International Journal of Selection and Assessment* 8: 41–53.

14. Kaplan, D. M., and Fisher, J. E. (2009). A rose by any other name: Identity and impression management in résumés. *Employee Responsibilities and Rights Journal* 21: 319–32.

15. Varma, A., Toh, S. M., and Pichler, S. (2006). Ingratiation in job applications: Impact on selection decisions. *Journal of Managerial Psychology* 21: 200–210.

16. Nicklin, J. M., and Roch, S. G. (2009). Letters of recommendation: Controversy and consensus from expert perspectives. *International Journal of Selection and Assessment* 17: 76–91.

17. Schmader, T., Whitehead, J., and Wysocki, V. H. (2007). A linguistic comparison of letters of recommendation for male and female chemistry and biochemistry job applicants. *Sex Roles* 57: 509–14.

18. Nicklin, J. M., and Roch, S. G. (2008). Biases influencing recommendation letter contents: Physical attractiveness and gender. *Journal of Applied Social Psychology* 38: 3053–74.

19. Madera, J. M., Hebl, M. R., and Martin, R. C. (2009). Gender and letters of recommendation for academia: Agentic and communal differences. *Journal of Applied Psychology* 94: 1591–99.

20. Dipboye, R. L. (1992). *Selection interviews: process perspectives.* Cincinnati: College Division South-Western Pub. Co.

Chapter 5

1. Bryant, A. (August 22, 2009). The C.E.O. must decide who swims. *The New York Times.* Retrieved from: www.nytimes.com.

2. Bryant, A. (February 20, 2010). Should I hire you? I'll ask the receptionist. *The New York Times.* Retrieved from: www.nytimes.com.

3. Ambady, N., Bernieri, F. J., and Richeson, J. A. (2000). Toward a histology of social behavior: Judgmental accuracy from thin slices of the behavioral stream. In M. P. Zanna (ed.). *Advances in Experimental Social Psychology* 32: 201–72. San Diego, CA: Academic Press.

4. Ambady, N., Krabbenhoft, M. A., and Hogan, D. (2006). The 30-sec sale: Using thin-slice judgments to evaluate sales effectiveness. *Journal of Consumer Psychology* 16: 4–13.

5. Ambady, N., and Rosenthal, R. (1992). Thin slices of expressive behavior as predictors of interpersonal consequences: A meta-analysis. *Psychological Bulletin* 111: 256–74.

6. Bryant, A. (January 23, 2010). High heels? They just don't fit. *The New York Times.* Retrieved from: www.nytimes.com.

7. DeGroot, T., and Motowidlo, S. J. (1999). Why visual and vocal interview cues can affect interviewers' judgments and predict job performance. *Journal of Applied Psychology* 84: 986–93.

8. DeGroot, T., and Gooty, J. (2009). Can nonverbal cues be used to make meaningful personality attributions in employment interviews? *Journal of Business and Psychology* 24: 179–92.

9. Stewart, G. L., Dustin, S. L., Barrick, M. R., and Darnold, T. C. (2008). Exploring the handshake in employment interviews. *Journal of Applied Psychology* 93: 1139–46.

10. Abel, M. H., and Deitz, M. (2008). Smiling, job qualifications, and ratings of job applicants. *American Journal of Psychological Research* 4.

11. Bryant, A. (July 4, 2009). Charisma? To her, it's overrated. *The New York Times*. Retrieved from: www.nytimes.com.

12. Bryant, A. (November 21, 2010). 68 rules? No, just 3 are enough. *The New York Times*. Retrieved from: www.nytimes.com.

13. Bryant, A. (March 5, 2010). An office? She'll pass on that. *The New York Times*. Retrieved from: www.nytimes.com.

14. Bryant, A. (July 4, 2009). Charisma? To her, it's overrated. *The New York Times*. Retrieved from: www.nytimes.com.

15. Schindler, E. (October 10, 2006). The best and worst tech interview questions. *DevSource*. Retrieved from: www.devsource.com.

16. Fisher, A. (February 4, 2010). Don't wear pajamas for a phone interview. CNN. Retrieved from: http://money.cnn.com.

17. Bryant, A. (December 26, 2009). Everything on one calendar, please. *The New York Times*. Retrieved from: www.nytimes.com.

18. Eagly, A. H., and Karau, S. J. (1991). Gender and the emergence of leaders. *Journal of Personality and Social Psychology* 60: 685–710.

19. Hoyt, C. L., Goethals, G. R., and Forsyth, D. R. (2008). *Leadership at the Crossroads, Volume 1: Leadership and Psychology*. Westport, CT: Praeger Publishers.

20. Hebl, M. R. (2000). Gender bias in leader selection. In L. T. Benjamin et al. (eds.). *Handbook for Teaching Introductory Psychology, Volume 2*. Hillsdale, NJ: Lawrence Erlbaum Associates.

21. Bryant, A. (May 14, 2010). If plan b fails, go through the alphabet. *The New York Times*. Retrieved from: www.nytimes.com.

22. Bryant, A. (April 9, 2010). Says rah-rah isn't for everyone. *The New York Times*. Retrieved from: http://www.nytimes.com.

23. Bryant, A. (November 14, 2009). Are you a Tigger, or an Eeyore? *The New York Times*. Retrieved from: www.nytimes.com.

24. Bryant, A. (January 9, 2010). On a scale of 1 to 10, how weird are you? *The New York Times*. Retrieved from: www.nytimes.com.

25. Bryant, A. (December 19, 2009). What makes you roar? He wants to know. *The New York Times*. Retrieved from: www.nytimes.com.

Chapter 6

1. Bryant, A. (March 19, 2010). Just give him 5 sentences, not *War and Peace*. *The New York Times*. Retrieved from: www.nytimes.com.

2. Davies, P. G., Spencer, S. J., and Steele, C. M. (2005). Clearing the air: Identity safety moderates the effects of stereotype threat on women's leadership aspirations. *Journal of Personality and Social Psychology* 8: 276–87.

3. Davies, P. G., Spencer, S. J., Quinn, D. M., and Gerhardstein, R. (2002). Consuming images: How television commercials that elicit stereotype threat can restrain women academically and professionally. *Personality and Social Psychology Bulletin* 28: 1615–28.

4. Cheryan, S., Plaut, V. C., Davies, P. G., and Steele, C. M. (2009). Ambient belonging: How stereotypical cues impact gender participation in computer science. *Journal of Personality and Social Psychology* 97: 1045–60.

5. Shapiro, J. R., and Neuberg, S. L. (2007). From stereotype threat to stereotype threats: Implications of a multi-threat framework for causes, moderators, mediators, consequences, and interventions. *Personality and Social Psychology Review* 11: 107–13.

6. McIntyre, R. B., Paulson, R. M., and Lord, C. G. (2003). Alleviating women's mathematics stereotype threat through salience of group achievements. *Journal of Experimental Social Psychology* 39: 83–90.

7. Ford, T. E., Ferguson, M. A., Brooks, J. L., and Hagadone, K. M. (2004). Coping sense of humor reduces effects of stereotype threat on women's math performance. *Personality and Social Psychology* 30: 643–53.

8. Hoyt, C., and Blascovich, J. (2007). Leadership efficacy and women leaders' responses to stereotype activation. *Group Processes and Intergroup Relations* 10: 595–616.

9. Bryant, A. (May 21, 2010). It's not a career ladder, it's an obstacle course. *The New York Times*. Retrieved from: www.nytimes.com.

10. Nosek, B. A., Banaji, M. R., and Greenwald, A. G. (2002b). Math = male, me = female, therefore math me. *Journal of Personality and Social Psychology* 83: 44–59.

11. Goldin, C., and Rouse, C. (2000). Orchestrating impartiality: The impact of "blind" auditions on female musicians. *The American Economic Review* 90: 715–41. Retrieved from: www.nber.org.

12. Major, B., Feinstein, J., and Crocker, J. (1994). Attributional ambiguity of affirmative action. *Basic and Applied Social Psychology* 15: 113–41.

13. Heilman, M. E., Rivero, J. C., and Brett, J. F. (1991). Skirting the competence issue: Effects of sex-based preferential selection on task choices of women and men. *Journal of Applied Psychology* 76: 99–105.

14. Ibid.

15. Knight, J. L., and Hebl, M. R. (2005). Affirmative reaction: The influence of type of justification on nonbeneficiary attitudes toward affirmative action plans in higher education. *Journal of Social Issues* 61: 547–68.

16. Bertrand, M., and Mullainathan, S. (2002). Are Emily and Brendan more employable than Lakisha and Jamal? A field experiment on labor market discrimination. Retrieved from: www.chicagobooth.edu/pdf/bertrand.pdf.

17. Singletary, S. L., and Hebl, M. R. (2009). Compensatory strategies for reducing interpersonal discrimination: The effectiveness of acknowledgments, increased positivity, and individuating information. *Journal of Applied Psychology* 94: 797–805.

Chapter 7

1. U.S. Department of Labor Bureau of Labor Statistics. (2009). Highlights of women's earnings in 2008. Washington, D.C.

2. Catalyst. (2010). Pipeline's broken promise. www.catalyst.org/publication/372/pipelines-broken-promise.

3. Duehr, E., and Bono, J. E. (2006). Men, women, and managers: Are stereotypes finally changing? *Personnel Psychology* 59: 815.

4. Amanatullah, E. T., and Morris, M. W. (2010). Negotiating gender roles: Gender differences in assertive negotiating are mediated by women's fear of backlash and attenuated when negotiating on behalf of others. *Journal of Personality and Social Psychology* 92: 256–67.

5. Major, B., McFarlin, D. B., and Gagnon, D. (1984). Overworked and underpaid: On the nature of gender differences in personal entitlement. *Journal of Personality and Social Psychology* 47: 1399–412.

6. Stuhlmacher, A. F., and Walters, A. E. (2006). Gender differences in negotiation outcome: A meta-analysis. *Personnel Psychology* 52: 653–77.

7. Bowles, H. R., Babcock, L., and Lai, L. (2007). Social incentives for gender differences in the propensity to initiate negotiations: Sometimes it does hurt to ask. *Organizational Behavior and Human Decision Processes* 103: 84–103.

8. Small, D. A., Gelfand, M., Babcock, L., and Gettman, H. (2007). Who goes to the bargaining table? The influence of gender and framing on the initiation of negotiation. *Journal of Personality and Social Psychology* 93: 600–613.

9. Bowles, H. R., Babcock, L., and McGinn, K. L. (2005). Constraints and triggers: Situational mechanics of gender in negotiation. *Journal of Personality and Social Psychology* 89: 951–65.

Chapter 8

1. Mantell, R. (April 21, 2010). U.S. women still earn less than men, but gap is narrowing. *The Wall Street Journal*. Retrieved from: http://online.wsj.com.

2. Mulligan, C. B. (February 5, 2010). In a first, women surpass men on U.S. payrolls. *The New York Times*. Retrieved from: http://economix.blogs.nytimes.com.

3. Mulligan, C. B. (January 14, 2009). A milestone for working women? *The New York Times*. Retrieved from: http://economix.blogs.nytimes.com.

4. Cullen, L. T. (October 6, 2002). Will manage for food. *Time Magazine*. Retrieved from: www.time.com.

5. King, E. B., Knight, J. L., and Hebl, M. R. (in press). The influence of economic threat on aspects of stigmatization. *Journal of Social Issues*.

6. Ask Amy. (May 1, 2010). Supervisor defers to snarky student. *The Chicago Tribune*. Retrieved from: www.chicagotribune.com.

7. Evans, K. (November 12, 2009). In downturn's wake, women hold half of U.S. jobs. *Wall Street Journal*. Retrieved from: http://online.wsj.com.

8. Crowley, M. S. (1998). Men's self-perceived adequacy as the family breadwinner: Implications for their psychological, marital and work-family well-being. *Journal of Family and Economic Issues* 19: 7–23.

9. Meisenbach, R. J. (2010). The female breadwinner: Phenomenological experience and gendered identity in work/family spaces. *Sex Roles* 62: 2–19.

10. Cha, Y., and Thébaud, S. (2009). Labor markets, breadwinning, and beliefs: How economic context shapes men's gender ideology. *Gender & Society* 23: 215–43.

11. Bittman, M., England, P., Folbre, N., Sayer, L., and Matheson, G. (2003). When does gender trump money? Bargaining and time in household work. *American Journal of Sociology* 109: 186–214.

12. Fry, R., and Cohn, D. (January 19, 2010). New economics of marriage: The rise of wives. Pew Research Center. Retrieved from: http://pewresearch.org/pubs/1466.

13. Zhao, H., Seibert, S. E., and Hills, G. E. (2005). The mediating role of self-efficacy in the development of entrepreneurial intentions. *Journal of Applied Psychology* 90: 1265–72.

14. Gupta, V. K., Turban, D. B., and Bhawe, N. M. (2008). The effect of gender stereotype activation on entrepreneurial intentions. *Journal of Applied Psychology* 93: 1053–61.

15. Wadhwa, V. (February 4, 2010). Addressing the dearth of female entrepreneurs. *Bloomberg Businessweek.* Retrieved from: www.businessweek.com.

16. Gardella, A. (June 11, 2010). Women don't help each other? *The New York Times.* Retrieved from: http://boss.blogs.nytimes.com.

Section 2

1. http://gmj.gallup.com/content/511/Item-10-Best-Friend-Work.aspx.

2. Schneider, B. (1987). The people make the place. *Personnel Psychology* 40: 437–53.

3. Ibarra, H. (1992). Homophily and differential returns: Sex differences in network structure and access in an advertising firm. *Administrative Sciences Quarterly* 37: 422–47.

Chapter 9

1. Society for Human Resource Management. (2002). Workplace Romance Survey. Alexandria, VA.

2. Brown, T. J., and Allgeier, E. R. (2006). The impact of participant characteristics, perceived motives, and job behaviors on co-workers' evaluations of workplace romances. *Journal of Applied Social Psychology* 26: 577–95.

3. Mainiero, (1986).

4. Quinn, R. E. (1977). Coping with cupid: The formation, impact, and management of romantic relationships in organizations. *Administrative Science Quarterly* 22: 30–45.

5. Foley, S., and Powell, G. N. (2000). Not all is fair in love and work: coworker preferences for and responses to managerial interventions regarding workplace romances. *Journal of Organizational Behavior* 20: 1043–56.

6. Jones, G. E. (1999). Hierarchical workplace romance: An experimental examination of team member perceptions. *Journal of Organizational Behavior* 20: 1057–72.

7. Pierce, C. A., Byrne, D., and Aguinis, H. (1996). Attraction in organizations: A model of workplace romance. *Journal of Organizational Behavior* 17: 5–32.

8. Data reported in Penn, M. J. (2007). *Microtrends: The Small Forces Behind Tomorrow's Big Changes*. New York: Twelve.

Chapter 10

1. Ryan, K. R., King, E. B., Adis, C., Gulick, L., and Peddie, C. (2009). Tokenism and the queen bee. Paper presented at the annual conference for the Society of Industrial Organizational Psychology, New Orleans, LA.

2. Adis, C., King, E. B., Gulick, L., Peddie, C., and Ryan, K. (2009). Self-esteem, social comparison, and undermining at work. Unpublished manuscript.

3. Rezvani, S. (2009). The next generation of women leaders: What you need to lead but won't learn in business school. Santa Barbara, CA: Praeger.

4. Workplace Bullying Institute. http://workplacebullying.org.

Chapter 11

1. Judge, T., and Ferris, G. (1993). Social context of performance evaluation decisions. *Academy of Management Journal* 36 (1): 80–105.

2. Zenger, T., and Lawrence, B. (1989). Organizational demography: The differential effects of age and tenure distributions on technical communications. *Academy of Management Journal* 32: 353–76.

3. Wagner, W. G., Pfeffer, J., and O'Reilly, C. A. (1984). Organizational demography and turnover in top management groups. *Administrative Science Quarterly* 29: 74–92.

4. *60 Minutes*. (November 11, 2007). The "Millennials" are coming.

5. Maurer, T. J., Barbeite, F. G., Weiss, E. M., and Lippstreu, M. (2008). New measures of stereotypical beliefs about otlder workers' ability and desire for development: Exploration among employees age 40 and over. *Journal of Managerial Psychology* 23: 395–418.

6. Ackerman, P. L. (2000). Domain-specific knowledge as the "dark matter" of adult intelligence: gf/gc, personality and interest correlates. *Journal of Gerontology: Psychological Sciences* 55: 69–84.

7. Schaie, K. W. (1996). Intellectual development in adulthood. In J. E. Birren and K. W. Schaie (eds.). *Handbook of the psychology of aging.* 4th ed. 266–86. San Diego: Academic Press.

8. Twenge, J. M., Campbell, S. M., Hoffman, B. J., and Lance, C. E. (2010). Generational differences in work values: Leisure and extrinsic values increasing, social and intrinsic values decreasing. *Journal of Management.*

9. Twenge, J. M., and Campbell, S. M. (2008). Generational differences in psychological traits and their impact on the workplace. *Journal of Managerial Psychology* 8: 862–77.

10. Twenge, J. M., and Campbell, W. K. (2001). Age and birth cohort differences in self-esteem: A cross-temporal meta-analysis. *Personality and Social Psychology Review* 5: 321–44.

Chapter 12

1. Milgram, S. (1967). The small world problem. *Psychology Today* 1: 61–67.

2. Baumeister, R. F., and Leary, M. R. (1995). The need to belong: Desire for interpersonal attachments as a fundamental human motivation. *Psychological Bulletin* 117: 497–529.

3. Ibarra, H. (1992). Homophily and differential returns: Sex differences in network structure access in an advertising firm. *Administrative Science Quarterly* 37: 422–47.

4. Brass, D. J. (1985). Men's and women's networks: A study of interaction patterns and influence in organizations. *Academy of Management Journal* 28: 327–43.

5. Brass, D. J. (1984). Being in the right place: A structural analysis of individual influence in an organization. *Administrative Science Quarterly* 29: 518–39.

6. Forret, M. L., and Dougherty, T. W. (2004). Networking behaviors and career outcomes: Differences for men and women? *Journal of Organizational Behavior* 25: 419–37.

Chapter 13

1. Swim, J. K., Aikin, K. J., Hall, W. S., and Hunter, B. A. (1995). Sexism and racism: Old-fashioned and modern prejudices. *Journal of Personality and Social Psychology* 68: 199–214.

2. Swim, J. K., Hyers, L. L., Cohen, L. L., and Ferguson, M. J. (2001). Everyday sexism: Evidence for its incidence, nature, and psychological impact from three daily diary studies. *Journal of Social Issues* 57: 31–54.

3. Hebl, M. R., King, E. B., Glick, P., Kazama, S., and Singletary, S. (2007). Hostile and benevolent reactions toward pregnant women: Complementary interpersonal punishments and rewards that maintain traditional roles. *Journal of Applied Psychology* 92: 1499–511.

4. Glick, P., and Fiske, S. T. (1996). The ambivalent sexism inventory: Differentiating hostile and benevolent sexism. *Journal of Personality and Social Psychology* 70: 491–512.

5. Singletary, S. L. B. (2009). The differential impact of formal and interpersonal discrimination on job performance. Unpublished dissertation. Rice University.

6. Stewart, K., King, E. B., Botsford, W., Hylton, K., Gilrane, V., and Jones, K. (2010). A dark side of seemingly civil behavior? Negative consequences of benevolent sexism on efficacy and performance. Unpublished manuscript. George Mason University.

7. Sechrist, G. B., Swim, J. K., and Stangor, C. (2004). When do the stigmatized make attributions to discrimination to the self and others? The roles of self-presentation and need for control. *Journal of Personality and Social Psychology* 87: 111–22.

8. Czopp, A. M., Monteith, M. J., and Mark, A. Y. (2006). Standing up for a change: Reducing bias through interpersonal confrontation. *Journal of Personality and Social Psychology* 90: 784–803.

9. Dodd, E. H., Giuliano, T. A., Boutell, J. M., and Moran, B. E. (2001). Respected or rejected: Perceptions of women who confront sexist remarks. *Sex Roles* 45: 567–77.

Chapter 14

1. www.eeoc.gov/eeoc/publications/fs-sex.cfm.

2. Berdahl, J. L., and Aquino, K. (2009). Sexual behavior at work: Fun or folly? *Journal of Applied Psychology* 94 (1): 34–47.

3. Willness, C. R., Steel, P. and Lee, K. (2006). A meta-analysis of the antecedents and consequences of workplace sexual harassment. *Personnel Psychology* 60: 127–62.

4. Parker, S. K., and Griffin, M. A. (2002). What is so bad about a little name-calling? Negative consequences of gender harassment for overperformance demands and distress. *Journal of Occupational Health Psychology* 7: 195–210.

5. Miner-Rubino, K., and Cortina, L. M. (2007). Beyond targets: Consequences of vicarious exposure to misogyny at work. *Journal of Applied Psychology* 92: 1254–69.

6. O'Leary-Kelly, A. M., Bowes-Sperry, L., Bates, C. A., and Lean, E. R. (2010). Sexual harassment at work: A decade (plus) of progress. *Journal of Management.*

7. Knapp, D. E., Faley, R. H., Ekeberg, S. E., and DuBois, C. L. Z. (1997). Determinants of target responses to sexual harassment: A conceptual framework. *Academy of Management Review* 22: 687–729.

8. Bingham, S. G., and Scherer, L. L. (1993). Factors associated with responses to sexual harassment and satisfaction with outcome. *Sex Roles* 29: 239–69.

9. Langelan, M. (1993). *Back Off! How to confront and stop sexual harassment and harassers.* New York: Simon & Schuster.

10. Bell, M. P., Quick, J. C., and Cycyota, C. S. (2002). Assessment and prevention of sexual harassment of employees: An applied guide to creating healthy organizations. *International Journal of Selection and Assessment* 10: 160–68.

Chapter 15

1. Allen, T. D., Eby, L. T., Poteet, M. L., Lentz, E., and Lima, L. (2004). Career Benefits Associated With Mentoring for Proteges: A Meta-Analysis. *Journal of Applied Psychology* 89: 127–36.

2. Eby, L. T., Lockwood, A. L., and Butts, M. (2006). Perceived support for mentoring: A multiple perspectives approach. *Journal of Vocational Behavior* 68: 267–91.

3. Eby, L. T., and McManus, S. E. (April, 2002). Protégés' most positive mentoring experience. In R. Day and T. D. Allen (cochairs). *Underlying processes responsible for beneficial mentorships: Implications of emerging research.* Annual meeting of the Society for Industrial and Organizational Psychology. Toronto, Canada.

4. Eby, L. T., Durley, J. R., Evans, S. C., and Ragins, B. R. (2006). The relationship between short-term mentoring benefits and long-term mentor outcomes. *Journal of Vocational Behavior* 69: 424–44.

5. Eby, L. T., and Lockwood, A. (2005). Protégés' and mentors' reactions to participating in formal mentoring programs: A qualitative investigation. *Journal of Vocational Behavior* 67: 441–458.

6. Ibarra, H. (March–April, 2000). Making partner: A mentor's guide to the psychological journey. *Harvard Business Review* 147–55.

7. Allen, T. D., Eby, L. T., and Lentz, E. (2006). Mentorship behaviors and mentorship quality associated with formal mentoring programs: Closing the gap between research and practice. *Journal of Applied Psychology* 91: 567–78.

8. Bryant, A. (March 5, 2010). An office? She'll pass on that. *The New York Times*. Retrieved from: www.nytimes.com.

9. Dreher, G. F., and Cox, T. H., Jr. (1996). Race, gender, and opportunity: A study of compensation attainment and the establishment of mentoring relationships. *Journal of Applied Psychology* 81: 297–308.

10. Lyness, K. S., and Thompson, D. E. (2000). Climbing the corporate ladder: Do female and male executives follow the same route? *Journal of Applied Psychology* 85: 86–101.

11. Ragins, B. R., and Cotton, J. L. (1999). Mentor functions and outcomes: a comparison of men and women in formal and informal mentoring relationships. *Journal of Applied Psychology* 84, 529–50.

12. Allen, T. D., and Eby, L. T. (2003). Relationship effectiveness for mentors: Factors associated with learning and quality. *Journal of Management* 29: 469–86.

13. Eby, L. T., and Allen, T. D. (2004). Factors related to mentor reports of mentoring functions provided: Gender and relational characteristics. *Sex Roles* 50: 129–39.

14. Bryant, A. (June 20, 2009). The divine, too, is in the details. *The New York Times*. Retrieved from: www.nytimes.com.

15. DeLong, T. J., Gabarro, J. J., and Lees, R. J. (January, 2008). Why mentoring matters in a hypercompetitive world. *Harvard Business Review*. 115–21.

16. Wang, S., Tomlinson, E. C., and Noe, R. A. (2010). The role of mentor trust and protégé internal locus of control in formal mentoring relationships. *Journal of Applied Psychology* 95: 358–67.

17. Lockwood, P., and Kunda, Z. (1997). Superstars and me: Predicting the impact of role models on the self. *Journal of Personality and Social Psychology* 73: 91–103.

18. Eby, L. T., Durley, J., Evans, S. C., and Ragins, B. R. (2008). Mentors' perceptions of negative mentoring experiences: Scale development and nomological validation. *Journal of Applied Psychology* 93: 358–73.

Section 3

1. Bryant, A. (April 18, 2009). Think "we" for best results. *The New York Times*. Retrieved from: www.nytimes.com.

2. http://dilbert.com/fast/1994-02-22.

3. *The Onion*. (December 12, 2008). Manager achieves full mastery of pointless managerial jargon. Retrieved from: www.theonion.com.

Chapter 16

1. Tannen, D. (1990). *You just don't understand: Women and men in conversation.* New York: William Morrow.

2. Tannen, D. (1994). *Talking from 9 to 5: How women's and men's conversational style affect who gets heard, who gets credit, and what gets done at work.* New York: William Morrow.

3. Tannen, D. (2004). *That's not what I meant: Language, culture, and meaning.* Los Angeles: Into the Classroom Media.

4. Grenberg, J., and Baron, R. A. (2003). *Behavior in organizations.* (8th ed). Upper Saddle River, NJ: Pearson.

5. Mehl, M. R., Vazire, S., Ramirez-Esparza, N., Slatcher, R. B., and Pennebaker, J. W. (2007). Are women really more talkative than men? *Science* 316: 82.

6. Tannen, D. (July 24, 1996). I'm sorry, I won't apologize. *The New York Times.* 34–35.

7. Mindell, P. (1995). *A Woman's Guide to the Language of Success.* Englewood Cliffs, NJ: Prentice Hall.

8. Ibid.

9. Tannen, D. (December 11, 1994). The talk of the sandbox; how Johnny and Suzy's playground chatter prepares them for life at the office. *The Washington Post.* Retrieved from: www9.georgetown.edu.

10. Bryant, A. (May 30, 2009). In praise of all that grunt work. *The New York Times.* Retrieved from: www.nytimes.com.

11. Tannen, *That's not what I meant.*

12. Farley, S. D. (2008). Attaining status at the expense of likeability: Pilfering power through conversational interruption. *Journal of Nonverbal Behavior* 32: 241–60.

13. Karakowsky, L., McBey, K., and Miller, D. L. (2004). Gender, perceived competence, and power displays: Examining verbal interruptions in a group context. *Small Group Research* 35: 407–39.

14. www.colbertnation.com/the-colbert-report-videos/313484/june-22-2010/gloria-steinem.

15. www.cbsnews.com.

16. Peters, J. W. (June 20, 2010). Elle, not camera shy, embraces reality TV. *The New York Times.* Retrieved from: www.nytimes.com.

17. Russell, B., Perkins, J., and Grinnell, H. (2008). Interviewees' overuse of the word "like" and hesitations: Effects in simulated hiring decisions. *Psychological Reports* 102: 111–18.

18. Mehl, M. R., and Pennebaker, J. W. (2003). The sounds of social life: A psychometric analysis of students' daily social environments and natural conversations. *Journal of Personality & Social Psychology* 84: 857–70.

19. Newman, M. L., Groom, C. J., Handelman, L. D., and Pennebaker, J. W. (2008). Gender differences in language use: An analysis of 14,000 text samples. *Discourse Processes*. 45: 211–36.

20. Jay, T. (2009). The utility and ubiquity of taboo words. *Perspectives on Psychological Science* 4: 153–61.

21. Baruch, Y., and Jenkins, S. (2007). Swearing at work and permissive leadership culture: When anti-social becomes social and incivility is acceptable. *Leadership & Organization Development Journal* 28: 492–507.

22. Reardon, K. K. (1995). *They don't get it, do they? Communication in the workplace—closing the gap between women and men.* New York: Little, Brown and Company.

23. Holmes, J. (2006). Sharing a laugh: Pragmatic aspects of humour and gender in the workplace. *Journal of Pragmatics* 38: 26–50.

24. Holmes, J., and Schnurr, S. (2005). Politeness, humor and gender in the workplace: Negotiating norms and identifying contestation. *Journal of Politeness Research* 1: 121–49.

25. Mindell, P. (1995). *A woman's guide to the language of success.* Englewood Cliffs, NJ: Prentice Hall.

26. Mulac, A., Wiemann, J. M., Widenmann, S. J., and Gibson, T. W. (1988). Male/female language differences and effects in same-sex and mixed-sex dyads: The gender-linked language affect. *Communication Monographs* 55: 315–35.

27. Tannen, D. (December 11, 1994). The talk of the sandbox; how Johnny and Suzy's playground chatter prepares them for life at the office. *The Washington Post*. Retrieved from: http://www9.georgetown.edu/faculty/tannend.

28. Tannen, *That's not what I meant.*

29. Kalbfleisch, P. J., and Cody, M. J. (1995). Gender, power, and communication in human relationships. Hillsdale, NJ: Lawrence Erlbaum Associates.

30. Mulrine, A. (November 1, 2009). A woman's place is at the Pentagon. *U.S. News & World Report*. Retrieved from: www.allbusiness.com.

31. LaFrance, M., Hecht, M., and Paluck, E. (2003). The contingent smile: A meta-analysis of sex differences in smiling. *Psychological Bulletin* 129: 305–34.

32. DeGroot, T., and Motowidlo, S. J. (1999). Why visual and vocal interview cues can affect interviewers' judgments and predict job performance. *Journal of Applied Psychology* 84: 986–93.

33. Guerrero, L. K. (1997). Nonverbal involvement across interactions with same-sex friends, opposite-sex friends, and romantic partners: Consistency or change. *Journal of Social and Personal Relationships* 14: 31–58.

34. Tannen, *That's not what I meant.*

35. DeGroot, and Motowidlo, *Journal of Applied Psychology.*

36. Tannen, *That's not what I meant.*

37. Giuliano, T. A., Barnes, L. C., Fiala, S. E., and Davis, D. M. (1998). An empirical investigation of Male Answer Syndrome. Poster presented at the 44th annual meeting of the Southwestern Psychological Association. New Orleans, LA.

38. Bryant, A. (April 23, 2010). What's wrong with saying "I don't know"? *The New York Times.* Retrieved from: www.nytimes.com.

Chapter 17

1. De Pillis, E., and Furumo, K. (2006). Virtual vs. face-to-face teams: Deadbeats, deserters, and other considerations. *SIGMIS-CPR.* 318–320. Claremont, CA: ACM Press.

2. Xiaoning, S. (2009). Why gender matters in CMC: Gender differences in remote trust and performance with initial social activities. Unpublished dissertation.

3. Furumo, K., and Pearson, J. M. (2007). Gender-based communication styles, trust, and satisfaction in virtual teams. *Journal of Information, Information Technology, and Organizations* 2: 47–60.

4. Greenberg, J., and Baron, R. A. (2003). *Behavior in Organizations.* (8th ed.) Upper Saddle River, NJ: Prentice Hall.

5. Ibid.

6. Goldstein, J. (June 14, 2010). Twenty-three things not to write in an e-mail. NPR. Retrieved from: www.npr.org.

7. Bryant, A. (January 23, 2010). High heels? they just don't fit. *The New York Times*. Retrieved from: www.nytimes.com.

8. Bryant, A. (April 23, 2010). What's wrong with saying "I don't know"? *The New York Times*. Retrieved from: www.nytimes.com.

9. Buchanan, L. (March 1, 2010). The e-mail zealot: Mark Cuban of the Dallas Mavericks. *Inc*. Retrieved from: www.inc.com.

10. Colley, A., Todd, Z., Bland, M., Holmes, M., Khanom, M., and Pike, H. (2004). Style and content in emails and letters to male and female friends. *Journal of Language and Social Psychology* 23: 369–78.

11. Thomson, R., and Murachver, T. (2001) Predicting gender from electronic discourse. *British Journal of Social Psychology* 40: 193–208.

12. Rosenwald, M. S. (June 20, 2010). Will iPhones edge out BlackBerrys in Washington? *The Washingon Post*. Retrieved from: www.washingtonpost.com.

13. Richtel, M. (June 6, 2010). Hooked on gadgets, and paying a mental price. *The New York Times*. Retrieved from: http://community.nytimes.com.

14. Goudreau, J. (June 29, 2010). Do computers really fry your brain? *Forbes*. Retrieved from: www.forbes.com.

15. Boswell, W. R., and Olson-Buchanan, J. B. (2007). The use of communication technologies after hours: The role of work attitudes and work-life conflict. *Journal of Management* 33: 592–610.

16. Fenner, G. H., and Renn, R. W. (2010). Technology-assisted supplemental work and work-to-family conflict: The role of instrumentality beliefs, organizational expectations and time management. *Human Relations* 63: 63–82.

17. Bryant, A. (August 8, 2009). The lesson of the 38 candy bars. *The New York Times*. Retrieved from: www.nytimes.com.

18. Bryant, A. (October 3, 2009). Want to talk to the chief? Book your half-hour. *The New York Times*. Retrieved from: www.nytimes.com.

19. Bryant, A. (March 13, 2009). Can you pass a C.E.O. test? *The New York Times*. Retrieved from: www.nytimes.com.

20. Bryant, A. (August 15, 2009). You want insights? Go to the front lines. *The New York Times*. Retrieved from: www.nytimes.com.

21. Derks, D., Bos, A. E. R., and von Grumbkow, J. (2008). Emoticons in computer-mediated communication: Social motives and social context. *Cyber Psychology & Behavior* 11: 99–101.

22. Wolf, A. (2000). Emotional expression online: Gender differences in emoticon use. *CyberPsychology & Behavior* 3: 827–33.

23. Greenberg, J. (2005). Managing behavior in organizations. (4th ed.) Upper Saddle River, NJ: Pearson.

24. Thompson, L. F., Mullins, A. K., Robinson, J. B., and Halberstadt, J. B. (April, 2010). *E-screening: The consequences of using "smileys" when e-mailing prospective employers.* Paper presented at the 25th annual meeting of the Society for Industrial and Organizational Psychology. Atlanta, GA.

25. Boutelle, C. (June 2, 2010). E-mail smiley faces not suitable for most business correspondence. Society for Industrial and Organizational Psychology. Retrieved from: www.siop.org.

Chapter 18

1. Granovetter, M. S. (1973). The strength of *Weak Ties. The American Journal of Sociology* 78: 1360–80.

2. Noon, M., and Delbridge, R. (1993). News from behind my hand: Gossip in organizations. *Organization Studies* 14: 23–36.

3. Poe, R., and Courter, C. L. (September, 1998). *The great coffee grapevine.* Across the Board.

4. Joyner, A. (May 1, 2010). How to keep your workers happy. *Inc.* Retrieved from: www.inc.com.

5. DiFonzo, N., and Bordia, P. (2007). *Rumor psychology: Social and organizational approaches.* Washington D.C.: American Psychological Association.

6. Kurland, N. B., and Pelled, L. H. (2000). Passing the word: Toward a model of gossip and power in the workplace. *Academy of Management Review* 25: 428–38.

7. Ganske, K. H., and Hebl, M. R. (2001). Once upon a time there was a math contest: gender stereotyping and memory. *Teaching of Psychology* 28: 266–68.

8. Allport, G. W., and Postman, L. (1947). *The psychology of rumor.* New York: Holt.

9. DiFonzo, and Bordia, *Rumor Psychology.*

10. www.printingforless.com/tsrteamdogs.html.

11. McKnight, S. (November 14, 2009). Workplace gossip? Keep it to yourself. *The New York Times.* Retrieved from: www.nytimes.com.

12. Kurland, and Pelled, Passing the word.

13. Lovell, J. (December 10, 2006). The 6th annual year in ideas: Workplace rumors are true. *The New York Times*. Retrieved from: http://query.nytimes.com.

Chapter 19

1. Stone, G., and Brady, J. (September 7, 2008). Are Palin's eyeglasses the new pantsuit? *ABC News*. Retrieved from: http://abcnews.go.com.

2. Givhan, R. (July 19, 2009). Opening a conventional closet in quest for a Supreme robe. *The Washington Post*. Retrieved from: www.washingtonpost.com.

3. Dana, R. (March 24, 2010). Nancy Pelosi, fashion icon. *The Daily Beast*. Retrieved from: www.thedailybeast.com.

4. Givhan, R. (May 23, 2010). Elena Kagan goes on Supreme Court confirmation offensive in drab D.C. clothes. *The Washington Post*. Retrieved from: www.washingtonpost.com.

5. Tanner, S. (July 15, 2009). President Obama's all-star game pitch: Dad jeans on display. *Entertainment Weekly*. Retrieved from: popwatch.ew.com.

6. Bryant, A. (December 12, 2009). Managing globally, and locally. *The New York Times*. Retrieved from: www.nytimes.com.

7. Glick, P., Larsen, S., Johnson, C., and Branstiter, H. (2005). Evaluations of sexy women in low- and high-status jobs. *Psychology of Women Quarterly* 29: 389–95.

8. Wookey, M. L., Graves, N. A., and Butler, J. C. (2009). Effects of a sexy appearance on perceived competence of women. *The Journal of Social Psychology* 149: 116–18.

9. Dwoskin, E. (2010, 1 June). Is this woman too hot to be a banker? *Village Voice*. Retrieved from: www.villagevoice.com.

10. Rucker, M. Anderson, E., and Kangas, A. (1999). Clothing, power, and the workplace. Appearance and power. In K. K. Johnson and S. J. Lennon (eds.). *Appearance and power: Dress, body, culture*. New York: Berg, 59–77.

11. Peluchette, J. V., and Karl, K. (2007). The impact of workplace attire on employee self-perceptions. *Human Resource Development Quarterly* 18: 345–60.

12. Hannover, B., and Kuhnen, U. (2002). "The clothing makes the self" via knowledge activation. *Journal of Applied Social Psychology* 32: 2513–25.

13. Rafaeli, A., Dutton, J., Harquali, C. V., and Mackie-Lewis, S. (1997). Navigating by attire: The use of dress by female administrative employees. *Academy of Management Journal* 40: 9–45.

14. Rucker, M., Anderson, E., and Kangas, A. (1999). Clothing, power, and the workplace: Appearance and power. In K. K. Johnson and S. J. Lennon (eds.). *Appearance and power: Dress, body, culture*. New York: Berg, 59–77

15. Marcus, R. (June 10, 2010). Carly Fiorina doesn't get a pass on comment about Boxer's hair. *The Washingotn Post*. Retrieved from: http://voices .washingtonpost.com.

16. Bryant, A. (September 19, 2009). Fitting in, and rising to the top. *The New York Times*. Retrieved from: www.nytimes.com.

17. Dress for Success Web site. Retrieved from: www.dressforsuccess.org.

Chapter 20

1. KUSI News (July 23, 2007). Sports clichés go from locker room to board-room. Retrieved from: hwww.kusi.com.

2. Mainstone, L. E., and Schroeder, D. M. (1999). Corporate hoop dreams: The power of metaphors in organizational transformation. *Consulting Psychology Journal: Practice and Research* 51: 198–208.

3. Lloyd, P. J., and Foster, S. L. (2006). Creating healthy, high-performance workplaces: Strategies from health and sports psychology. *Consulting Psychology Journal: Practice and Research* 58: 23–39.

4. Bryant, A. (May 28, 2010). For the chief of Saks, it's culture that drives results. *The New York Times*. Retrieved from: www.nytimes.com.

5. Totterdell, P. (2000). Catching moods and hitting runs: Mood linkage and subjective performance in professional sport teams. *Journal of Applied Psychology* 85: 848–59.

6. Bryant, A. (July 25, 2009). No doubts: Women are better managers. *The New York Times*. Retrieved from: www.nytimes.com.

7. Bryant, A. (May 7, 2010). On her team, it's all about bench strength. *The New York Times*. Retrieved from: www.nytimes.com.

8. Women's Sports Foundation (2009). Benefits—Why Sports Participation for Girls and Women: The Foundation Position. Retrieved from: www .womenssportsfoundation.org.

Chapter 21

1. Richeson, J. A., and Trawalter, S. (2005). Why do interracial interactions impair executive function? A resource depletion account. *Journal of Personality and Social Psychology* 88: 934–47.

2. Carlson, E. N., and Furr, R. M. (2009). Evidence of differential meta-accuracy: People understand the different impressions they make. *Psychological Science*.

3. Carlson, E. N., Furr, R. M., and Vazire, S. (2010). Do we know the first impressions we make? Evidence for idiographic meta-accuracy and calibration of first impressions. *Social Psychological and Personality Science* 1: 94–98.

4. Vorauer, J. D., and Sakamoto, Y. (2006). I thought we could be friends, but . . . Systematic miscommunication and defensive distancing as obstacles to cross-group friendship formation. *Psychological Science*.

5. Vorauer, J. D., Cameron, J. J., Holmes, J. G., and Pearce, D. G. (2003). Invisible overtures: Fears of rejection and the signal amplification bias. *Journal of Personality and Social psychology* 84: 793–812.

6. Watkins, M. B., Kaplan, S., Brief, A. P., Shulld, A., Dietz, J., Mansfield, M., and Cohen, R. (2006). Does it pay to be a sexist? The relationship between modern sexism and career outcomes. *Journal of Vocational Behavior* 69: 524–37.

7. Hebl, M., and Dovidio, J. F. (2005). Promoting the "social" in the examination of social stigmas. *Personality and Social Psychological Review* 9: 156–82.

8. Trawalter, S., and Richeson, J. A. (2006). Regulatory focus and executive function after interracial interactions. *Journal of Experimental Social Psychology* 42: 406–12.

9. Collins, N. L., and Miller, L. C. (1991). Self-disclosure and liking: A meta-analysis. *Psychological Bulletin* 116: 457–75.

Chapter 22

1. Morand, D. A. (1995). The role of behavioral formality and informality in the enactment of bureaucratic versus organic organizations. *Academy of Management* 20: 831–72.

2. Becker, F., and Sims, W. (2001). *Offices that Work: Balancing Communication, Flexibility, and Cost*. International Workplace Studies Program.

3. McCusker, J. A. (2002). *Individuals and open space office design: The relationship between personality and satisfaction in an open space work environment*. Dissertation from Alliant University.

4. Zalesny, M. D., and Farace, R. V. (1987). Traditional versus open offices: A comparison of sociotechnical, social relations, and symbolic meaning perceptions. *Academy of Management Journal* 30: 240–59.

5. Schlosser, J. (2006). *Cubicles: The great mistake. FORTUNE Magazine*.

6. Back, M. D., Stopfer, J. M., Vazire, S., Gaddis, S., Schmukle, S. C., Egloff, B., and Gosling, S. D. (2010). Facebook profiles reflect actual personality not self-idealization. *Psychological Science* 21: 372–74.

7. Naumann, L. P., Vazire, S., Rentfrow, P. J., and Gosling, S. D. (2009). Personality judgments based on physical appearance. *Personality and Social Psychology Bulletin* 35: 1661–71.

8. Rentfrow, P. J., and Gosling, S. D. (2003). The do re mi's of everyday life: The structure and personality correlates of music preferences. *Journal of Personality and Social Psychology* 84: 1236–56.

9. Vazire, S. and Gosling, S. D. (2004). E-perceptions: Personality impressions based on personal websites. *Journal of Personality and Social Psychology* 87: 123–32.

10. Conan, N. (May 26, 2008). What your stuff says about you. *National Public Radio*. Retrieved from: www.npr.org.

Section 4

1. Scherer, M. (May 13, 2010). The new sheriffs of Wall Street. *Time Magazine*. Retrieved from: www.time.com.

2. Bennhold, K. (March 5, 2010). Risk and opportunity for women in 21st century. *The New York Times*. Retrieved from: www.nytimes.com.

Chapter 23

1. Holland, K. (September 10, 2006). Performance reviews: many need improvement. *The New York Times*.

2. Parker-Pope, T. (May 17, 2010). Time to review workplace reviews? *The New York Times*.

3. Kluger, A. N., and DeNisi, A. (1996). The effects of feedback interventions on performance: A historical review, a meta-analysis, and a preliminary feedback intervention theory. *Psychological Bulletin* 119: 254–84.

4. McCauley, C. D. (1999). *Learning from work experience: Job challenge profile*. San Francisco: John Wiley & Sons, Inc.

5. Bowen, C. C., Swim, J. K., and Jacobs, R. R. (2000). Evaluating gender biases on actual job performance of real people: A meta-analysis. *Journal of Applied Social Psychology* 30: 2194–215.

6. Heilman, M. E. and Chen, J. J. (2005). Same behavior, different consequences: Reactions to men's and women's altruistic citizenship behavior. *Journal of Applied Psychology* 90: 431–41.

7. Lyness, K. S., and Heilman, M. E. (2006). When fit is fundamental: Performance evaluations and promotions of upper-female and male managers. *Journal of Applied Psychology* 91: 777–85.

8. Rudman, L. A. and Fairchild, K. (2004). Reactions to counterstereotypic behavior: The role of backlash in cultural stereotype maintenance. *Journal of Personality and Social Psychology* 87: 157–76.

9. King, E. B., Morgan, W. B., Kazama, S. T., Hebl, M. R., Dawson, J. F., and Perkins, A. (In press). Benevolent sexism at work: Gender differences in the distribution of challenging work experiences. *Journal of Management.*

10. Roberts, T. A., and Nolen-Hoeksema, S. (1989). Sex differences in reactions to evaluative feedback. *Sex Roles* 21: 725–47.

11. Johnson, M., and Helgeson, V. S. (2002). Sex differences in response to evaluative feedback: A field study. *Psychology of Women Quarterly* 26: 242–51.

12. LaPlante, D., and Ambady, N. (2002). Saying it like it isn't: Mixed messages from men and women in the workplace. *Journal of Applied Social Psychology* 32: 2435–57.

13. Brewer, N., Socha, L., and Potter, R. (1996). Gender differences in supervisors' use of performance feedback. *Journal of Applied Social Psychology* 26: 786–803.

14. Lizzio, A., Wilson, K. L., Gilchrist, J., and Gallois, C. (2003). The role of gender in the construction and evaluation of feedback effectiveness. *Management Communication Quarterly* 16: 341–79.

15. Latham, G., and Locke, E. A. (2002). Building a practically useful theory of goal setting and task motivation. *The American Psychologist* 57: 705–17.

Chapter 24

1. Speitzer, G. M., McCall, M. W., and Mahoney, J. D. (1997). Early identification of international executive potential. *Journal of Applied Psychology* 82: 6–29.

2. McCauley, C. D. (1999). *Learning from work experience: Job challenge profile.* San Francisco, CA: John Wiley & Sons, Inc.

3. govleaders.org/development.htm.

4. Van Velsor, E., McCauley, C. D., and Moxley, R. S. (1998). Introduction: Our view of leadership development. *Handbook of Leadership Development.* San Francisco: Jossey-Bass Publishers, 1–28.

5. Ohlott, P. J., Ruderman, M. N., and McCauley, C. D. (1994). Gender differences in managers' developmental job experiences. *Academy of Management Journal* 37: 46–67.

6. Lyness, K. S., and Thompson, D. E. (2000). Climbing the corporate ladder: Do female and male executives follow the same route? *Journal of Applied Psychology* 85: 86–101.

7. King, E. B., Morgan, W. B., Kazama, S. T., Hebl, M. R., Dawson, J. F., and Perkins, A. (In press). Benevolent sexism at work: Gender differences in the distribution of challenging work experiences. *Journal of Management.*

8. De Pater, I. E., Van Vianen, A. E. M., Fischer, A. H., and Van Ginkel, W. P. (2009). Challenging experiences: Gender differences in task choice. *Journal of Managerial Psychology* 24: 4–28.

9. Ryan, M. K., and Haslam, S. (2007). The glass cliff: Exploring the dynamics surrounding the appointment of women to precarious leadership positions. *Academy of Management Review* 32: 549–72.

10. govleaders.org/development.htm.

Chapter 25

1. www.google.com/corporate/execs.html#marissa.

2. Judge, T. A., and Cable, D. M. (2004). The effect of physical height on workplace success and income: Preliminary test of a theoretical model. *Journal of Applied Psychology* 89: 428–41.

3. Ng, T. W. H., Eby, L. T., Sorensen, K. L., and Feldman, D. C. (2005). Predictors of objective and subjective career success: A meta-analysis. *Personnel Psychology* 58: 367–408.

4. www.sanfranmag.com/story/adventures-marissa.

5. Eagly, A. H., and Karau, S. J. (1991). Gender and the emergence of leaders: A meta-analysis. *Journal of Personality and Social Psychology* 60: 685–710.

6. Eagly, A. H., and Karau, S. J. (2002). Role congruity theory of prejudice toward female leaders. *Psychological Review* 109: 573–98.

7. Judge, T. A., and Hurst, C. (2008). How the rich (and happy) get richer (and happier): Relationship of core self-evaluations to trajectories in attaining work success. *Journal of Applied Psychology* 93: 849–63.

8. www.businessweek.com.

9. www.nytimes.com.

Chapter 26

1. Porter, N., and Geis, F. (1983). Are women invisible as leaders? *Sex Roles* 9: 1035–49.

2. Jackson, D., Engstrom, E., and Emmers-Sommer, T. (2007). Think leader, think male and female: Sex vs. seating arrangement as leadership cues. Sex Roles 57: 713–23.

3. Butler, D., and Geis, F. L. (1990). Nonverbal affect responses to male and female leaders: Implications for leadership evaluations. *Journal of Personality and Social Psychology* 58: 48–59.

4. Brescoll, V. L., and Uhlmann, E. L. (2008). Can an angry woman get ahead? Status conferral, gender, and expression of emotion in the workplace. *Psychological Science* 19: 268–75.

5. Heilman, M. E., Wallen, A. S., Fuchs, D., and Tamkins, M. M. (2004). Penalties for success: Reactions to women who succeed at male gender-typed tasks. *Journal of Applied Psychology* 89: 416–27.

6. Heilman, M. E., and Okimoto, T. G. (2007). Why are women penalized for success at male tasks? The implied communality deficit. *Journal of Applied Psychology* 92: 81–92.

7. Eagly, A. H., Johannesen-Schmidt, M. C., and van Engen, M. L. (2003). Transformational, transactional, and laissez-faire leadership styles. A meta-analysis comparing women and men. *Psychological Bulletin* 129: 569–91.

8. Rosette, A. S., and Tost, L. P. (2010). Agentic women and communal leadership: How role prescriptions confer advantage to top women leaders. *Journal of Applied Psychology* 95: 221–235.

Chapter 27

1. Macan, T. H., Shahani, C., Dipboye, R. L., and Phillips, A. P. (1990). College students' time management: correlations with academic performance and stress. *Journal of Educational Psychology* 82: 760–68.

2. Macan, T. H. (1994). Time management: test of a process model. *Journal of Applied Psychology*, 79: 381–91.

3. Zampetakis, L. A., Bouranta, N., and Moustakis, V. S. (2010). On the relationship between individual creativity and time management. *Thinking Skills and Creativity* 5: 23–32.

4. Liu, O. L., Rijmen, F., MacCann, C., and Roberts, R. (2009). The assessment of time management in middle-school students. *Personality and Individual Differences* 47: 174–79.

5. Classens, B. J. C., Van Erde, W., Rutte, C. G., and Roe, R. A. (2007). A review of the time management literature. *Personnel Review* 36: 255–76.

6. Peeters, M. A. G., and Rutte, C. G. (2005). Time management behavior as a moderator for the job demand-control interaction. *Journal of Occupational Health Psychology* 10: 64–75.

7. Adams, G. A., and Jex, S. M. (1999). Relationships between time management, control, work-family conflict, and strain. *Journal of Occupational Health Psychology* 4: 72–77.

8. Bryant, A. (December 26, 2009). Everything on one calendar, please. *The New York Times*. Retrieved from: www.nytimes.com.

9. Bryant, A. (August 22, 2009). The C.E.O. must decide who swims. *The New York Times*. Retrieved from: www.nytimes.com.

10. Bryant, A. (May 7, 2010). On her team, it's all about bench strength. *The New York Times*. Retrieved from: www.nytimes.com.

11. Bryant, A. (March 21, 2009). The keeper of that tapping pen. *The New York Times*. Retrieved from: www.nytimes.com.

12. Bryant, A. (July 25, 2009). No doubts: women are better managers. *The New York Times*. Retrieved from: www.nytimes.com.

13. Buchanan, L. (March 1, 2010). 15 ways to be more productive. *Inc.* Retrieved from: www.inc.com.

14. Ibid.

15. Ibid.

16. Bryant, A. (April 25, 2009). He wants subjects, verbs and objects. *The New York Times*. Retrieved from: www.nytimes.com.

17. Big rocks first: double your productivity this week. Retrieved from: http://zenhabits.net/big-rocks-first-double-your-productivity-this-week.

Chapter 28

1. Hackman, J. R., and Oldham, G. R. (1978). Development of the job diagnostic survey. *Journal of Applied Psychology* 60: 159–70.

2. DeNisi, A. S., and Griffin, R. W. (2001). *Human resource management*. Boston: Houghton Mifflin Company.

3. DuBrin, A. J. (2004). *Applying psychology: Individual and organizational effectiveness*. Upper Saddle River, NJ: Pearson.

4. Johnson, T. (July 17, 2006). Dealing with a bad boss. *ABC News*. Retrieved from: http://abcnews.go.com.

5. Mulligan, C. B. (May 26, 2010). Gender segregation by the clock. *The New York Times*. Retrieved from: http://economix.blogs.nytimes.com.

6. Taylor, S. E., Klein, L. C., Lewis, B. P., Gruenewald, T. L., Gurung, R. A. R., and Updegraff, J. A. (2000). Biobehavioral responses to stress in females: Tend-and-befriend, not fight-or-flight. *Psychological Review* 107: 411–29.

7. Kosslyn, S. M., and Rosenberg, R. S. (2004). *Psychology: The brain, the person, the world*. (2nd ed.) New York: Pearson.

8. Grenberg, J. (2005). *Managing behavior in organizations*. (4th ed). Upper Saddle River, NJ: Pearson.

9. Maslach, C., Jackson, S. E, and Leiter, M. P. (1996). *MBI: The Maslach burnout inventory: Manual*. Palo Alto: Consulting Psychologists Press.

10. DuBrin, *Applying psychology*.

11. Pennebaker, J. W., Kiecolt-Glaser, J. K., and Glaser, R. (2004). Disclosure of traumas and immune function: health implications for psychotherapy. In R. M. Kowalski and M. R. Leary (eds.). *The Interface of social and clinical psychology: Key readings*. New York: Psychology Press, 301–12.

12. Sexton, J. D., and Pennebaker, J. W. (2009). The healing powers of expressive writing. In S. B. Kaufman and J. C. Kaufman (eds.). *The psychology of creative writing*. New York: Cambridge University Press, 264–73.

13. Niederhoffer, K. G., and Pennebaker, J. W. (2009). Sharing one's story: On the benefits of writing or talking about emotional experience. In S. J. Lopez and C. R. Snyder (eds.). *Oxford handbook of positive psychology* (2nd ed.). New York: Oxford University Press, 621–32.

14. Eagly, A. H., Carli, L. L. (2007). *Through the labyrinth: The truth about how women become leaders*. Cambridge: Harvard Business School Press.

15. Warner, L., and Shields, S. (2007). The perception of crying in women and men: angry tears, sad tears, and the "right way" to cry. In U. Hess and P. Philippot (eds.). *Group dynamics and emotional expression*. New York: Cambridge University Press.

Section 5

1. http://www.channelinsider.com/c/a/Spotlight/10-iPad-Apps-for-WorkLife -Balance-799676/.

2. www.channelinsider.com.

3. U.S. Department of Labor, Bureau of Labor Statistics (2006). Retrieved from: www.bls.gov/news.release/famee.t04.htm.

4. Bianchi, D. M., Milkie, M. A., Sayer, L. C., and Robinson, J. P. (2000). Is anyone doing the housework? Trends in the gender division of household labor. *Social Forces* 79: 191–228.

5. Craig, L. (2006). Does father care mean fathers share? A comparison of how mothers and fathers in intact families spend time with children. *Gender & Society* 20: 259–81.

6. Johnson, T. D. (2008). *Maternity leave and employment: Patterns of first-time mothers 1961–2003*. United States Census Bureau. Retrieved from: www.census.gov.

Chapter 29

1. Lucy Stone League. Retrieved from: www.lucystoneleague.org.

2. Kopelman, R. E., Shea-Van Fossen, R. J., Paraskevas, E., Lawter, L., and Prottas, D. J. (2009). The bride is keeping her name: A 35-year retrospective analysis of trends and correlates. *Social Behavior and Personality* 37: 687–700.

3. Noordewier, M. K., Horen, F., Ruys, K. I., and Stapel, D. (2010). What's in a name? 361.708 euros: The effects of marital name change. *Basic and Applied Social Psychology* 32: 17–25.

4. Etaugh, C. E., Bridges, J. S., Cummings-Hill, M., and Cohen, Joseph. (1999). "Names can never hurt me?": The effects of surname use on perceptions of married women. *Psychology of Women Quarterly* 23: 819–23.

5. Forbes, G. B., Adam-Curtis, L. E., White, K. B., and Hamm, N. R. (2002). Perceptions of married women and married men with hyphenated surnames. *Sex roles* 46: 167–75.

6. Parigoris, C. G. (2002). Marital surnames and gender roles of contemporary women. Dissertation Abstracts International: Section B: The Sciences and Engineering.

7. Hoffnung, M. (2006). What's in a name? Marital name choice revisited. *Sex roles* 55: 817–25.

8. Twenge, J. M. (1997). "Mrs. his name": Women's preferences for married names. *Psychology of Women Quarterly* 21: 417–29.

9. Jayson, S. (May 30, 2005). Hyphenated names less-and-less used. *USA Today*. Retrieved from: www.usatoday.com.

10. Scheuble, L. K., and Johnson, D. R. (2005). Married women's situational use of last names: an empirical study. *Sex Roles* 53: 143–51.

Chapter 30

1. Clair, J., Beatty, J., and MacLean, T. (2005). Out of sight but not out of mind: Managing invisible social identities in the workplace. *Academy of Management Review*, 30, 78–95.

2. http://mason.gmu.edu/~eking6/pregnancy.html.

3. Fox, C. (2008). Telling the boss you're pregnant.: AJC Jobs. Retrieved from: www.ajc.com.

4. King, E. B., and Botsford, W. (2009). Managing pregnancy disclosures: Understanding and overcoming the challenges of expectant motherhood at work. *Human Resource Management Review* 19: 314–23.

5. Ellison, M. A. (2003). Authoritative knowledge and single women's unintentional pregnancies, abortions, adoption, and single motherhood: Social stigma and structural violence. *Medical Anthropology Quarterly* 17: 322–47.

6. Queneau, H., and Marmo, M. (2001). Tensions between employment and pregnancy: A workable balance. *Family Relations* 50: 59–66.

7. www.workingmother.com/BestCompanies/hall-of-fame/2009/08/american-express.

8. Zimmerman, E. (November 21, 2009). Expecting a baby, but not the stereotypes. *New York Times*. Retrieved from: www.nytimes.com.

9. Buzanell, P., and Liu, M. (2007). It's "give and take": Maternity leave as a conflict management process. *Human Relations* 60: 463–95.

10. Gueutal, H. G., Luciano, J., and Michaels, C. A. (1995). Pregnancy in the workplace: Does pregnancy affect performance appraisal ratings? *Journal of Business and Psychology* 10: 155–67.

11. Gueutal, H. G., and Taylor, E. M. (1991). Employee pregnancy: The impact on organizations, pregnant employees and co-workers. *Journal of Business and Psychology* 5: 459–76.

12. U.S. Department of Labor. (1998). *A workable balance: Report to congress on family and medical leave policies*. Washington, D.C.

13. Lyness, K. S., Thompson, C. A., Francesco, A. M., and Judiesch, M. K. (1999). Work and pregnancy: Individual and organizational factors influencing organizational commitment, timing of maternity leave, and return to work. *Sex Roles* 41: 485–508.

14. Klein, M. H., Hyde, J. S., Essex, M. J., and Clark, R. (1998). Maternity leave, role quality, work involvement, and mental health one year after delivery. *Psychology of Women Quarterly* 22: 239–66.

15. Judiesch, M. K., and Lyness, K. S. (1999). Left behind? The impact of leaves of absence on managers' career success. *Academy of Management Journal* 42: 641–51.

16. Major, V. S. (2004). Pregnancy in the workplace: Stigmatization and work identity management among pregnant employees. Doctoral Dissertation, University of Maryland, College Park.

Chapter 31

1. Cohany, S. R. and Sok, E. (2007). Trends in labor force participation of married mothers and infants. *Monthly Labor Review* 130: 9–16.

2. Davis, J. A., and Smith, T. W. (2007). National Opinion Research Center, General Social Surveys, 1972–2006. Online: http://www.norc.org/GSS+Website.

3. Eby, L. T., Casper, W. J., Lockwood, A., Bordeaux, C., and Brinley, A. (2005). Work and family research in IO/OB: Content analysis and review of the literature (1980–2002). *Journal of Vocational Behavior* 66: 124–97.

4. Williams, J. C., & Boushey, H. (2010). The three faces of work-family conflict: The poor, the professionals, and the missing middle. The Center for Work Life Progress for WorkLife Law.

5. Byron, K. (2005). A meta-analytic review of work–family conflict and its antecedents. *Journal of Vocational Behavior* 67: 169–98.

6. Hammer, L. B., Bauer, T. N., and Grandey, A. A. (2003). Work-family conflict and work-related withdrawal behaviors. *Journal of Business and Psychology* 17: 419–36.

7. Hammer, L. B., Kossek, E. E., Yragui, N. L., Bodner, T. E., and Hanson, G. C. (2009). Development and validation of a multidimensional measure of family supportive supervisor behaviors (FSSB). *Journal of Managemen*, 35: 837–57.

8. Shockley, K., and Allen, T. (2007). When flexibility helps: Another look at the availability of flexible work arrangements and work-family conflict. *Journal of Vocational Behavior* 71: 479–93.

9. Rothbard, N. P., Phillips, K. W., and Dumas, T. L. (2005). Managing multiple roles: Work-family policies and individuals' desires for segmentation. *Organization Science* 16: 243–58.

10. Rotondo, D. M., Carlson, D. S., and Kincaid, J. F. (2003). Coping with multiple dimensions of work-family conflict. *Personnel Review* 32: 275–97.

Chapter 32

1. www.worklifelaw.org.

2. Chadwick v. Wellpoint, Inc. (2009). Appeal from the U.S. District Court.

3. Waldfogel, J. (1998). Understanding the "family gap" in pay for women with children. *Journal of Economic Perspective* 12: 137–56.

4. Cuddy, A. J. C., Fiske, S. T., and Glick, P. (2004). When professionals become mothers, warmth doesn't cut the ice. *Journal of Social Issues* 60: 701–18.

5. Correll, S. J., Benard, S., and Paik, I. (2007). Getting a job: Is there a motherhood penalty? *American Journal of Sociology* 112: 1297–338.

6. Heilman, M. E., and Okimoto, T. (2008). Motherhood: A potential source of bias in employment decisions. *Journal of Applied Psychology* 93, 189–98.

7. Hoobler, J. M., Wayne, S. J., and Lemmon, G. (2009). Bosses' perceptions of family-work conflict and women's promotability: Glass ceiling effects. *Academy of Management Journal* 52: 939–57.

8. King, E. B. (2008). The effect of bias on the advancement of working mothers: Disentangling legitimate concerns from inaccurate stereotypes as predictors of career success. *Human Relations* 61: 1677–711.

9. Michelle Obama (April 14, 2010). *The New York Times*. Retrieved from: http://topics.nytimes.com.

10. Belkin, L. (May 17, 2010). Judging women. *The New York Times*. Retrieved from: www.nytimes.com.

Chapter 33

1. Calvert, C. (2010). Family responsibilities discrimination: Litigation update 2010. Center for WorkLife Law.

2. Spillman, B. C., and Pezzin, L. E. (2000). Potential and active family caregivers: Changing networks and the "sandwich generation." *The Milbank Quarterly* 78: 347–74.

3. Neal, M. B., Ingersoll-Dayton, B., and Starrels, M. E. (1997). Gender and relationship differences in caregiving patterns and consequences among employed caregivers. *The Gerontologist* 37: 804–16.

4. Pierret, C. R. (2006). The "sandwich generation": Women caring for parents and children. *Monthly Labor Review* 9: 3–9.

5. Kramer, B. J., and Kipnis, S. (1995). Eldercare and work-role conflict: Toward an understanding of gender differences in caregiver burden. *The Gerontologist* 35: 340–48.

6. Haslanger, K. (June 22, 2010). Caregiving advice: Finding work-life balance as a caregiver. *The Huffington Post.* www.huffingtonpost.com.

7. Kossek, E. E., Colquitt, J. A., and Noe, R. A. (2001). Caregiving decisions, well-being, and performance: The effects of place and provider as a function of dependent type and work-family climates. *Academy of Management Journal* 44: 29–44.

8. Williams, J. C., and Bornstein, S. (2007). The evolution of "FReD": Family responsibilities discrimination and developments in the law of stereotyping and implict bias. *Hastings Law Journal* 59: 1310–58.

9. www.seniorhousingnet.com/care-selection/evaluate.aspx.

10. www.caregiver.org.

11. www.homefair.com/articles.

12. Calvert, Family responsibilities discrimination.

Chapter 34

1. Evans, G. W., and Wener, R. E. (2006). Rail commuting duration and passenger stress. *Health Psychology* 25: 408–12.

2. Van Rooy, D. L. (2006). Effects of automobile commute characteristics on affect and job candidate evaluations: A field experiment. *Environment and Behavior* 38: 626–55

3. Data reported in Penn, M. J. (2007). *Microtrends: The small forces behind tomorrow's big changes.* New York: Twelve.

4. Koslowsky, M., Kluger, A. N., and Reich, M. (1995). *Commuting stress: Causes, effects, and methods of coping.* New York: Plenum Press.

5. Gajendran, R. S., and Harrison, D. A. (2007). The good, the bad, and the unknown about telecommuting: Meta-analysis of psychological mediators and individual consequences. *Journal of Applied Psychology* 92: 1524–41.

6. Ibid.

7. Koslowsky, M., Kluger, A. N., and Reich, M. (1995). *Commuting stress: Causes, effects, and methods of coping.* New York: Plenum Press.

8. Bake, L. (October, 2009). How to get more bicyclists on the road: To boost urban bicycling, figure out what women want. *Scientific American Magazine.* Accessible: www.scientificamerican.com.

Chapter 35

1. Aycan, Z., and Kanungo, R. N. (1997). Current issues and future challenges in expatriate management. In Z. Aycan (ed.). *New approaches to employee management* (Vol. 4). Greenwich, CT: JAI Press.

2. Mol, S. T., Born, M. P. H., Willemsen, M. E., and Van Der Molen, H. T. (2005). Predicting Expatriate Job Performance for Selection Purposes: A Quantitative Review. *Journal of Cross-Cultural Psychology* 36: 590–620.

3. Caligiuri, P. M. (2006). The big five personality characteristics as predictors of expatriate's desire to terminate the assignment and supervisor-rated performance. *Personnel Psychology* 53: 67–88.

4. Shaffer, M. A., Harrison, D. A., Gregersen, H., Black, J., and Ferzandi, L. A. (2006). You can take it with you: Individual differences and expatriate effectiveness. *Journal of Applied Psychology* 91: 109–25.

5. House, R. J., Hanges, P. J., Javidan, M., Dorfman, P. W., and Gupta, V. (2004). *Culture, leadership, and organizations: The GLOBE study of 62 societies.* Thousand Oaks, CA: Sage Publications.

6. Ibid.

7. Takeuchi, R., Yun, S., and Tesluk, P. E. (2002). An examination of crossover and spillover effects of spousal and expatriate cross-cultural adjustment on expatriate outcomes. *Journal of Applied Psychology* 87: 655–66.

8. Harvey, M., and Wiese, D (1998). The dual-career couple: female expatriates and male trailing spouses. *Thunderbird International Business Review* 40: 359–88.

9. Shaffer, M. A., and Harrison, D. A. (2001). Forgotten partners of international assignments: development and test of a model of spouse adjustment. *Journal of Applied Psychology* 86: 238–54.

10. Bryant, A. (February 6, 2010). Now, put yourself in my shoes. *The New York Times*. Retrieved from: www.nytimes.com.

11. Valian, V. (1999). The cognitive bases of gender bias. *Brooklyn Law Revie*, 65: 1037–62.

12. Brookfield Global Relocation Services (2010). The global recession forced a record number of companies to cut back on overseas assignments of employees in 2009. Retrieved from: www.brookfieldgrs.com.

13. Insch, G. S., McIntyre, N., and Napier, N. K. (2008). The expatriate glass ceiling: The second layer of glass. *Journal of Business Ethics*, 83: 19–28.

14. Axtell, R. E., Briggs, T., Corcoran, M., and Lamb, M. B. (1997). *Do's and taboos around the world for women in business.* New York: John Wiley & Sons.

15. Stroh, L., Varma, A., and Valy-Durbin, S. J. (2000). Why are women left at home: Are they unwilling to go on international assignments? *Journal of World Business* 35: 241–55.

16. Burrus, K. (2009). Coaching women managers in multinational companies. The Routledge companion to international business coaching. In M. Moral and G. Abbott (eds.). *The Routledge companion to international business coaching.* New York: Routledge/Taylor & Francis Group, 218–29.

17. Lyness, K. S., and Thompson, D. E. (2000). Climbing the corporate ladder: do female and male executives follow the same route? *Journal of Applied Psychology* 85: 86–101.

18. Sinangil, H. K., and Ones, D. S. (2003). Gender differences in expatriate job performance. *Applied Psychology: An International Review* 52: 461–75.

19. Caligiuri, P. M., and Tung, R. L. (1999). Comparing the success of male and female expatriates from a US-based multinational company. *International Journal of Human Resource Management* 10: 763–82.

Section 6

1. EEOC v. Campbell Concrete of Nevada, Inc. (D. Nev. May 18, 2004).

2. EEOC v. Milgard Manufacturing, Inc. (D. Col. May 19, 2004).

3. Berdahl, J. L., and Moore, C. (2006). Workplace harassment: Double jeopardy for minority women. *Journal of Applied Psychology* 91: 426–36.

4. Raver, J. L., and Nishii, L. H. (2010). Once, twice, or three times as harmful? Ethnic harassment, gender harassment, and generalized workplace harassment. *Journal of Applied Psychology* 95: 236–54.

Chapter 36

1. Jans, L., and Stoddard, S. (1999). *Chartbook on women and disability in the United States.* Berkeley, CA: InfoUse.

2. Miller, B. K., and Werner, S. (2005). Factors influencing the inflation of task performance ratings for workers with disabilities and contextual performance. *Human Performance* 18: 309–29.

3. Braithwaite, D. O., and Thompson, T. L. (2000). *Handbook of communication and people with disabilities: Research and application.* Hillsdale, NJ: Lawrence Erlbaum.

4. Charles, K. K. (2003). The longitudinal structure of earnings losses among work-limited disabled workers. *Journal of Human Resources.*

5. Block. L. Stereotypes about people with disabilities. www.npr.org/programs/disability.

6. Colella, A., DeNisi, A. S., and Varma, A. (1997). Appraising the performance of employees with disabilities: A review and model. *Human Resource Management Review* 7: 27–53.

7. http://federaljobs.net/disabled.htm.

8. Hebl, M. R., and Skorinko, J. L. (2005). Acknowledging one's disability in the interview: Does "when" make a difference? *Journal of Applied Social Psychology* 35: 2477–92.

9. Davison, H. K., O'Leary, B. J., Schlosberg, J. A., and Bing, M. N. (2009). Don't ask and you shall not receive: Why future American workers with disability are reluctant to demand legally required accommodations. *Journal of Workplace Rights* 14: 49–73.

10. Paetzold, R. L., Garcia, M. F., Colella, A., Ren, L. R., Triana, M. C., and Ziebro, M. (2008). Perceptions of people with disabilities: When is accommodation fair? *Basic and Applied Social Psychology* 30: 27–35.

11. Balser, D. B., and Harris, M. M. (2008). Factors affecting employee satisfaction with disability accommodation: A field study. *Employee Rights and Responsibilities Journal* 20: 13–28.

12. Jans, and Stoddard, *Chartbook on women and disability.*

Chapter 37

1. Steinem, G. (January 8, 2008). Women are never the front-runners. *The New York Times.* www.nytimes.com.

2. U.S. Department of Labor (2010). Quick stats on women workers, 2009. www.dol.gov/wb/stats/main.htm.

3. Bendick, M., Jackson, C., and Reinoso, V. (1994). Measuring employment discrimination through controlled experiments. *Review of Black Political Economy* 23: 25–48.

4. Landau, J. (1995). The relationship of race and gender to managers' ratings of promotion potential. *Journal of Organizational Behavior* 16: 391–400.

5. Kraiger, K., and Ford, J. K. (1985). A meta-analysis of ratee tace effects in performance ratings. *Journal of Applied Psychology* 70: 56–65.

6. Rosette, A. S., Leonardelli, G. J., and Phillips, K. W. (2008). The white standard: Racial bias in leader categorization. *Journal of Applied Psychology* 93: 758–77.

7. Greenhaus, J. H., Parasuraman, S., and Wormley, W. M. (1990). Effects of race on organizational experiences, job performance evaluations, and career outcomes. *Academy of Management Journal* 33: 64–86.

8. Tucker, J., Viruell, E. A., and Wolfe, L. R. (1995). Workplace cultures: A reality check—Listening to the voices of women of color. Center for Women Policy Studies. www.centerwomenpolicy.org.

9. Shuter, R., and Turner, L. H. (1997). African American and European American women in the workplace. *Management Communication Quarterly* 11: 74.

10. Cortina, L. M., Fitzgerald, L. F., and Drasgow, F. (2002). Contextualizing Latina experiences of sexual harassment: Preliminary tests of a structural model. *Basic and Applied Social Psychology* 24: 295–311.

11. Taylor, C. R., and Stern, B. B. (1997). Television advertising and the "model minority" stereotype. *Journal of Advertising* 26: 47–61.

12. Crocker, J. and Major, B. (1989). Social stigma and self-esteem: the self-protective properties of stigma. *Psychological Review* 96: 608–30.

13. Tucker, J., Viruell, E. A., and Wolfe, L. R. (1995). Workplace cultures: A reality check—Listening to the voices of women of color. Center for Women Policy Studies. www.centerwomenpolicy.org.

14. African American women step up in the business world (August 24, 2006). *USA Today*. www.usatoday.com.

15. Gardella, A. (June 18, 2010). Preparing women to build growing businesses. *The New York Times*. Retrieved from: http://boss.blogs.nytimes.com.

16. Dwyer, C. E., Stevens, D., Sullivan, J. L., and Allen, B. (2009). Racism, sexism, and candidate evaluations in the 2008 U.S. Presidential election. *Analyses of Social Issues and Public Policy* 9: 223–40.

17. Conrad, C. A. (September 22, 2008). Black women: The unfinished agenda. *The American Prospect*. www.prospect.org.

Chapter 38

1. Savin-Williams, R. C. (2006). Who's gay? Does it matter? *Current Directions in Psychological Science* 15: 40–44.

2. King, E. B., Reilly, C., and Hebl, M. R. (2008). The best and worst of times: Dual perspectives of coming out in the workplace. *Group and Organization Management* 33: 566–601.

3. Gallup (2010). Americans' acceptance of gay relations crosses 50% threshold. www.gallup.com/poll/135764.

4. Hebl, M., Foster, J. M., Mannix, L. M., and Dovidio, J. F. (2002). Formal and interpersonal discrimination: A field study examination of applicant bias. *Personality and Social Psychological Bulletin* 28: 815–25.

5. Ragins, B. R. and Cornwell, J. M. (2001). Pink triangles: Antecedents and consequences of perceived workplace discrimination against gay and lesbian employees. *Journal of Applied Psychology* 86: 1244.

6. Schneider, B. E. (1991). Put up and shut up: Workplace sexual assaults. *Gender and Society* 5: 533–48.

7. Crocker, J., Major, B., and Steele, C. (1998). Social Stigma. In Gilbert, D., Fiske, S. T., and Lindzey, G. (eds.), *The handbook of social psychology* (4th ed., Vol. 2.). New York: McGraw Hill, 504–53.

8. Ragins, B. R. and Cornwell, J. M. (2001). Pink triangles: Antecedents and consequences of perceived workplace discrimination against gay and lesbian employees. *Journal of Applied Psychology* 86: 1244.

9. Gedro, J. A., Cervero, R. M., and Johnson-Bailey, J. (2004). How lesbians learn to negotiate the heterosexism of corporate America. *HRDI* 7: 181–95.

Chapter 39

1. Quinn, P., and Allen, K. R. (1989). Facing challenges and making compromises: How single mothers endure. *Family Relations* 38: 390–95.

2. Harris, G. (May 13, 2009). Out-of-wedlock birthrates are soaring, U.S. reports. *The New York Times*. Retrieved from: www.nytimes.com.

3. U.S. Census Bureau (2009). Custodial mothers and fathers and their child support: 2007.

4. McManus, K., Korabik, K., Rosin, H. M., and Kelloway, E. K. (2002). Employed mothers and the work-family interface: Does family structure matter? *Human Relations* 55: 1295–311.

5. Quinn, P., and Allen, K. R. (1989). Facing challenges and making compromises: How single mothers endure. *Family Relations* 38: 390–95.

6. Ibid.

7. Hertz, R. (1999). Working to place family at the center of life: Dual-earner and single-parent strategies. *Annals* 562: 16.

8. Hertz, R., and Ferguson, F. I. (1998). Only one pair of hands: Ways that single mothers stretch work and family resources. *Community, Work, and Family* 1: 13–37.

9. Parker, L. (1994). The role of workplace support in facilitating self-sufficiency among single mothers on welfare. *Family Relations* 43: 168–73.

10. Robbins, L. R., and McFadden, J. R. (2003). Single mothers: The impact of work on home and the impact of home on work. *Journal of Family and Consumer Sciences Education* 21.

Chapter 40

1. Ashburn-Nardo, L., Morris, K. A., and Goodwin, S. A. (2008). The confronting prejudiced responses (CPR) model: Applying CPR in organizations. *Academy of Management Learning and Education* 7: 332–42.

2. Blanchard, F. A., Crandall, C. S., Brigham, J. C., and Vaughn, L. A. (1996). Condemning and condoning racism: A social context approach to interracial settings. *Journal of Applied Psychology* 79: 993–99.

3. Czopp, A. M., Monteith, M. J., and Mark, A. Y. (2006). Standing up for a change: Reducing bias through interpersonal confrontation. *Journal of Personality and Social Psychology* 90: 784–803.

4. Shelton, N., and Stewart, R. E. (2004). Confront perpetrators of prejudice: The inhibitory effects of social costs. *Psychology of Women Quarterly* 3: 215–22.

Index